Indexes for Worship Planning

Revised Common Lectionary
Lutheran Book of Worship
With One Voice

Augsburg Fortress
Minneapolis

INDEXES FOR WORSHIP PLANNING

Compilers: Marilyn Kay Stulken, Martin A. Seltz
Additional contributors: Craig M. Mueller, Kristine Oberg, Paul Schuessler, Frank Stoldt, Samuel Torvend

Material from the following sources is acknowledged:
Lutheran Book of Worship, © 1978 Lutheran Church in America, The American Lutheran Church, The Evangelical Lutheran Church of Canada, and The Lutheran Church–Missouri Synod.
Lutheran Book of Worship: Ministers Edition, © 1978 Lutheran Church in America, The American Lutheran Church, The Evangelical Lutheran Church of Canada, and The Lutheran Church–Missouri Synod.
Hymnal Companion to the Lutheran Book of Worship, © 1981 Fortress Press.
With One Voice: Leaders Edition, © 1995 Augsburg Fortress.
The Revised Common Lectionary, © 1992 Consultation on Common Texts.
Lectionary for Worship: Ritual Edition, © 1996 Augsburg Fortress.

The paper used in this publication meets the minimum requirements of American National Standard for Information Sciences–Permanence for Printed Library Materials, ANSI Z329.48–1984.

♾

Manufactured in U.S.A.   ISBN 0–8066–2348–9   AF   3–400
03   02   01   00   99   98   97   96   1   2   3   4   5   6   7   8   9   0

CONTENTS

Also available:

LECTIONARY TABLES

Readings and Prayers (3–388)
> A table of Revised Common Lectionary readings with LBW Prayers of the Day.

With One Voice Leaders Edition (3–302)
> This supplementary Lutheran worship resource contains a table of
> Revised Common Lectionary readings paired with propers from LBW.

LECTIONARY VOLUMES

Lectionary for Worship, Cycle A (3–381), B (3–382), and C (3–383)
> Complete Revised Common Lectionary readings,
> sense-lined to facilitate public reading. NRSV translation.

Lectionary for Worship, Ritual Edition (3–384)
> Hardcover volume containing complete Revised Common Lectionary readings
> for all three lectionary cycles (A, B, C), sense-lined. NRSV.

Readings for the Assembly, Cycle A (3–396), B (3–397), and C (3–398)
> Complete Revised Common Lectionary readings, sense-lined to facilitate public
> reading. Based on the NRSV and incorporating inclusive language for God.
> Edited by Gail Ramshaw and Gordon Lathrop.

WORSHIP PLANNING RESOURCES FOR CONGREGATIONAL USE

Sundays and Seasons Worship Planning Guide
> Calendar-dated guide providing materials needed to prepare worship for Sundays
> and seasons. Based on the Revised Common Lectionary. Published annually.

INTRODUCTION

Recent developments in Lutheran resources for worship have provided the impetus for the present volume. The publication of *With One Voice* has made available a sizeable collection of hymns and liturgical material supplementing *Lutheran Book of Worship*. Furthermore, the *Revised Common Lectionary* has come into widespread use in North American churches. *Indexes for Worship Planning* is an integrated guide to these three core resources presently in use among Lutherans. Others who use the *Revised Common Lectionary* or a similar system of readings should find the contents useful as well.

The most substantial index in this volume is the section titled "Hymns for the Church Year." Hymn suggestions are provided for Sundays and principal festivals as well as lesser festivals and occasions. The recommendations are correlated to the readings appointed by the Revised Common Lectionary and to the days and seasons of the church year. For calendar observances not covered by RCL, the readings appointed by *Lutheran Book of Worship* are used. "Hymns for the Church Year" is a significant adaptation and expansion of an index originally prepared by Marilyn Kay Stulken for *Hymnal Companion to the Lutheran Book of Worship* (Fortress, 1981). It takes into account not only RCL but also the additional hymns and songs available in *With One Voice*. Texts of the appointed propers (Prayer of the Day, Verse, Offertory), brief reading summaries, and an expanded list of recommendations for Hymn of the Day have all been included so that key information helpful to the worship preparation process is consolidated in one place. For the Season after Pentecost, suggestions are provided for both Old Testament "tracks" of RCL: the series of readings correlated with the Gospels, as well as the alternate, "semi-continuous" series.

The section which follows is a complete index to the three-year *Revised Common Lectionary* (including *Lutheran Book of Worship* additions for lesser festivals and occasions). Arranged in biblical order, the index includes not only the complete list of appointed readings, but also a listing of all the appointed psalms.

The remaining indexes in this volume are integrated reference tools to the hymns, songs, and canticles in *Lutheran Book of Worship* and *With One Voice*. Both the scriptural index and the topical index are augmented versions of the corresponding indexes prepared for *Lutheran Book of Worship: Ministers Edition* and *With One Voice*. In contrast to the "Hymns for the Church Year" listing (based on lectionary and season), the scriptural index traces biblical images, references, and allusions contained in the hymns; thus a hymn listed in this index may not always be seasonally fitting for the related reading's place in the lectionary. The topical index includes listings related to particular themes and images in alphabetical order, as well as abbreviated listings for days and seasons of the year.

Integrated alphabetical and metrical tune indexes follow. Included also is a listing of alternate tunes. Many fine hymn texts that are presently paired with music a congregation has not yet learned can be immediately useful when combined with familiar melodies. This list provides an expanded set of examples of how this can be done; other combinations are possible using the metrical tune index.

Indexes for Worship Planning is a primary reference to several core Lutheran resources for worship. Users are invited to use free page space to jot down additional hymns and songs from the many worship resources presently available. Paired with a comprehensive seasonal planning guide such as *Sundays and Seasons* (Augsburg Fortress, annual), this volume is intended as one key opening the treasures of the church's hymnody so that the song of God's people might be enriched.

HYMNS FOR THE CHURCH YEAR
SUNDAYS AND PRINCIPAL FESTIVALS

FIRST SUNDAY IN ADVENT

Prayer of the day

Stir up your power, O Lord, and come. Protect us by your strength and save us from the threatening dangers of our sins, for you live and reign with the Father and the Holy Spirit, one God, now and forever. (1)

Verse

Alleluia. Show us your mercy, O LORD, and grant us your salvation. Alleluia. (Ps. 85:7)

Offertory

Truly, the LORD's salvation is very near to those who fear him, that his glory may dwell in our land. The LORD will indeed grant prosperity, and our land will yield its increase. Righteousness shall go before him, and peace shall be a pathway for his feet. (Ps. 85:9, 12–13)

YEAR A

Hymn of the day

28	Savior of the nations, come
31	Wake, awake, for night is flying
37	Hark! A thrilling voice is sounding!
628	Each winter as the year grows older

Hymns related to the readings

First Reading: Isaiah 2:1–5
Weapons of war transformed into instruments of peace

22	The advent of our God
23	O Lord, how shall I meet you
28	Savior of the nations, come
33	The King shall come
322	The clouds of judgment gather
414	O God of love, O King of peace
630	Light one candle to watch for Messiah
762	O day of peace

Psalmody: Psalm 122
I was glad when they said to me, "Let us go to the house of the LORD." (Ps. 122:1)

Second Reading: Romans 13:11–14
Salvation is near; time to wake from sleep

22	The advent of our God
37	Hark! A thrilling voice is sounding!
31	Wake, awake, for night is flying
382	Awake, O Spirit of the watchmen

Gospel: Matthew 24:36–44
The sudden coming of the Son of Man

31	Wake, awake, for night is flying
244	Lord our God, with praise we come
321	The day is surely drawing near
627	My Lord, what a morning
628	Each winter as the year grows older

Additional hymns for the day/season

25	Rejoice, rejoice, believers
27	Lo! He comes with clouds descending
32	Fling wide the door
38	O Savior, rend the heavens wide
312	Once he came in blessing
318	The Lord will come and not be slow
323	O Lord of light, who made the stars
332	Battle Hymn of the Republic
397	O Zion, haste
443	Rise, my soul, to watch and pray
462	God the omnipotent!
471	Grant peace, we pray, in mercy, Lord
631	Lift up your heads, O gates
744	Soon and very soon

Year B

Hymn of the day

38 O Savior, rend the heavens wide
27 Lo! He comes with clouds descending
627 My Lord, what a morning

Hymns related to the readings

First Reading: Isaiah 64:1–9
Prayer that God would come with power and compassion

38 O Savior, rend the heavens wide
266 Maker of the earth and heaven
414 O God of love, O King of peace

Psalmody: Psalm 80:1–7, 16–18*
Show the light of your countenance, and we shall be saved. (Ps. 80:7)

Second Reading: 1 Corinthians 1:3–9
Gifts of grace sustain those who wait for the end

23 O Lord, how shall I meet you
800 Each morning brings us fresh outpoured

Gospel: Mark 13:24–37
The sudden coming of the Son of Man

31 Wake, awake, for night is flying
37 Hark! A thrilling voice is sounding!
244 Lord our God, with praise we come
321 The day is surely drawing near
627 My Lord, what a morning
628 Each winter as the year grows older

Additional hymns for the day/season

24 Come, O precious Ransom
25 Rejoice, rejoice, believers
28 Savior of the nations, come
32 Fling wide the door
33 The King shall come
312 Once he came in blessing
318 The Lord will come and not be slow
323 O Lord of light, who made the stars
443 Rise, my soul, to watch and pray
630 Light one candle to watch for Messiah
631 Lift up your heads, O gates
744 Soon and very soon

Year C

Hymn of the day

31 Wake, awake, for night is flying
33 The King shall come
626 People, look east

Hymns related to the readings

First Reading: Jeremiah 33:14–16
A righteous branch springing up from David

22 The advent of our God
23 O Lord, how shall I meet you
34 Oh, come, oh, come, Emmanuel

Psalmody: Psalm 25:1–9**
To you, O LORD, I lift up my soul. (Ps. 25:1)

Second Reading: 1 Thessalonians 3:9–13
Strengthen hearts of holiness for the coming of the Lord

745 Awake, O sleeper
800 Each morning brings us fresh outpoured

Gospel: Luke 21:25–36
Be alert for the coming of the Son of Man

31 Wake, awake, for night is flying
37 Hark! A thrilling voice is sounding!
244 Lord our God, with praise we come
321 The day is surely drawing near
355 Through the night of doubt and sorrow
627 My Lord, what a morning
628 Each winter as the year grows older

Additional hymns for the day/season

24 Come, O precious Ransom
25 Rejoice, rejoice, believers
27 Lo! He comes with clouds descending
28 Savior of the nations, come
32 Fling wide the door
312 Once he came in blessing
318 The Lord will come and not be slow
323 O Lord of light, who made the stars
394 Lost in the night
630 Light one candle to watch for Messiah
631 Lift up your heads, O gates
725 Blessed be the God of Israel
744 Soon and very soon

*Psalm 80:1–7, 17–19 (NRSV)
**Psalm 25:1–10 (NRSV)

Second Sunday in Advent

Prayer of the day

Stir up our hearts, O Lord, to prepare the way for your only Son. By his coming give us strength in our conflicts and shed light on our path through the darkness of this world; through your Son, Jesus Christ our Lord, who lives and reigns with you and the Holy Spirit, one God, now and forever. (2)

Verse

Alleluia. Prepare the way of the Lord, make his paths straight; all flesh shall see the salvation of our God. Alleluia. (Luke 3:4, 6)

Offertory

Then people will come from east and west, from north and south, and will eat in the kingdom of God. Blessed is the one who will eat bread in the kingdom of God! (Luke 13:29; 14:15)

YEAR A

Hymn of the day

36	On Jordan's banks the Baptist's cry
29	Comfort, comfort now my people
762	O day of peace

Hymns related to the readings

First Reading: Isaiah 11:1–10
From David's line, a ruler bringing justice and peace

34	Oh, come, oh, come, Emmanuel
35	Hark, the glad sound!
58	Lo, how a rose is growing
172	Lord, enthroned in heavenly splendor
762	O day of peace

Psalmody: Psalm 72:1–7, 18–19
In his time the righteous shall flourish. (Ps. 72:7)

87	Hail to the Lord's anointed (paraphrase)
530	Jesus shall reign (paraphrase)

Second Reading: Romans 15:4–13
Live in harmony, welcoming one another

25	Rejoice, rejoice, believers
704	Father, we thank you
708	Grains of wheat
710	One bread, one body

Gospel: Matthew 3:1–12
A voice cries: Prepare the way of the Lord

29	Comfort, comfort now my people
36	On Jordan's banks the Baptist's cry
37	Hark! A thrilling voice is sounding!
556	Herald, sound the note of judgment

Additional hymns for the day/season

22	The advent of our God
26	Prepare the royal highway
387	Spirit of God, unleashed on earth
630	Light one candle to watch for Messiah
725	Blessed be the God of Israel
763	Let justice flow like streams

Year B

Hymn of the day
629   All earth is hopeful
26   Prepare the royal highway
29   Comfort, comfort now my people

Hymns related to the readings

First Reading: Isaiah 40:1–11
Good news of God's coming to a people in exile

26   Prepare the royal highway
29   Comfort, comfort now my people
629   All earth is hopeful
630   Light one candle to watch for Messiah

Psalmody: Psalm 85:1–2, 8–13
Righteousness and peace shall go before the LORD.
(Ps. 85:13)

Second Reading: 2 Peter 3:8–15a
Waiting for and hastening the day of God

244   Lord our God, with praise we come
320   O God, our help in ages past

Gospel: Mark 1:1–8
John appears from the wilderness

26   Prepare the royal highway
29   Comfort, comfort now my people
36   On Jordan's banks the Baptist's cry
556   Herald, sound the note of judgment

Additional hymns for the day/season
22   The advent of our God
25   Rejoice, rejoice, believers
35   Hark, the glad sound!
507   How firm a foundation
626   People, look east
630   Light one candle to watch for Messiah

Year C

Hymn of the day
631   Lift up your heads, O gates
36   On Jordan's banks the Baptist's cry
418   Judge eternal, throned in splendor

Hymns related to the readings

First Reading: Malachi 3:1–4
My messenger is a refiner and purifier

318   The Lord will come and not be slow
462   God the omnipotent!
507   How firm a foundation

OR

First Reading: Baruch 5:1–9
The return of scattered Israel

224   Soul, adorn yourself with gladness
626   People, look east
629   All earth is hopeful

Psalmody: Luke 1:68–79
In the tender compassion of our God, the dawn from
on high shall break upon us. (Luke 1:78)

725   Blessed be the God of Israel (paraphrase)

Second Reading: Philippians 1:3–11
A harvest of righteousness on the day of Jesus Christ

312   Once he came in blessing

Gospel: Luke 3:1–6
Prepare the way of the Lord

26   Prepare the royal highway
29   Comfort, comfort now my people
36   On Jordan's banks the Baptist's cry
556   Herald, sound the note of judgment

Additional hymns for the day/season
22   The advent of our God
25   Rejoice, rejoice, believers
35   Hark, the glad sound!
630   Light one candle to watch for Messiah
704   Father, we thank you

Prayer of the day

Almighty God, you once called John the Baptist to give witness to the coming of your Son and to prepare his way. Grant us, your people, the wisdom to see your purpose today and the openness to hear your will, that we may witness to Christ's coming and so prepare his way; through Jesus Christ our Lord, who lives and reigns with you and the Holy Spirit, one God, now and forever. (3)

OR

Lord, hear our prayers and come to us, bringing light into the darkness of our hearts; for you live and reign with the Father and the Holy Spirit, one God, now and forever. (4)

Verse

Alleluia. See, I am sending my messenger ahead of you, who will prepare your way before you. Alleluia. (Matt. 11:10)

Offertory

The LORD says, I will make a covenant of peace with them; it shall be an everlasting covenant with them. My dwelling place shall be with them; and I will be their God, and they shall be my people. (Ezek. 37:26–27)

YEAR A

Hymn of the day

26   Prepare the royal highway
556   Herald, sound the note of judgment
629   All earth is hopeful

Hymns related to the readings

First Reading: Isaiah 35:1–10
The desert blooms as God's people return from exile

87   Hail to the Lord's anointed
384   Your kingdom come, O Father
394   Lost in the night
402   Look from your sphere of endless day
626   People, look east
629   All earth is hopeful
633   Awake, awake, and greet the new morn
635   Surely it is God who saves me
716   Word of God, come down on earth

Psalmody: Psalm 146:4–9*
The LORD lifts up those who are bowed down. (Ps. 146:7)

538   Oh, praise the Lord, my soul! (paraphrase)
539   Praise the Almighty (paraphrase)

OR

Canticle: Luke 1:47–55
My spirit rejoices in God my Savior. (Luke 1:47)

6   My soul proclaims the greatness of the Lord
180   My soul now magnifies the Lord (paraphrase)
730   My soul proclaims your greatness (paraphrase)

Second Reading: James 5:7–10
Patience until the coming of the Lord

318   The Lord will come and not be slow
453   If you but trust in God to guide you
662   Restore in us, O God

Gospel: Matthew 11:2–11
The forerunner of Christ

26   Prepare the royal highway
36   On Jordan's banks the Baptist's cry
556   Herald, sound the note of judgment

Additional hymns for the day/season

29   Comfort, comfort now my people
35   Hark, the glad sound!
630   Light one candle to watch for Messiah
723   The Spirit sends us forth to serve
768   He comes to us as one unknown

YEAR B

Hymn of the day
37 Hark! A thrilling voice is sounding!
87 Hail to the Lord's anointed
628 Each winter as the year grows older

Hymns related to the readings

First Reading: Isaiah 61:1–4, 8–11
Righteousness and praise flourish like a garden

29 Comfort, comfort now my people
203 Now we join in celebration
224 Soul, adorn yourself with gladness
530 Jesus shall reign
723 The Spirit sends us forth to serve

Psalmody: Psalm 126
The LORD has done great things for us. (Ps. 126:4)

OR

Canticle: Luke 1:47–55
The Lord has lifted up the lowly. (Luke 1:52)
6 My soul proclaims the greatness of the Lord
180 My soul now magnifies the Lord (paraphrase)
730 My soul proclaims your greatness (paraphrase)

Second Reading: 1 Thessalonians 5:16–24
Kept in faith until the coming of Christ

498 All who would valiant be
553 Rejoice, O pilgrim throng

Gospel: John 1:6–8, 19–28
A witness to the light

29 Comfort, comfort now my people
36 On Jordan's banks the Baptist's cry
556 Herald, sound the note of judgment
649 I want to walk as a child of the light

Additional hymns for the day/season
25 Rejoice, rejoice, believers
35 Hark, the glad sound!
396 O God, O Lord of heaven and earth
630 Light one candle to watch for Messiah

YEAR C

Hymn of the day
32 Fling wide the door
635 Surely it is God who saves me
715 Open your ears, O faithful people

Hymns related to the readings

First Reading: Zephaniah 3:14–20
Rejoice, the LORD is in your midst

23 O Lord, how shall I meet you
34 Oh, come, oh, come, Emmanuel
35 Hark, the glad sound!
742 Come, we that love the Lord

Psalmody: Isaiah 12:2–6
In your midst is the Holy One of Israel. (Isa. 12:6)

635 Surely it is God who saves me (paraphrase)

Second Reading: Philippians 4:4–7
Rejoice, the Lord is near

171 Rejoice, the Lord is king!
516 Arise, my soul, arise!
633 Awake, awake, and greet the new morn

Gospel: Luke 3:7–18
One more powerful is coming, baptizing with fire

36 On Jordan's banks the Baptist's cry
556 Herald, sound the note of judgment

Additional hymns for the day/season
25 Rejoice, rejoice, believers
29 Comfort, comfort now my people
37 Hark! A thrilling voice is sounding!
630 Light one candle to watch for Messiah

*Psalm 146:5–10 (NRSV)

Prayer of the day

Stir up your power, O Lord, and come. Take away the hindrance of our sins and make us ready for the celebration of your birth, that we may receive you in joy and serve you always; for you live and reign with the Father and the Holy Spirit, now and forever. (5)

Verse

Alleluia. The virgin shall conceive and bear a son, and they shall name him Emmanuel. Alleluia. (Matt. 1:23)

Offertory

Sing aloud, O daughter Zion; shout, O Israel! Rejoice and exult with all your heart, O daughter Jerusalem! The LORD, your God, is in your midst; he will renew you in his love; he will exult over you with loud singing as on a day of festival. (Zeph. 3:14, 17)

YEAR A

Hymn of the day

34	Oh, come, oh, come, Emmanuel
28	Savior of the nations, come
641	Peace came to earth

Hymns related to the readings

First Reading: Isaiah 7:10–16
The sign of Immanuel

34	Oh, come, oh, come, Emmanuel
629	All earth is hopeful
632	The angel Gabriel from heaven came
641	Peace came to earth

Psalmody: Psalm 80:1–7, 16–18*
Show the light of your countenance and we shall be saved. (Ps. 80:7)

Second Reading: Romans 1:1–7
Paul's greeting to the church at Rome

24	Come, O precious Ransom
86	The only Son from heaven

Gospel: Matthew 1:18–25
A God near at hand

28	Savior of the nations, come
64	From east to west
641	Peace came to earth

Additional hymns for the day/season

30	Come, thou long-expected Jesus
32	Fling wide the door
38	O Savior, rend the heavens wide
198	Let all mortal flesh keep silence
315	Love divine, all loves excelling
630	Light one candle to watch for Messiah
631	Lift up your heads, O gates
633	Awake, awake, and greet the new morn
634	Sing of Mary, pure and lowly
768	He comes to us as one unknown

Year B

Hymn of the day

634 Sing of Mary, pure and lowly
28 Savior of the nations, come
34 Oh, come, oh, come, Emmanuel

Hymns related to the readings

First Reading: 2 Samuel 7:1–11, 16
The LORD's promise to David

87 Hail to the Lord's anointed

Canticle: Luke 1:47–55
The Lord has lifted up the lowly. (Luke 1:52)

6 My soul proclaims the greatness of the Lord
180 My soul now magnifies the Lord (paraphrase)
730 My soul proclaims your greatness (paraphrase)

OR

Psalmody: Psalm 89:1–4, 19–26
Your love, O LORD, forever will I sing. (Ps. 89:1)

Second Reading: Romans 16:25–27
The mystery revealed in Jesus Christ

28 Savior of the nations, come
42 Of the Father's love begotten
47 Let all together praise our God

Gospel: Luke 1:26–38
The angel appears to Mary

64 From east to west
86 The only Son from heaven
632 The angel Gabriel from heaven came
692 For all the faithful women

Additional hymns for the day/season

30 Come, thou long-expected Jesus
198 Let all mortal flesh keep silence
315 Love divine, all loves excelling
630 Light one candle to watch for Messiah
633 Awake, awake, and greet the new morn

Year C

Hymn of the day

730 My soul proclaims your greatness
86 The only Son from heaven
180 My soul now magnifies the Lord

Hymns related to the readings

First Reading: Micah 5:2–5a
From Bethlehem comes a ruler

41 O little town of Bethlehem
86 The only Son from heaven
643 Once in royal David's city

Canticle: Luke 1:47–55
The Lord has lifted up the lowly. (Luke 1:52)

6 My soul proclaims the greatness of the Lord
180 My soul now magnifies the Lord (paraphrase)
730 My soul proclaims your greatness (paraphrase)

OR

Psalmody: Psalm 80:1–7
Show the light of your countenance and we shall be saved. (Ps. 80:7)

Second Reading: Hebrews 10:5–10
I have come to do your will

323 O Lord of light, who made the stars
489 Wide open are your hands

Gospel: Luke 1:39–45 [46–55]
Blessed are you among women/My soul magnifies the Lord

6 My soul proclaims the greatness of the Lord
64 From east to west
180 My soul now magnifies the Lord
632 The angel Gabriel from heaven came
635 Surely it is God who saves me
730 My soul proclaims your greatness

Additional hymns for the day/season

28 Savior of the nations, come
30 Come, thou long-expected Jesus
34 Oh, come, oh, come, Emmanuel
198 Let all mortal flesh keep silence
315 Love divine, all loves excelling
630 Light one candle to watch for Messiah
633 Awake, awake, and greet the new morn
634 Sing of Mary, pure and lowly

*Psalm 80:1–7, 17–19 (NRSV)

THE NATIVITY OF OUR LORD

CHRISTMAS EVE (I)
YEARS A,B,C

Prayer of the day

Almighty God, you made this holy night shine with the brightness of the true Light. Grant that here on earth we may walk in the light of Jesus' presence and in the last day wake to the brightness of his glory; through your only Son, Jesus Christ our Lord, who lives and reigns with you and the Holy Spirit, one God, now and forever. (6)

Verse

Alleluia. To you is born this day a Savior, who is the Messiah, the Lord. Alleluia. (Luke 2:11)

Offertory

The people who walked in darkness have seen a great light; those who lived in a land of deep darkness—on them light has shined. For a child has been born for us, a son given to us; authority rests upon his shoulders, and he is named Wonderful Counselor, Mighty God, Everlasting Father, Prince of Peace. (Isa. 9:2, 6)

Hymn of the day

51	From heaven above
47	Let all together praise our God
636	Before the marvel of this night

Hymns related to the readings

First Reading: Isaiah 9:2–7
Light shines: a child is born for us

8	The people who walked in darkness
39	Joy to the world
54	It came upon the midnight clear
636	Before the marvel of this night
641	Peace came to earth

Psalmody: Psalm 96
Let the heavens rejoice and the earth be glad. (Ps. 96:11)

Second Reading: Titus 2:11–14
The grace of God has appeared

45	Oh, come, all ye faithful
65	Silent night, holy night!

Gospel: Luke 2:1–14 [15–20]
God with us

41	O little town of Bethlehem
42	Of the Father's love begotten
44	Infant holy, infant lowly
46	Once again my heart rejoices
48	All praise to you, eternal Lord
51	From heaven above
52	Your little ones, dear Lord
58	Lo, how a rose is growing
63	From shepherding of stars
67	Away in a manger
68	He whom shepherds once came praising
71	Angels we have heard on high
72	'Twas in the moon of wintertime
74	A stable lamp is lighted
636	Before the marvel of this night
643	Once in royal David's city
644	Away in a manger

See Christmas Dawn

Additional hymns for the day/season

69	I am so glad each Christmas Eve
198	Let all mortal flesh keep silence
638	Holy child within the manger

See Christmas Dawn, Christmas Day

CHRISTMAS DAWN (II)
YEARS A,B,C

Prayer of the day

Almighty God, you have made yourself known in your Son, Jesus, redeemer of the world. We pray that his birth as a human child will set us free from the old slavery of our sin; through Jesus Christ our Lord, who lives and reigns with you and the Holy Spirit, one God, now and forever. (7)

Verse

Alleluia. The LORD said to me, You are my son; this day have I begotten you. Alleluia. (Ps. 2:7)

Offertory

The LORD said to me, You are my son; this day have I begotten you. Princely state has been yours from the day of your birth; in the beauty of holiness have I begotten you, like dew from the womb of the morning. (Ps. 2:7; Ps. 110:3)

Hymn of the day

70 Go tell it on the mountain
55 Good Christian friends, rejoice
643 Once in royal David's city

Hymns related to the readings

First Reading: Isaiah 62:6–12
God comes to restore the people

39 Joy to the world
70 Go tell it on the mountain

Psalmody: Psalm 97
Light has sprung up for the righteous. (Ps. 97:11)

Second Reading: Titus 3:4–7
Saved through water and the Spirit

60 Hark! The herald angels sing

Gospel: Luke 2:[1–7] 8–20
The birth of the Messiah revealed to shepherds

40 What child is this

43 Rejoice, rejoice this happy morn
44 Infant holy, infant lowly
45 Oh, come, all ye faithful
55 Good Christian friends, rejoice
56 The first Noel
59 When Christmas morn is dawning
64 From east to west
66 Come rejoicing, praises voicing
70 Go tell it on the mountain
See Christmas Eve

Additional hymns for the day/season

73 All hail to you, O blessed morn!
640 Gloria (Taizé)
641 Peace came to earth
645 There's a star in the East
637 Gloria, gloria, gloria
787 Glory to God, we give you thanks
788 Glory to God, glory in the highest
See Christmas Eve, Christmas Day

CHRISTMAS DAY (III)
YEARS A,B,C

Prayer of the day

Almighty God, you wonderfully created and yet more wonderfully restored the dignity of human nature. In your mercy, let us share the divine life of Jesus Christ who came to share our humanity, and who now lives and reigns with you and the Holy Spirit, one God, now and forever. (8)

Verse

Alleluia. When the fullness of time had come, God sent his Son. Alleluia. (Gal. 4:4)

Offertory

The LORD said to me, You are my son; this day have I begotten you. Ask of me, and I will give you the nations for your inheritance and the ends of the earth for your possession. (Ps. 2:7–8)

Hymn of the day

42 Of the Father's love begotten
60 Hark! The herald angels sing
638 Holy child within the manger

Hymns related to the readings

First Reading: Isaiah 52:7–10
Heralds announce God's salvation

55 Good Christian friends, rejoice
60 Hark! The herald angels sing
70 Go tell it on the mountain

Psalmody: Psalm 98
All the ends of the earth have seen the victory of our God. (Ps. 98:4)

39 Joy to the world (paraphrase)

Second Reading: Hebrews 1:1–4 [5–12]
God has spoken by a Son

42 Of the Father's love begotten

62 The bells of Christmas
66 Come rejoicing, praises voicing

Gospel: John 1:1–14
The Word became flesh

40 What child is this
42 Of the Father's love begotten
45 Oh, come, all ye faithful
47 Let all together praise our God
48 All praise to you, eternal Lord
49 O Savior of our fallen race
57 Let our gladness have no end
64 From east to west
641 Peace came to earth
716 Word of God, come down on earth

Additional hymns for the day/season

73 All hail to you, O blessed morn!
701 What feast of love
See Christmas Eve, Christmas Dawn

FIRST SUNDAY AFTER CHRISTMAS

Prayer of the day

Almighty God, you have made yourself known in your Son, Jesus, redeemer of the world. We pray that his birth as a human child will set us free from the old slavery of our sin; through Jesus Christ our Lord, who lives and reigns with you and the Holy Spirit, one God, now and forever. (7)

OR

Almighty God, you wonderfully created and yet more wonderfully restored the dignity of human nature. In your mercy, let us share the divine life of Jesus Christ who came to share our humanity, and who now lives and reigns with you and the Holy Spirit, one God, now and forever. (8)

Verse

Alleluia. Let the peace of Christ rule in your hearts. Alleluia. (Col. 3:15)

Offertory

In the beginning was the Word, and the Word was with God, and the Word was God. And the Word became flesh and lived among us, and we have seen his glory, the glory as of the Father's only Son, full of grace and truth. (John 1:1, 14)

YEAR A

Hymn of the day

47	Let all together praise our God
74	A stable lamp is lighted
639	Oh, sleep now, holy baby

Hymns related to the readings

First Reading: Isaiah 63:7–9
Israel saved by God's own presence

| 43 | Rejoice, rejoice this happy morn |
| 49 | O Savior of our fallen race |

Psalmody: Psalm 148
The splendor of the LORD is over earth and heaven. (Ps. 148:13)

| 540 | Praise the Lord! O heavens (paraphrase) |
| 541 | Praise the Lord of heaven! (paraphrase) |

Second Reading: Hebrews 2:10–18
Christ shares flesh and blood to free humankind

55	Good Christian friends, rejoice
60	Hark! The herald angels sing
88	Oh, love, how deep

Gospel: Matthew 2:13–23
The slaughter of innocent children

85	When Christ's appearing was made known
639	Oh, sleep now, holy baby
642	I wonder as I wander

Additional hymns for the day/season

40	What child is this
48	All praise to you, eternal Lord
52	Your little ones, dear Lord
53	Cold December flies away
54	It came upon the midnight clear
61	The hills are bare at Bethlehem
63	From shepherding of stars
72	'Twas in the moon of wintertime
643	Once in royal David's city

See Christmas Eve, Dawn, and Day

YEAR B

Hymn of the day

40   What child is this
62   The bells of Christmas
641 Peace came to earth

Hymns related to the readings

First Reading: Isaiah 61:10—62:3
Clothed in garments of salvation

53   Cold December flies away
61   The hills are bare at Bethlehem
203 Now we join in celebration

Psalmody: Psalm 148
The splendor of the LORD is over earth and heaven.
(Ps. 148:13)

540 Praise the Lord! O heavens (paraphrase)
541 Praise the Lord of heaven! (paraphrase)

Second Reading: Galatians 4:4–7
Children and heirs of God

47   Let all together praise our God
48   All praise to you, eternal Lord
52   Your little ones, dear Lord

Gospel: Luke 2:22–40
The presentation of the child

184 In his temple now behold him
259 Lord, dismiss us with your blessing
339 O Lord, now let your servant
349 I leave, as you have promised, Lord
357 Our Father, by whose name
417 In a lowly manger born

Additional hymns for the day/season

50   Angels from the realms of glory
55   Good Christian friends, rejoice
71   Angels we have heard on high
198 Let all mortal flesh keep silence
634 Sing of Mary, pure and lowly
642 I wonder as I wander
See Christmas Eve, Dawn, and Day

YEAR C

Hymn of the day

53   Cold December flies away
417 In a lowly manger born
638 Holy child within the manger

Hymns related to the readings

First Reading: 1 Samuel 2:18–20, 26
The boy Samuel grew in favor with the LORD and the people

Psalmody: Psalm 148
The splendor of the LORD is over earth and heaven.
(Ps. 148:13)

540 Praise the Lord! O heavens (paraphrase)
541 Praise the Lord of heaven! (paraphrase)

Second Reading: Colossians 3:12–17
Clothe yourselves in love; let the peace of Christ rule your hearts

203 Now we join in celebration
267 Father, we praise you
545, 546 When morning gilds the skies
553 Rejoice, O pilgrim throng!
790 Praise to you, O God of mercy

Gospel: Luke 2:41–52
The boy Jesus increased in wisdom, and in divine and human favor

357 Our Father, by whose name
417 In a lowly manger born
634 Sing of Mary, pure and lowly

Additional hymns for the day/season

47   Let all together praise our God
48   All praise to you, eternal Lord
52   Your little ones, dear Lord
55   Good Christian friends, rejoice
642 I wonder as I wander
See Christmas Eve, Dawn, and Day

Prayer of the day

Almighty God, you have filled us with the new light of the Word who became flesh and lived among us. Let the light of our faith shine in all that we do; through your Son, Jesus Christ our Lord, who lives and reigns with you and the Holy Spirit, one God, now and forever. (9)

Verse

Alleluia. All the ends of the earth have seen the victory of our God. Alleluia. (Ps. 98:4)

Offertory

God is light, and in him there is no darkness at all. If we walk in the light as he is in the light, we have fellowship with one another, and the blood of Jesus cleanses us from all sin. (1 John 1:5, 7)

YEARS A, B, C

Hymn of the day

57	Let our gladness have no end
64	From east to west
641	Peace came to earth

Hymns related to the readings

First Reading: Jeremiah 31:7–14
Joy at the gathering of God's scattered flock

14	Listen! You nations
39	Joy to the world
242	Let the whole creation cry
638	Holy Child within the manger

OR

First Reading: Sirach 24:1–12
Wisdom lives among God's people

64	From east to west

Psalmody: Psalm 147:13–21*
Worship the LORD, O Jerusalem; praise your God, O Zion. (Ps. 147:13)

OR

Psalmody: Wisdom of Solomon 10:15–21
We sing, O Lord, to your holy name; we praise with one accord your defending hand. (Wis. of Sol. 10:20)

Second Reading: Ephesians 1:3–14
The will of God made known in Christ

48	All praise to you, eternal Lord

76	O Morning Star, how fair and bright!
693	Baptized in water

Gospel: John 1:[1–9] 10–18
God with us: the incarnation of the Word

40	What child is this
42	Of the Father's love begotten
45	Oh, come, all ye faithful
49	O Savior of our fallen race
57	Let our gladness have no end
77	O one with God the Father
271	O Splendor of the Father's light
716	Word of God, come down on earth

Additional hymns for the day/season

47	Let all together praise our God
50	Angels, from the realms of glory
55	Good Christian friends, rejoice
56	The first Noel
73	All hail to you, O blessed morn!
198	Let all mortal flesh keep silence
641	Peace came to earth
642	I wonder as I wander
701	What feast of love

*Psalm 147:12–20 (NRSV)

THE EPIPHANY OF OUR LORD

Prayer of the day

Lord God, on this day you revealed your Son to the nations by the leading of a star. Lead us now by faith to know your presence in our lives, and bring us at last to the full vision of your glory, through your Son, Jesus Christ our Lord, who lives and reigns with you and the Holy Spirit, one God, now and forever. (10)

Verse

Alleluia. We observed his star in the East, and have come to pay him homage. Alleluia. (Matt. 2:2)

Offertory

Arise, shine; for your light has come, and the glory of the LORD has risen upon you. They shall bring gold and frankincense, and shall proclaim the praise of the LORD. We observed his star in the East, and have come to pay him homage. (Isa. 60:1, 6; Matt. 2:2)

YEARS A, B, C

Hymn of the day

76   O Morning Star, how fair and bright!
84   Brightest and best of the stars of the morning
649   I want to walk as a child of the light

Hymns related to the readings

First Reading: Isaiah 60:1–6
Nations come to the light

77   O one with God the Father
274   The day you gave us, Lord, has ended
518   Beautiful Savior
652   Arise, your light has come!

Psalmody: Psalm 72:1–7, 10–14
All kings shall bow down before him. (Ps. 72:11)

87   Hail to the Lord's anointed (paraphrase)
530   Jesus shall reign (paraphrase)

Second Reading: Ephesians 3:1–12
The gospel's promise extends to all

237   O God of light
516   Arise, my soul, arise!

Gospel: Matthew 2:1–12
Revelation of Christ to the nations of the earth

40   What child is this
50   Angels, from the realms of glory
56   The first Noel
75   Bright and glorious is the sky
81   O chief of cities, Bethlehem
82   As with gladness men of old

84   Brightest and best of the stars of the morning
85   When Christ's appearing was made known
646   We three kings of Orient are

Additional hymns for the day/season

86   The only Son from heaven
271   O Splendor of the Father's light

THE BAPTISM OF OUR LORD

Prayer of the day

Father in heaven, at the baptism of Jesus in the River Jordan you proclaimed him your beloved Son and anointed him with the Holy Spirit. Make all who are baptized into Christ faithful in their calling to be your children and inheritors with him of everlasting life; through your Son, Jesus Christ our Lord, who lives and reigns with you and the Holy Spirit, one God, now and forever. (11)

Verse

Alleluia. You are my Son, the Beloved; with you I am well pleased. Alleluia. (Mark 1:11)

Offertory

Ascribe to the LORD the glory due his name: worship the LORD in the beauty of holiness. The voice of the LORD is upon the waters; the God of glory thunders. The voice of the LORD is a powerful voice; the voice of the LORD is a voice of splendor. (Ps. 29:2–4)

YEAR A

Hymn of the day

188	I bind unto myself today
76	O Morning Star, how fair and bright!
647	When Jesus came to Jordan

Hymns related to the readings

First Reading: Isaiah 42:1–9
The servant of the LORD brings justice

87	Hail to the Lord's anointed
400	God, whose almighty word
530	Jesus shall reign

Psalmody: Psalm 29
The voice of the LORD is upon the waters. (Ps. 29:3)

Second Reading: Acts 10:34–43
Jesus' ministry after his baptism

140	With high delight let us unite
696	I've just come from the fountain
723	The Spirit sends us forth to serve

Gospel: Matthew 3:13–17
Revelation of Christ as God's servant

79	To Jordan came the Christ, our Lord
85	When Christ's appearing was made known
88	Oh, love, how deep
90	Songs of thankfulness and praise
188	I bind unto myself today
647	When Jesus came to Jordan

Additional hymns for the day/season

77	O one with God the Father
83	From God the Father, virgin-born
189	We know that Christ is raised
192	Baptized into your name most holy
194	All who believe and are baptized
195	This is the Spirit's entry now
373	Eternal Ruler of the ceaseless round
376	Your kingdom come!
486	Spirit of God, descend upon my heart
557	Let all things now living
652	Arise, your light has come!
693	Baptized in water
698	We were baptized in Christ Jesus
721	Go, my children, with my blessing
741	Thy holy wings

YEAR B

Hymn of the day

647   When Jesus came to Jordan
83   From God the Father, virgin-born
88   Oh, love, how deep

Hymns related to the readings

First Reading: Genesis 1:1–5
God creates light

233   Thy strong Word
271   O Splendor of the Father's light
400   God, whose almighty word
523   Holy Spirit, ever dwelling
557   Let all things now living
726   Oh, sing to God above
757   Creating God, your fingers trace
794   Many and great, O God, are your works
799   When long before time

Psalmody: Psalm 29
The voice of the LORD is upon the waters. (Ps. 29:3)

Second Reading: Acts 19:1–7
Baptized in the name of the Lord Jesus

192   Baptized into your name most holy
683   Loving Spirit

693   Baptized in water

Gospel: Mark 1:4–11
Revelation of Christ as God's servant

79   To Jordan came the Christ, our Lord
85   When Christ's appearing was made known
88   Oh, love, how deep
90   Songs of thankfulness and praise
188   I bind unto myself today
647   When Jesus came to Jordan

Additional hymns for the day/season

76   O Morning Star, how fair and bright!
See Year A

YEAR C

Hymn of the day

85   When Christ's appearing was made known
79   To Jordan came the Christ, our Lord
647   When Jesus came to Jordan

Hymns related to the readings

First Reading: Isaiah 43:1–7
*When you pass through the waters, do not fear, for
I am with you*

359   In Christ there is no east or west
463   God, who stretched the spangled heavens
507   How firm a foundation
550   From all that dwell below the skies

Psalmody: Psalm 29
The voice of the LORD is upon the waters. (Ps. 29:3)

Second Reading: Acts 8:14–17
Prayer and laying on of hands for the Holy Spirit

693   Baptized in water
697   Wash, O God, our sons and daughters

Gospel: Luke 3:15–17, 21–22
The baptism of Jesus with the descent of the Holy Spirit

79   To Jordan came the Christ, our Lord
85   When Christ's appearing was made known
88   Oh, love, how deep
90   Songs of thankfulness and praise
188   I bind unto myself today
647   When Jesus came to Jordan

Additional hymns for the day/season

76   O Morning Star, how fair and bright!
See Year A

Prayer of the day

Lord God, you showed your glory and led many to faith by the works of your Son. As he brought gladness and healing to his people, grant us these same gifts and lead us also to perfect faith in him, Jesus Christ our Lord. (12)

Verse

Alleluia. The LORD said to me: You are my servant in whom I will be glorified. Alleluia. (Isa. 49:3)

Offertory

Jesus revealed his glory, and his disciples believed in him. Everyone serves the good wine first, but you have kept the good wine until now. (John 2:11, 10)

YEAR A

Hymn of the day

87	Hail to the Lord's anointed
86	The only Son from heaven
648	Jesus, come! for we invite you

Hymns related to the readings

First Reading: Isaiah 49:1–7
The servant brings light to the nations

14	Listen! you nations
376	Your kingdom come!
432	We worship you, O God of might

Psalmody: Psalm 40:1–12*
I love to do your will, O my God. (Ps. 40:9)

Second Reading: 1 Corinthians 1:1–9
Paul's greeting to the church at Corinth

263	Abide with us, our Savior
364	Son of God, eternal Savior

Gospel: John 1:29–42
Revelation of Christ as the Lamb of God

103	O Christ, thou Lamb of God
354	Eternal God, before your throne
494	Jesus calls us; o'er the tumult
536	O God of God, O Light of light

Additional hymns for the day/season

76	O Morning Star, how fair and bright!
77	O one with God the Father
205	Now the silence
237	O God of light
248	Dearest Jesus, at your word
265	Christ, whose glory fills the skies
393	Rise, shine, you people!
650	We are marching in the light of God
652	Arise, your light has come!
752	I, the Lord of sea and sky
768	He comes to us as one unknown

Year B

Hymn of the day

434 The Son of God, our Christ
503 O Jesus, I have promised
752 I, the Lord of sea and sky

Hymns related to the readings

First Reading: 1 Samuel 3:1–10 [11–20]
The calling of Samuel

403 Lord, speak to us, that we may speak
503 O Jesus, I have promised
752 I, the Lord of sea and sky
768 He comes to us as one unknown

Psalmody: Psalm 139:1–5, 12–17**
You have searched me out and known me. (Ps. 139:1)

311 Wondrous are your ways, O God (paraphrase)

Second Reading: 1 Corinthians 6:12–20
Glorify God in your body

164 Creator Spirit, by whose aid

Gospel: John 1:43–51
The calling of the first disciples

178 By all your saints in warfare (stanza 17)
283 O God, send heralds
434 The Son of God, our Christ
494 Jesus calls us; o'er the tumult
506 Dear Lord and Father of mankind
782 All my hope on God is founded

Additional hymns for the day/season
See Year A

Year C

Hymn of the day

648 Jesus, come! for we invite you
78 All praise to you, O Lord
224 Soul, adorn yourself with gladness

Hymns related to the readings

First Reading: Isaiah 62:1–5
As bridegroom and bride rejoice, so shall God rejoice over you

16 I will sing the story of your love
31 Wake, awake, for night is flying
76 O Morning Star, how fair and bright!
224 Soul, adorn yourself with gladness
529 Praise God. Praise him

Psalmody: Psalm 36:5–10
We feast on the abundance of your house, O LORD. (Ps. 36:8)

Second Reading: 1 Corinthians 12:1–11
There are a variety of gifts but the same Spirit

381 Hark, the voice of Jesus calling
737 There is a balm in Gilead
755 We all are one in mission

Gospel: John 2:1–11
The wedding at Cana

76 O Morning Star, how fair and bright!
78 All praise to you, O Lord
90 Songs of thankfulness and praise
205 Now the silence
748 Bind us together
751 As man and woman we were made

Additional hymns for the day/season

85 When Christ's appearing was made known
211 Here, O my Lord, I see thee
513 Come, my way, my truth, my life
516 Arise, my soul, arise!
701 What feast of love
789 Now the feast and celebration

*Psalm 40:1–11 (NRSV)
**Psalm 139:1–6, 13–18 (NRSV)

Prayer of the day

Almighty God, you sent your Son to proclaim your kingdom and to teach with authority. Anoint us with the power of your Spirit, that we, too, may bring good news to the afflicted, bind up the brokenhearted, and proclaim liberty to the captive; through your Son, Jesus Christ our Lord. (13)

Verse

Alleluia. Jesus went throughout Galilee, teaching, proclaiming the good news, and curing every disease. Alleluia. (Matt. 4:23)

Offertory

I sought the LORD, and he answered me and delivered me out of all my terror. Look upon him and be radiant, and let not your faces be ashamed. I called in my affliction, and the LORD heard me and saved me from all my troubles. (Ps. 34:4–6)

YEAR A

Hymn of the day

233 Thy strong Word
562 Lift every voice and sing
784 You have come down to the lakeshore

Hymns related to the readings

First Reading: Isaiah 9:1–4
Light shines for those in darkness

8 The people who walked in darkness
77 O one with God the Father
651 Shine, Jesus, shine
652 Arise, your light has come!

Psalmody: Psalm 27:1, 5–13*
The LORD is my light and my salvation. (Ps. 27:1)

Second Reading: 1 Corinthians 1:10–18
Appeal for unity in the gospel

126 Where charity and love prevail
369 The Church's one foundation
373 Eternal Ruler of the ceaseless round
523 Holy Spirit, ever dwelling
710 One bread, one body
755 We all are one in mission

Gospel: Matthew 4:12–23
Revelation of Christ as a prophet

434 The Son of God, our Christ
449 They cast their nets
455 "Come, follow me," the Savior spake

492 O Master, let me walk with you
494 Jesus calls us; o'er the tumult
506 Dear Lord and Father of mankind
649 I want to walk as a child of the light
712 Listen, God is calling
754 Let us talents and tongues employ
784 You have come down to the lakeshore

Additional hymns for the day/season

76 O Morning Star, how fair and bright!
83 From God the Father, virgin-born
205 Now the silence
237 O God of light
248 Dearest Jesus, at your word
252 You servants of God
265 Christ, whose glory fills the skies
393 Rise, shine, you people!
397 O Zion, haste
400 God, whose almighty word
503 O Jesus, I have promised
650 We are marching in the light of God
752 I, the Lord of sea and sky
761 Now we offer
800 Each morning brings us

Year B

Hymn of the day

784 You have come down to the lakeshore
380 O Christ, our light, O Radiance true
449 They cast their nets

Hymns related to the readings

First Reading: Jonah 3:1–5, 10
Repentance at Ninevah

380 O Christ, our light, O Radiance true
508 Come down, O Love divine

Psalmody: Psalm 62:6–14**
In God is my safety and my honor. (Ps. 62:8)

Second Reading: 1 Corinthians 7:29–31
Living in the end times

244 Lord our God, with praise we come
318 The Lord will come and not be slow

Gospel: Mark 1:14–20
The calling of the disciples at the sea

434 The Son of God, our Christ
449 They cast their nets
455 "Come, follow me," the Savior spake
494 Jesus calls us; o'er the tumult
503 O Jesus, I have promised
506 Dear Lord and Father of mankind
649 I want to walk as a child of the light
712 Listen, God is calling
754 Let us talents and tongues employ
784 You have come down to the lakeshore

Additional hymns for the day/season
See Year A

Year C

Hymn of the day

35   Hark, the glad sound!
87   Hail to the Lord's anointed
755 We all are one in mission

Hymns related to the readings

First Reading: Nehemiah 8:1–3, 5–6, 8–10
Ezra reads the law of Moses before the people

240 Father of mercies, in your Word
715 Open your ears, O faithful people

Psalmody: Psalm 19
The law of the LORD revives the soul.(Ps. 19:7)

Second Reading: 1 Corinthians 12:12–31a
You are the body of Christ

189 We know that Christ is raised
369 The Church's one foundation
381 Hark, the voice of Jesus calling
708 Grains of wheat
710 One bread, one body

Gospel: Luke 4:14–21
Jesus reads from the scroll of the prophet Isaiah

35   Hark, the glad sound!
230 O Word of God incarnate
396 O God, O Lord of heaven and earth
716 Word of God, come down on earth

Additional hymns for the day/season

87   Hail to the Lord's anointed
119 Nature with open volume stands
205 Now the silence
239 God's Word is our great heritage
397 O Zion, haste
410 We give thee but thine own
530 Jesus shall reign
559 Oh, for a thousand tongues to sing
680 O Spirit of life
723 The Spirit sends us forth to serve

*Psalm 27:1, 4–9 (NRSV)
**Psalm 62:5–12 (NRSV)

Fourth Sunday after the Epiphany

Prayer of the day

O God, you know that we cannot withstand the dangers which surround us. Strengthen us in body and spirit so that, with your help, we may be able to overcome the weakness that our sin has brought upon us; through Jesus Christ, your Son our Lord. (14)

Verse

Alleluia. The Spirit of the Lord is upon me, because he has anointed me to bring good news to the poor. Alleluia. (Luke 4:18)

Offertory

Make your face to shine upon your servant; and in your lovingkindness save me. How great is your goodness, O Lord, which you have laid up for those who fear you; which you have done in the sight of all for those who put their trust in you. (Ps. 31:16, 19)

Year A

Hymn of the day

429   Where cross the crowded ways of life
425   O God of mercy, God of light
764   Blest are they

Hymns related to the readings

First Reading: Micah 6:1–8
The offering of justice, kindness, humility

203   Now we join in celebration
423   Lord, whose love in humble service

Psalmody: Psalm 15
Lord, who may abide upon your holy hill? (Ps. 15:1)

Second Reading: 1 Corinthians 1:18–31
Christ crucified, the wisdom and power of God

104   In the cross of Christ I glory
119   Nature with open volume stands
464   You are the way
482   When I survey the wondrous cross
782   All my hope on God is founded

Gospel: Matthew 5:1–12
The teaching of Christ: Beatitudes

17   How blest are those who know their need of God
316   Jesus, the very thought of you
689   Rejoice in God's saints
764   Blest are they

Additional hymns for the day/season

90   Songs of thankfulness and praise
248   Dearest Jesus, at your word
270   God of our life, all-glorious Lord
415   God of grace and God of glory
493   Hope of the world
537   O Jesus, king most wonderful!
723   The Spirit sends us forth to serve
750   Oh, praise the gracious power
763   Let justice flow like streams
776   Be thou my vision
790   Praise to you, O God of mercy

YEAR B

Hymn of the day
90   Songs of thankfulness and praise
393 Rise, shine, you people!
737 There is a balm in Gilead

Hymns related to the readings

First Reading: Deuteronomy 18:15–20
The prophet speaks with God's authority

237 O God of light
238 God has spoken by his prophets
715 Open your ears, O faithful people

Psalmody: Psalm 111
The fear of the LORD is the beginning of wisdom.
(Ps. 111:10)

Second Reading: 1 Corinthians 8:1–13
Limits to liberty: the case of food offered to idols

504 O God, my faithful God
542 Sing praise to God, the highest good

Gospel: Mark 1:21–28
The healing of one with an unclean spirit

360 O Christ, the healer, we have come
393 Rise, shine, you people!
716 Word of God, come down on earth
738 Healer of our every ill

Additional hymns for the day/season
86   The only Son from heaven
87   Hail to the Lord's anointed
242 Let the whole creation cry
299 Dear Christians, one and all
364 Son of God, eternal Savior
400 God, whose almighty word
431 Your hand, O Lord, in days of old
493 Hope of the world
550 From all that dwell below the skies
559 Oh, for a thousand tongues to sing

YEAR C

Hymn of the day
237 O God of light
397 O Zion, haste
768 He comes to us as one unknown

Hymns related to the readings

First Reading: Jeremiah 1:4–10
I appointed you a prophet to the nations

406 Take my life, that I may be
510 O God of youth
460 I am trusting you, Lord Jesus

Psalmody: Psalm 71:1–6
From my mother's womb you have been my strength.
(Ps. 71:6)

Second Reading: 1 Corinthians 13:1–13
If I speak without love, I am a noisy gong

126 Where charity and love prevail
336 Jesus, thy boundless love to me
508 Come down, O Love divine
551 Joyful, joyful we adore thee
665 Ubi caritas et amor
721 Go, my children, with my blessing

Gospel: Luke 4:21–30
Jesus says a prophet is not accepted in his hometown

237 O God of light
402 Look from your sphere of endless day

Additional hymns for the day/season
90   Songs of thankfulness and praise
248 Dearest Jesus, at your word
379 Spread, oh, spread, almighty Word
403 Lord, speak to us that we may speak
415 God of grace and God of glory
493 Hope of the world
550 From all that dwell below the skies

Prayer of the day

Almighty God, you sent your only Son as the Word of life for our eyes to see and our ears to hear. Help us to believe with joy what the Scriptures proclaim, through Jesus Christ our Lord. (15)

Verse

Alleluia. Jesus said: I am the light of the world. Whoever follows me will never walk in darkness but will have the light of life. Alleluia. (John 8:12)

Offertory

Blessed are the poor in spirit, for theirs is the kingdom of heaven. Blessed are the meek, for they will inherit the earth. Blessed are those who hunger and thirst for righteousness, for they will be filled. (Matt. 5:3, 5–6)

YEAR A

Hymn of the day

393 Rise, shine, you people!
237 O God of light
753 You are the seed

Hymns related to the readings

First Reading: Isaiah 58:1–9a [9b–12]
The fast God chooses

383 Rise up, O saints of God!
393 Rise, shine, you people!
405 Lord of light
420 Lord, save your world
423 Lord, whose love in humble service
433 The Church of Christ, in every age
716 Word of God, come down on earth
763 Let justice flow like streams

Psalmody: Psalm 112:1–9 [10]
Light shines in the darkness for the upright. (Ps. 112:4)

Second Reading: 1 Corinthians 2:1–12 [13–16]
God's wisdom revealed through the Spirit

464 You are the way
524 My God, how wonderful thou art

Gospel: Matthew 5:13–20
The teaching of Christ: salt and light

405 Lord of light
718 Here in this place
753 You are the seed

Additional hymns for the day/season

87   Hail to the Lord's anointed
232 Your Word, O Lord, is gentle dew
233 Thy strong Word
265 Christ, whose glory fills the skies
400 God, whose almighty word
505 Forth in thy name, O Lord, I go
523 Holy Spirit, ever dwelling
649 I want to walk as a child of the light
650 We are marching in the light of God

Year B

Hymn of the day
543   Praise to the Lord, the Almighty
493   Hope of the world
779   You who dwell in the shelter of the Lord

Hymns related to the readings

First Reading: Isaiah 40:21–31
The creator of all cares for the powerless

519   My soul, now praise your maker!
548   Oh, worship the King
652   Arise, your light has come!
757   Creating God, your fingers trace

Psalmody: Psalm 147:1–12, 21c*
The LORD heals the brokenhearted. (Ps. 147:3)

Second Reading: 1 Corinthians 9:16–23
A servant for the sake of the gospel

390   I love to tell the story
393   Rise, shine, you people!
765   Jesu, Jesu, fill us with your love

Gospel: Mark 1:29–39
The healing of Peter's mother–in–law

360   O Christ, the healer, we have come
393   Rise, shine, you people!
400   God, whose almighty word
431   Your hand, O Lord, in days of old
506   Dear Lord and Father of mankind
666   Great God, your love has called us

Additional hymns for the day/season
232   Your Word, O Lord, is gentle dew
265   Christ, whose glory fills the skies
435   O God, whose will is life and good
484   God, my Lord, my strength
559   Oh, for a thousand tongues to sing
738   Healer of our every ill

Year C

Hymn of the day
752   I, the Lord of sea and sky
403   Lord, speak to us, that we may speak
432   We worship you, O God of might

Hymns related to the readings

First Reading: Isaiah 6:1–8 [9–13]
Isaiah says, Here am I; send me

198   Let all mortal flesh keep silence
381   Hark, the voice of Jesus calling
432   We worship you, O God of might
528   Isaiah in a vision did of old
535   Holy God, we praise your name
631   Lift up your heads, O gates
752   I, the Lord of sea and sky
773   Send me, Jesus

Psalmody: Psalm 138
I will bow down toward your holy temple. (Ps. 138:2)

Second Reading: 1 Corinthians 15:1–11
I am the least of the apostles

140   With high delight let us unite
448   Amazing grace, how sweet the sound
800   Each morning brings us fresh outpoured

Gospel: Luke 5:1–11
Jesus calls the disciples to fish for people

434   The Son of God, our Christ
494   Jesus calls us; o'er the tumult
506   Dear Lord and Father of mankind
784   You have come down to the lakeshore

Additional hymns for the day/season
87   Hail to the Lord's anointed
214   Come, let us eat
242   Let the whole creation cry
247   Holy Majesty, before you
253   Lord Jesus Christ, be present now
265   Christ, whose glory fills the skies
397   O Zion, haste
449   They cast their nets
503   O Jesus, I have promised
723   The Spirit sends us forth to serve

*Psalm 147:1–11, 20c (NRSV)

Sixth Sunday after the Epiphany

Proper 1

Prayer of the day
Lord God, mercifully receive the prayers of your people. Help us to see and understand the things we ought to do, and give us grace and power to do them; through your Son, Jesus Christ our Lord. (16)

Verse
Alleluia. Lord, to whom shall we go? You have the words of eternal life. Alleluia. (John 6:68)

Offertory
Behold, God is my helper; it is the LORD who sustains my life. I will offer you a freewill sacrifice and praise your name, O LORD, for it is good. For you have rescued me from every trouble. (Ps. 54:4, 6–7)

Year A

Hymn of the day
300   O Christ, our hope
480   Oh, that the Lord would guide my ways
738   Healer of our every ill

Hymns related to the readings

First Reading: Deuteronomy 30:15–20
Choose life

270   God of our life, all-glorious Lord
353   May we your precepts, Lord, fulfill
475   Come, gracious Spirit, heavenly dove

OR

First Reading: Sirach 15:15–20
Choose between life and death

270   God of our life, all-glorious Lord
353   May we your precepts, Lord, fulfill
475   Come, gracious Spirit, heavenly dove

Psalmody: Psalm 119:1–8
Happy are they who walk in the law of the LORD. (Ps. 119:1)

Second Reading: 1 Corinthians 3:1–9
God gives the growth

227   How blest are they who hear God's Word
523   Holy Spirit, ever dwelling
658   The Word of God is source and seed
685   Like the murmur of the dove's song

Gospel: Matthew 5:21–37
The teaching of Christ: forgiveness

126   Where charity and love prevail
196   Praise the Lord, rise up rejoicing
268   Now that the daylight fills the sky
307   Forgive our sins as we forgive
735   God! When human bonds are broken
739   In all our grief

Additional hymns for the day/season
373   Eternal Ruler of the ceaseless round
386   Christ is the king!
441   Eternal Spirit of the living Christ
487   Let us ever walk with Jesus
504   O God, my faithful God
508   Come down, O Love divine
524   My God, how wonderful thou art
527   All creatures of our God and King
551   Joyful, joyful we adore thee
745   Awake, O sleeper
746   Day by day

Year B

Hymn of the day
360   O Christ the healer, we have come
90   Songs of thankfulness and praise
737   There is a balm in Gilead

Hymns related to the readings

First Reading: 2 Kings 5:1–14
Naaman is healed of leprosy

431   Your hand, O Lord, in days of old
435   O God, whose will is life and good

Psalmody: Psalm 30
My God, I cried out to you, and you restored me to health. (Ps. 30:2)

Second Reading: 1 Corinthians 9:24–27
Run the race for an imperishable prize

308   God the Father, be our stay
461   Fight the good fight
502   Thee will I love, my strength

Gospel: Mark 1:40–45
The healing of one with leprosy

90   Songs of thankfulness and praise
360   O Christ, the healer, we have come
431   Your hand, O Lord, in days of old
435   O God, whose will is life and good

Additional hymns for the day/season
83   From God the Father, virgin-born
86   The only Son from heaven
300   O Christ, our hope
309   Lord Jesus, think on me
400   God, whose almighty word
441   Eternal Spirit of the living Christ
480   Oh, that the Lord would guide my ways
559   Oh, for a thousand tongues to sing
738   Healer of our every ill

Year C

Hymn of the day
562   Lift every voice and sing
232   Your Word, O Lord, is gentle dew
764   Blest are they

Hymns related to the readings

First Reading: Jeremiah 17:5–10
Blessed are those who trust the LORD, they are like trees by water

232   Your Word, O Lord, is gentle dew
250   Open now thy gates of beauty
378   Amid the world's bleak wilderness

Psalmody: Psalm 1
They are like trees planted by streams of water. (Ps. 1:3)

Second Reading: 1 Corinthians 15:12–20
Christ has been raised, the first fruits of those who have died

140   With high delight let us unite
172   Lord, enthroned in heavenly splendor
671   Alleluia, alleluia, give thanks

Gospel: Luke 6:17–26
Jesus speaks blessings on the poor and hungry; woes on the rich and full

17   How blest are those who know their need of God
316   Jesus, the very thought of you
689   Rejoice in God's saints
764   Blest are they

Additional hymns for the day/season
221   Sent forth by God's blessing
415   God of grace and God of glory
441   Eternal Spirit of the living Christ
539   Praise the Almighty
668   There in God's garden
750   Oh, praise the gracious power
763   Let justice flow like streams
790   Praise to you, O God of mercy

Seventh Sunday after Epiphany

Proper 2

Prayer of the day

God of compassion, keep before us the love you have revealed in your Son, who prayed even for his enemies; in our words and deeds help us to be like him through whom we pray, Jesus Christ our Lord. (18)

OR

(Year B) Lord God, we ask you to keep your family, the Church, always faithful to you, that all who lean on the hope of your promises may gain strength from the power of your love; through your Son, Jesus Christ our Lord. (17)

Verse

Alleluia. Sanctify us in the truth; your word is truth. Alleluia. (John 17:17)

Offertory

I appeal to you, therefore, by the mercies of God, to present your bodies as a living sacrifice, holy and acceptable to God, which is your spiritual worship. (Rom. 12:1)

Year A

Hymn of the day

433 The Church of Christ, in every age
356 O Jesus, joy of loving hearts
762 O day of peace

Hymns related to the readings

First Reading: Leviticus 19:1–2, 9–18
Holiness revealed in acts of mercy and justice

404 As saints of old
422 O God, empower us to stem
441 Eternal Spirit of the living Christ

Psalmody: Psalm 119:33–40
Teach me, O Lord, the way of your statutes. (Ps. 119:33)

Second Reading: 1 Corinthians 3:10–11, 16–23
Allegiance to Christ, not human leaders

164 Creator Spirit, by whose aid
367 Christ is made the sure foundation
369 The Church's one foundation
459 O Holy Spirit, enter in
747 Christ is made the sure foundation
750 Oh, praise the gracious power
782 All my hope on God is founded

Gospel: Matthew 5:38–48
The teaching of Christ: love

307 Forgive our sins as we forgive
419 Lord of all nations, grant me grace
422 O God, empower us to stem
424 Lord of glory, you have bought us
441 Eternal Spirit of the living Christ
666 Great God, your love has called us
765 Jesu, Jesu, fill us with your love

Additional hymns for the day/season

88   Oh, love, how deep
271 O Splendor of the Father's light
396 O God, O Lord of heaven and earth
421 Lord Christ, when first you came to earth
423 Lord, whose love in humble service
551 Joyful, joyful we adore thee
745 Awake, O sleeper
757 Creating God, your fingers trace

Year B

Hymn of the day
549   Praise, my soul, the King of heaven
519   My soul, now praise your maker!
737   There is a balm in Gilead

Hymns related to the readings

First Reading: Isaiah 43:18–25
Like rivers in the desert, God makes new

384   Your kingdom come, O Father
635   Surely it is God who saves me
727   Lord, your hands have formed

Psalmody: Psalm 41
Heal me, for I have sinned against you. (Ps. 41:4)

Second Reading: 2 Corinthians 1:18–22
Every promise of God is a "Yes"

540   Praise the Lord! O heavens
693   Baptized in water

Gospel: Mark 2:1–12
The healing of a paralyzed man

90   Songs of thankfulness and praise
290   There's a wideness in God's mercy
360   O Christ, the healer, we have come
434   The Son of God, our Christ
519   My soul, now praise your maker!
549   Praise, my soul, the king of heaven

Additional hymns for the day/season
88   Oh, love, how deep
305   I lay my sins on Jesus
393   Rise, shine, you people!
396   O God, O Lord of heaven and earth
400   God, whose almighty word
402   Look from your sphere of endless day
504   O God, my faithful God
721   Go, my children, with my blessing
781   My life flows on in endless song

Year C

Hymn of the day
307   Forgive our sins as we forgive
422   O God, empower us
739   In all our grief

Hymns related to the readings
First Reading: Genesis 45:3–11, 15
Joseph forgives his brothers

126   Where charity and love prevail
307   Forgive our sins as we forgive

Psalmody: Psalm 37:1–12, 41–42*
The lowly shall possess the land; they will delight in abundance of peace. (Ps. 37:12)

Second Reading: 1 Corinthians 15:35–38, 42–50
The mystery of the resurrection of the body

372   In Adam we have all been one
470   Praise and thanks and adoration
769   Mothering God, you gave me birth

Gospel: Luke 6:27–38
Love your enemies

126   Where charity and love prevail
307   Forgive our sins as we forgive
419   Lord of all nations, grant me grace
422   O God, empower us
424   Lord of glory, you have bought us
442   O thou, who hast of thy pure grace
735   God! When human bonds are broken
765   Jesu, Jesu, fill us with your love

Additional hymns for the day/season
88   Oh, love, how deep
268   Now that the daylight fills the sky
271   O Splendor of the Father's light
309   Lord Jesus, think on me
396   O God, O Lord of heaven and earth
423   Lord, whose love in humble service
527   All creatures of our God and King
716   Word of God, come down on earth

*Psalm 37:1–11, 39–40 (NRSV)

PROPER 3

Prayer of the day

Almighty and everlasting God, ruler of heaven and earth: Hear our prayer and give us your peace now and forever; through your Son, Jesus Christ our Lord. (19)

Verse

Alleluia. The steadfast love of the LORD never ceases; his mercies never come to an end. Alleluia. (Lam. 3:22)

Offertory

I put my trust in your mercy; my heart is joyful because of your saving help. I will sing to you, O LORD, for you have dealt with me richly. (Ps. 13:5–6)

YEAR A

Hymn of the day

542   Sing praise to God, the highest good
714   The thirsty fields drink in the rain
783   Seek ye first the kingdom of God

Hymns related to the readings

First Reading: Isaiah 49:8–16a
God's motherly compassion for the people

313   A multitude comes from the east and the west
519   My soul, now praise your maker!
524   My God, how wonderful thou art
714   The thirsty fields drink in the rain
800   Each morning brings us

Psalmody: Psalm 131
Like a child upon its mother's breast, my soul is quieted within me. (Ps. 131:3)

Second Reading: 1 Corinthians 4:1–5
Servants accountable to God for their stewardship

283   O God, send heralds
405   Lord of light

Gospel: Matthew 6:24–34
The teaching of Christ: trust in God

474   Children of the heavenly Father
783   Seek ye first the kingdom of God
790   Praise to you, O God of mercy

Additional hymns for the day/season

447   All depends on our possessing
453   If you but trust in God to guide you
457, 458 Jesus, priceless treasure
469   Lord of all hopefulness
477   O God of Jacob
543   Praise to the Lord, the Almighty
552   In thee is gladness
769   Mothering God, you gave me birth

Year B

Hymn of the day
542 Sing praise to God, the highest good
298 One there is, above all others
790 Praise to you, O God of mercy

Hymns related to the readings

First Reading: Hosea 2:14–20
The covenant renewed by God's persistent love

369 The Church's one foundation
762 O day of peace

Psalmody: Psalm 103:1–13, 22
The Lord is full of compassion and mercy. (Ps. 103:8)

519 My soul, now praise your maker! (paraphrase)
543 Praise to the Lord, the Almighty (paraphrase)
549 Praise, my soul, the King of heaven (paraphrase)
798 Bless the Lord, O my soul (Ps. 103:1)

Second Reading: 2 Corinthians 3:1–6
Equipped as ministers of God's new covenant

680 O Spirit of life

Gospel: Mark 2:13–22
Eating and drinking with tax collectors and prostitutes

290 There's a wideness in God's mercy
291 Jesus sinners will receive
360 O Christ, the healer, we have come
434 The Son of God, our Christ

Additional hymns for the day/season
297 Salvation unto us has come
375 Only-begotten, Word of God eternal
465 Evening and morning
478 Come, oh, come, O quickening Spirit

Year C

Hymn of the day
542 Sing praise to God, the highest good
293, 294 My hope is built on nothing less
781 My life flows on in endless song

Hymns related to the readings

First Reading: Isaiah 55:10–13
The word goes forth from the mouth of God

530 Jesus shall reign
695 O blessed spring
714 The thirsty fields drink in the rain

OR

First Reading: Sirach 27:4–7
Wisdom rules both heaven and earth

403 Lord, speak to us, that we may speak

Psalmody: Psalm 92:1–4, 11–14*
The righteous shall flourish like a palm tree. (Ps. 92:11)

Second Reading: 1 Corinthians 15:51–58
The mystery of the resurrection

133 Jesus lives! The victory's won!
140 With high delight let us unite
340 Jesus Christ, my sure defense
790 Praise to you, O God of mercy

Gospel: Luke 6:39–49
Take the speck from your eye; build your house on a firm foundation

293, 294 My hope is built on nothing less
413 Father eternal, ruler of creation
454 If God himself be for me
459 O Holy Spirit, enter in
552 In thee is gladness

Additional hymns for the day/season
425 O God of mercy, God of light
446 Whatever God ordains is right
507 How firm a foundation
520 Give to our God immortal praise!
793 Shout for joy loud and long

*Psalm 92:1–4, 12–15 (NRSV)

THE TRANSFIGURATION OF OUR LORD

LAST SUNDAY AFTER THE EPIPHANY

Prayer of the day

Almighty God, on the mountain you showed your glory in the transfiguration of your Son. Give us the vision to see beyond the turmoil of our world and to behold the king in all his glory; through your Son, Jesus Christ our Lord, who lives and reigns with you and the Holy Spirit, one God, now and forever. (20)

OR

O God, in the transfiguration of your Son you confirmed the mysteries of the faith by the witness of Moses and Elijah, and in the voice from the bright cloud you foreshadowed our adoption as your children. Make us with the king heirs of your glory, and bring us to enjoy its fullness, through Jesus Christ our Lord, who lives and reigns with you and the Holy Spirit, one God, now and forever. (21)

Verse

Alleluia. You are the fairest of men; grace flows from your lips. Alleluia. (Ps. 45:2)

Offertory

Beloved, we are God's children now; what we will be has not yet been revealed. What we do know is this: when he is revealed we will be like him, for we will see him as he is. And all who have this hope in him purify themselves, just as he is pure. (1 John 3:2–3)

YEAR A

Hymn of the day

315 Love divine, all loves excelling
76 O Morning Star, how fair and bright!
653 Jesus on the mountain peak

Hymns related to the readings

First Reading: Exodus 24:12–18
Moses enters the cloud of God's glory on Mount Sinai

526 Immortal, invisible, God only wise

Psalmody: Psalm 2
You are my son; this day have I begotten you. (Ps. 2:7)

OR

Psalmody: Psalm 99
Proclaim the greatness of the LORD; worship upon God's holy hill. (Ps. 99:4)

Second Reading: 2 Peter 1:16–21
The apostle's message confirmed on the mount of transfiguration

86 The only Son from heaven
237 O God of light
800 Each morning brings us

Gospel: Matthew 17:1–9
Revelation of Christ as God's beloved Son

80 Oh, wondrous type! Oh, vision fair
89 How good, Lord, to be here!
653 Jesus on the mountain peak

Additional hymns for the day/season

77 O one with God the Father
172 Lord, enthroned in heavenly splendor
233 Thy strong Word
264 When all your mercies, O my God
271 O Splendor of the Father's light
511 Renew me, O eternal Light
514 O Savior, precious Savior
518 Beautiful Savior
536 O God of God, O Light of light
545, 546 When morning gilds the skies
552 In thee is gladness
649 I want to walk as a child of the light
651 Shine, Jesus, shine
654 Alleluia, song of gladness
797 O God beyond all praising

Year B

Hymn of the day

653 Jesus on the mountain peak
80 Oh, wondrous type! Oh, vision fair
518 Beautiful Savior

Hymns related to the readings

First Reading: 2 Kings 2:1–12
Elijah taken up to heaven and succeeded by Elisha

233 Thy strong Word

Psalmody: Psalm 50:1–6
Out of Zion, perfect in beauty, God shines forth in glory. (Ps. 50:2)

Second Reading: 2 Corinthians 4:3–6
God's light seen clearly in the face of Christ

222 O Bread of life from heaven
317 To God the Holy Spirit let us pray

Gospel: Mark 9:2–9
Revelation of Christ as God's beloved Son

80 Oh, wondrous type! Oh, vision fair
89 How good, Lord, to be here!
653 Jesus on the mountain peak

Additional hymns for the day/season

See Year A

Year C

Hymn of the day

80 Oh, wondrous type! Oh, vision fair
315 Love divine, all loves excelling
651 Shine, Jesus, shine

Hymns related to the readings

First Reading: Exodus 34:29–35
Coming down from Mount Sinai, Moses' face shone

526 Immortal, invisible, God only wise

Psalmody: Psalm 99
Proclaim the greatness of the LORD; worship upon God's holy hill. (Ps. 99:9)

Second Reading: 2 Corinthians 3:12—4:2
With unveiled faces we see the Lord's glory as we are transformed

199 Thee we adore, O hidden Savior
400 God, whose almighty word

Gospel: Luke 9:28–36 [37–43]
Jesus is transfigured on the mountain

80 Oh, wondrous type! Oh, vision fair
89 How good, Lord, to be here!
653 Jesus on the mountain peak

Additional hymns for the day/season

See Year A

Prayer of the day

Almighty and ever-living God, you hate nothing you have made and you forgive the sins of all who are penitent. Create in us new and honest hearts, so that, truly repenting of our sins, we may obtain from you, the God of all mercy, full pardon and forgiveness; through your Son, Jesus Christ our Lord, who lives and reigns with you and the Holy Spirit, one God, now and forever. (22)

Verse

Return to the LORD, your God, who is gracious and merciful, slow to anger, and abounding in steadfast love. (Joel 2:13)

Offertory

Create in me a clean heart, O God, and renew a right spirit within me. Cast me not away from your presence, and take not your Holy Spirit from me. Restore to me the joy of your salvation, and uphold me with your free Spirit. (Ps. 51:10–12)

Years A, B, C

Hymn of the day

295	Out of the depths I cry to you
91	Savior, when in dust to you
659	O Sun of justice

Hymns related to the readings

First Reading: Joel 2:1–2, 12–17
Return to the Lord, your God

303	When in the hour of deepest need

OR

First Reading: Isaiah 58:1–12
The fast that God chooses

420	Lord, save your world
423	Lord, whose love in humble service

Psalmody: Psalm 51:1–18*
Have mercy on me, O God, according to your lovingkindness. (Ps. 51:1)

732	Create in me a clean heart, O God (Ps. 51:10–12)

Second Reading: 2 Corinthians 5:20b—6:10
Now is the day of salvation

304	Today your mercy calls us
659	O Sun of justice

Gospel: Matthew 6:1–6, 16–21
The practice of faith

310	To you, omniscient Lord of all
776	Be thou my vision

Additional hymns for the day/season

99	O Lord, throughout these forty days
295	Out of the depths I cry to you
296	Just as I am, without one plea
302	Jesus, your blood and righteousness
309	Lord Jesus, think on me
438	Lord, teach us how to pray aright
508	Come down, O Love divine
511	Renew me, o eternal Light
656	By the Babylonian rivers
657	The glory of these forty days
662	Restore in us, O God
733	Our Father, we have wandered
734	Softly and tenderly Jesus is calling

*Psalm 51:1–17 (NRSV)

Prayer of the day

Lord God, you led your ancient people through the wilderness and brought them to the promised land. Guide now the people of your Church, that, following our Savior, we may walk through the wilderness of this world toward the glory of the world to come; through your Son, Jesus Christ our Lord, who lives and reigns with you and the Holy Spirit, one God, now and forever. (24)

OR

Lord God, our strength, the battle of good and evil rages within and around us, and our ancient foe tempts us with his deceits and empty promises. Keep us steadfast in your Word and, when we fall, raise us again and restore us through your Son, Jesus Christ our Lord, who lives and reigns with you and the Holy Spirit, one God, now and forever. (25)

Verse

One does not live by bread alone, but by every word that comes from the mouth of God. (Matt. 4:4)

Offertory

Repent and turn from all your transgressions; otherwise iniquity will be your ruin. Cast away from you all the transgressions that you have committed against me, and get yourselves a new heart and a new spirit! For I have no pleasure in the death of anyone, says the Lord GOD. Turn, then, and live. (Ezek. 18:30–32)

YEAR A

Hymn of the day

228   A mighty fortress is our God
230   Lord, keep us steadfast in your Word
660   I want Jesus to walk with me

Hymns related to the readings

First Reading: Genesis 2:15–17; 3:1–7
Eating of the tree of the knowledge of good and evil

372   In Adam we have all been one

Psalmody: Psalm 32
Mercy embraces those who trust in the LORD. (Ps. 32:11)

Second Reading: Romans 5:12–19
Death came through one; life comes through one

470   Praise and thanks and adoration
484   God, my Lord, my strength

Gospel: Matthew 4:1–11
The temptation of Jesus in the wilderness for forty days

88   Oh, love, how deep
99   O Lord, throughout these forty days
228, 229 A mighty fortress is our God
341   Jesus, still lead on
657   The glory of these forty days

Additional hymns for the day/season

230   Lord, keep us steadfast in your Word
343   Guide me ever, great Redeemer
366   Lord of our life
450   Who trusts in God, a strong abode
454   If God himself be for me
478   Come, oh, come, O quickening Spirit
484   God, my Lord, my strength
503   O Jesus, I have promised
511   Renew me, O eternal Light
655   As the sun with longer journey
660   I want Jesus to walk with me
733   Our Father, we have wandered
779   You who dwell in the shelter of the Lord

Year B

Hymn of the day

230   Lord, keep us steadfast in your Word
366   Lord of our life
741   Thy holy wings

Hymns related to the readings

First Reading: Genesis 9:8–17
The rainbow, sign of God's covenant

324   O Love that will not let me go
741   Thy holy wings

Psalmody: Psalm 25:1–9*
Your paths are love and faithfulness to those who keep your covenant. (Ps. 25:9)

Second Reading: 1 Peter 3:18–22
Saved through water

192   Baptized into your name most holy
741   Thy holy wings

Gospel: Mark 1:9–15
The temptation of Jesus in the wilderness for forty days

88   Oh, love, how deep
99   O Lord, throughout these forty days
228, 229   A mighty fortress is our God
341   Jesus, still lead on
657   The glory of these forty days

Additional hymns for the day/season
See Year A

Year C

Hymn of the day

660   I want Jesus to walk with me
228, 229   A mighty fortress is our God
341   Jesus, still lead on

Hymns related to the readings

First Reading: Deuteronomy 26:1–11
The LORD brought us out of Egypt with a mighty hand

533, 534   Now thank we all our God
562   Lift every voice and sing

Psalmody: Psalm 91:1–2, 9–16
God shall charge the angels to keep you in all your ways. (Ps. 91:11)

779   You who dwell in the shelter of the Lord (paraphrase)

Second Reading: Romans 10:8b–13
If you confess that Jesus is Lord, you will be saved

292   God loved the world
312   Once he came in blessing

Gospel: Luke 4:1–13
The temptation of Jesus in the wilderness for forty days

88   Oh, love, how deep
99   O Lord, throughout these forty days
228, 229   A mighty fortress is our God
341   Jesus, still lead on
657   The glory of these forty days

Additional hymns for the day/season
See Year A

*Psalm 25:1–10 (NRSV)

Prayer of the day

Eternal God, it is your glory always to have mercy. Bring back all who have erred and strayed from your ways; lead them again to embrace in faith the truth of your Word and to hold it fast; through Jesus Christ your Son our Lord, who lives and reigns with you and the Holy Spirit, one God, now and forever. (26)

Verse

God so loved the world that he gave his only Son, so that everyone who believes in him may not perish but may have eternal life. (John 3:16)

Offertory

What shall I render to the Lord for all his benefits to me? I will offer the sacrifice of thanksgiving and will call on the name of the Lord. I will take the cup of salvation and will call on the name of the Lord. I will pay my vows to the Lord now in the presence of all his people, in the courts of the Lord's house, in the midst of you, O Jerusalem. (Ps. 116:10–12, 16–17)

Year A

Hymn of the day

292   God loved the world
194   All who believe and are baptized
698   We were baptized in Christ Jesus

Hymns related to the readings

First Reading: Genesis 12:1–4a
The blessing of God upon Abram

485   Lord, as a pilgrim
544   The God of Abraham praise
660   I want Jesus to walk with me

Psalmody: Psalm 121
It is the Lord who watches over you. (Ps. 121:5)

445   Unto the hills (paraphrase)

Second Reading: Romans 4:1–5, 13–17
The promise to those who share Abraham's faith

297   Salvation unto us has come
544   The God of Abraham praise
725   Blessed be the God of Israel

Gospel: John 3:1–17
The mission of Christ: to save the world

292   God loved the world
377   Lift high the cross
693   Baptized in water
769   Mothering God, you gave me birth

Additional hymns for the day/season

93   Jesus, refuge of the weary
325   Lord, thee I love with all my heart
356   O Jesus, joy of loving hearts
425   O God of mercy, God of light
453   If you but trust in God to guide you
479   My faith looks up to thee
507   How firm a foundation
659   O Sun of justice
662   Restore in us, O God
683   Loving Spirit
697   Wash, O God, our sons and daughters
699   Blessed assurance

Year B

Hymn of the day

496   Around you, O Lord Jesus
325   Lord, thee I love with all my heart
660   I want Jesus to walk with me

Hymns related to the readings

First Reading: Genesis 17:1–7, 15–16
God blesses Abraham and Sarah

544   The God of Abraham praise
730   My soul proclaims your greatness

Psalmody: Psalm 22:22–30*
All the ends of the earth shall remember and turn to the Lord. (Ps. 22:26)

Second Reading: Romans 4:13–25
The promise to those who share Abraham's faith

507   How firm a foundation
544   The God of Abraham praise
725   Blessed be the God of Israel

Gospel: Mark 8:31–38
The passion prediction

105   A lamb goes uncomplaining forth
398   "Take up your cross," the Savior said
455   "Come, follow me," the Savior spake
487   Let us ever walk with Jesus
504   O God, my faithful God

Additional hymns for the day/season

88   Oh, love, how deep
93   Jesus, refuge of the weary
406   Take my life, that I may be
662   Restore in us, O God
782   All my hope on God is founded
785   Weary of all trumpeting

Year C

Hymn of the day

421   Lord Christ, when first you came to earth
427   O Jesus Christ, may grateful hymns be rising
663   When twilight comes

Hymns related to the readings

First Reading: Genesis 15:1–12, 17–18
The covenant with Abram and his descendants

343   Guide me ever, great Redeemer
544   The God of Abraham praise

Psalmody: Psalm 27
In the day of trouble, the Lord shall keep me safe. (Ps. 27:7)

Second Reading: Philippians 3:17—4:1
Our citizenship is in heaven from where we expect a Savior

102   On my heart imprint your image
662   Restore in us, O God

Gospel: Luke 13:31–35
I have desired to gather Jerusalem as a hen gathers her brood

421   Lord Christ, when first you came to earth
427   O Jesus Christ, may grateful hymns be rising
436   All who love and serve your city
496   Around you, O Lord Jesus
663   When twilight comes
741   Thy holy wings

Additional hymns for the day/season

105   A lamb goes uncomplaining forth
325   Lord, thee I love with all my heart
402   Look from your sphere of endless day
660   I want Jesus to walk with me
725   Blessed be the God of Israel

*Psalm 22:23–31 (NRSV)

Prayer of the day

Eternal Lord, your kingdom has broken into our troubled world through the life, death, and resurrection of your Son. Help us to hear your Word and obey it, so that we become instruments of your redeeming love; through your Son, Jesus Christ our Lord, who lives and reigns with you and the Holy Spirit, one God, now and forever. (28)

OR

(Year A) Almighty God, your Son once welcomed an outcast woman because of her faith. Give us faith like hers, that we also may trust only in your love for us and may accept one another as we have been accepted by you; through your Son, Jesus Christ our Lord, who lives and reigns with you and the Holy Spirit, one God, now and forever. (27)

Verse

Jesus humbled himself and became obedient to the point of death—even death on a cross. (Phil. 2:8)

Offertory

In those days and in that time, says the LORD, the people of Israel and the people of Judah shall come; they shall come weeping as they seek the LORD their God. They shall ask the way to Zion, with faces turned toward it, and they shall come and join themselves to the LORD by an everlasting covenant that will never be forgotten. (Jer. 50:4–5)

YEAR A

Hymn of the day

497   I heard the voice of Jesus say
356   O Jesus, joy of loving hearts
695   O blessed spring

Hymns related to the readings

First Reading: Exodus 17:1–7
Water from the rock in the wilderness

327   Rock of Ages, cleft for me
343   Guide me ever, great Redeemer
358   Glories of your name are spoken

Psalmody: Psalm 95
Let us shout for joy to the rock of our salvation. (Ps. 95:1)

Second Reading: Romans 5:1–11
Reconciled to God by Christ's death

292   God loved the world
326   My heart is longing
385   What wondrous love is this
750   Oh, praise the gracious power

Gospel: John 4:5–42
Baptismal image: the woman at the well

356   O Jesus, joy of loving hearts
497   I heard the voice of Jesus say

Additional hymns for the day/season

93   Jesus, refuge of the weary
222   O Bread of life from heaven
226   Draw near and take the body of the Lord
301   Come to Calvary's holy mountain
340   Jesus Christ, my sure defense
452   As pants the hart for cooling streams
459   O Holy Spirit, enter in
499   Come, thou Fount of every blessing
635   Surely it is God who saves me
655   As the sun with longer journey
696   I've just come from the fountain
772   The Lord is my song

YEAR B

Hymn of the day
782 All my hope on God is founded
104 In the cross of Christ I glory
415 God of grace and God of glory

Hymns related to the readings

First Reading: Exodus 20:1–17
The commandments given at Sinai

480 Oh, that the Lord would guide my ways
504 O God, my faithful God

Psalmody: Psalm 19
The commandment of the LORD gives light to the eyes. (Ps. 19:8)

Second Reading: 1 Corinthians 1:18–25
Christ crucified, the wisdom of God

119 Nature with open volume stands
464 You are the way

Gospel: John 2:13–22
The cleansing of the temple

421 Lord Christ, when first you came to earth
428 O God of earth and altar

Additional hymns for the day/season
104 In the cross of Christ I glory
250 Open now thy gates of beauty
335 May God bestow on us his grace
377 Lift high the cross
415 God of grace and God of glory
668 There in God's garden
750 Oh, praise the gracious power
776 Be thou my vision
796 My Lord of light

YEAR C

Hymn of the day
662 Restore in us, O God
326 My heart is longing
343 Guide me ever, great Redeemer

Hymns related to the readings

First Reading: Isaiah 55:1–9
Everyone who thirsts, come to the water; seek the Lord

15 Seek the Lord
214 Come, let us eat
226 Draw near and take the body of the Lord
497 I heard the voice of Jesus say
711 You satisfy the hungry heart

Psalmody: Psalm 63:1–8
O God, eagerly I seek you; my soul thirsts for you. (Ps. 63:1)

Second Reading: 1 Corinthians 10:1–13
Israel, baptized in cloud and seas, ate the same spiritual food as Christians

341 Jesus, still lead on
343 Guide me ever, great Redeemer
498 All who would valiant be
504 O God, my faithful God

Gospel: Luke 13:1–9
Unless you repent, you will perish: parable of the fig tree

655 As the sun with longer journey
662 Restore in us, O God

Additional hymns for the day/season
104 In the cross of Christ I glory
197 O living Bread from heaven
212 Let us break bread together
290 There's a wideness in God's mercy
327 Rock of Ages, cleft for me
385 What wondrous love is this
446 Whatever God ordains is right
452 As pants the hart for cooling streams
499 Come, thou Fount of every blessing
706 Eat this bread, drink this cup

Prayer of the day

God of all mercy, by your power to heal and to forgive, graciously cleanse us from all sin and make us strong; through your Son, Jesus Christ our Lord, who lives and reigns with you and the Holy Spirit, one God, now and forever. (29)

Verse

Just as Moses lifted up the serpent in the wilderness, so must the Son of Man be lifted up, that whoever believes in him may have eternal life. (John 3:14–15)

Offertory

Come, let us return to the LORD; for it is he who has torn, and he will heal us; he has struck down, and he will bind us up. After two days he will revive us; on the third day he will raise us up. (Hos. 6:1–2)

YEAR A

Hymn of the day

248 Dearest Jesus, at your word
400 God, whose almighty word
716 Word of God, come down on earth

Hymns related to the readings

First Reading: 1 Samuel 16:1–13
David is chosen and anointed

505 Forth in thy name, O Lord, I go

Psalmody: Psalm 23
You have anointed my head with oil. (Ps. 23:5)

451 The Lord's my shepherd (paraphrase)
456 The King of love my shepherd is (paraphrase)

Second Reading: Ephesians 5:8–14
Awake from sleep, live as children of light

649 I want to walk as a child of the light
659 O Sun of justice
745 Awake, O sleeper

Gospel: John 9:1–41
Baptismal image: the man born blind

400 God, whose almighty word
446 Whatever God ordains is right
448 Amazing grace, how sweet the sound
716 Word of God, come down on earth
776 Be thou my vision

Additional hymns for the day/season

96 Your heart, O God, is grieved
97 Christ, the life of all the living
102 On my heart imprint your image
265 Christ, whose glory fills the skies
380 O Christ, our light, our Radiance true
385 What wondrous love is this
405 Lord of light
431 Your hand, O Lord, in days of old
497 I heard the voice of Jesus say
520 Give to our God immortal praise
668 There in God's garden
737 There is a balm in Gilead
738 Healer of our every ill

YEAR B

Hymn of the day

385   What wondrous love is this
448   Amazing grace, how sweet the sound
668   There in God's garden

Hymns related to the readings

First Reading: Numbers 21:4–9
The lifting up of the serpent

377   Lift high the cross
479   My faith looks up to thee

Psalmody: Psalm 107:1–3, 17–22
The LORD delivered them from their distress.
(Ps. 107:19)

Second Reading: Ephesians 2:1–10
Saved by grace through faith for good works

297   Salvation unto us has come
448   Amazing grace, how sweet the sound
513   Come, my way, my truth, my life

Gospel: John 3:14–21
The lifting up of the Son of Man

100   Deep were his wounds
101   O Christ, our king, creator, Lord
292   God loved the world
377   Lift high the cross
489   Wide open are your hands

Additional hymns for the day/season

96   Your heart, O God, is grieved
104   In the cross of Christ I glory
420   Lord, save your world
520   Give to our God immortal praise
524   My God, how wonderful thou art

YEAR C

Hymn of the day

733   Our Father, we have wandered
304   Today your mercy calls us
448   Amazing grace, how sweet the sound

Hymns related to the readings

First Reading: Joshua 5:9–12
Israel eats bread and grain, the produce of the land

341   Jesus, lead thou on
477   O God of Jacob

Psalmody: Psalm 32
Be glad, you righteous, and rejoice in the LORD.
(Ps. 32:12)

Second Reading: 2 Corinthians 5:16–21
The mystery and ministry of reconciliation

194   All who believe and are baptized
315   Love divine, all loves excelling
385   What wondrous love is this
511   Renew me, O eternal Light
781   My life flows on in endless song

Gospel: Luke 15:1–3, 11b–32
The parable of the prodigal father and the repentant son

290   There's a wideness in God's mercy
291   Jesus sinners will receive
298   One there is above all others
304   Today your mercy calls us
499   Come, thou Fount of every blessing
524   My God, how wonderful thou art
733   Our Father, we have wandered
734   Softly and tenderly Jesus is calling

Additional hymns for the day/season

96   Your heart, O God, is grieved
102   On my heart imprint your image
372   In Adam we have all been one
438   Lord, teach us how to pray aright
659   O Sun of justice
698   We were baptized in Christ Jesus

Prayer of the day

Almighty God, our redeemer, in our weakness we have failed to be your messengers of forgiveness and hope in the world. Renew us by your Holy Spirit, that we may follow your commands and proclaim your reign of love; through your Son, Jesus Christ our Lord, who lives and reigns with you and the Holy Spirit, one God, now and forever. (30)

Verse

The Son of Man came not to be served but to serve, and to give his life a ransom for many. (Mark 10:45)

Offertory

Remember Jesus Christ, raised from the dead, a descendant of David. If we have died with him, we will also live with him; if we endure, we will also reign with him. If we are faithless, he remains faithful—for he cannot deny himself. (2 Tim. 2:8, 11–13)

YEAR A

Hymn of the day

385	What wondrous love is this
325	Lord, thee I love with all my heart
658	The Word of God is source and seed

Hymns related to the readings

First Reading: Ezekiel 37:1–14
The dry bones of Israel brought to life

488	Breathe on me, breath of God
656	By the Babylonian rivers
658	The Word of God is source and seed
686	Veni Sancte Spiritus

Psalmody: Psalm 130
With the LORD there is mercy and plenteous redemption. (Ps. 130:6–7)

295	Out of the depths I cry to you (paraphrase)

Second Reading: Romans 8:6–11
Life in the Spirit

192	Baptized into your name most holy
508	Come down, O Love divine

Gospel: John 11:1–45
Baptismal image: the raising of Lazarus

340	Jesus Christ, my sure defense
658	The Word of God is source and seed
702	I am the Bread of life

Additional hymns for the day/season

95	Glory be to Jesus
96	Your heart, O God, is grieved
207	We who once were dead
272	Abide with me
342	I know of a sleep in Jesus' name
399	We are the Lord's
464	You are the way
479	My faith looks up to thee
487	Let us ever walk with Jesus
513	Come, my way, my truth, my life

YEAR B

Hymn of the day
658   The Word of God is source and seed
101   O Christ, our king, creator, Lord
479   My faith looks up to thee

Hymns related to the readings

First Reading: Jeremiah 31:31–34
A new covenant written on the heart

301   Come to Calvary's holy mountain
701   What feast of love

Psalmody: Psalm 51:1–13*
Create in me a clean heart, O God. (Ps. 51:11)

732   Create in me a clean heart (Ps. 51:10–12)

OR

Psalmody: Psalm 119:9–16
I treasure your promise in my heart. (Ps. 119:11)

Second Reading: Hebrews 5:5–10
Through suffering Christ becomes the source of salvation

202   Victim Divine, your grace we claim

Gospel: John 12:20–33
The grain of wheat dying in the earth

105   A lamb goes uncomplaining forth
148   Now the green blade rises
658   The Word of God is source and seed
769   Mothering God, you gave me birth

Additional hymns for the day/season
104   In the cross of Christ I glory
326   My heart is longing
344   We sing the praise of him who died
377   Lift high the cross
385   What wondrous love is this
482   When I survey the wondrous cross
655   As the sun with longer journey
668   There in God's garden

YEAR C

Hymn of the day
482   When I survey the wondrous cross
336   Jesus, thy boundless love to me
655   As the sun with longer journey

Hymns related to the readings

First Reading: Isaiah 43:16–21
The LORD gives water in the wilderness to the chosen people

293, 294   My hope is built on nothing less
343   Guide me ever, great Redeemer
384   Your kingdom come, O Father

Psalmody: Psalm 126
Those who sowed with tears will reap with songs of joy. (Ps. 126:6)

Second Reading: Philippians 3:4b–14
To know Christ and his resurrection, to share in his sufferings

107   Beneath the cross of Jesus
344   We sing the praise of him who died
482   When I survey the wondrous cross
785   Weary of all trumpeting

Gospel: John 12:1–8
Mary anoints Jesus for his burial

105   A lamb goes uncomplaining forth
336   Jesus, thy boundless love to me
406   Take my life, that I may be

Additional hymns for the day/season
97   Christ, the life of all the living
106   In the hour of trial
316   Jesus, the very thought of you
326   My heart is longing
385   What wondrous love is this
706   Eat this bread, drink this cup

*Psalm 51:1–12 (NRSV)

Prayer of the day

Almighty God, you sent your Son, our Savior Jesus Christ, to take our flesh upon him and to suffer death on the cross. Grant that we may share in his obedience to your will and in the glorious victory of his resurrection; through your Son, Jesus Christ our Lord, who lives and reigns with you and the Holy Spirit, one God, now and forever. (31)

Verse

The hour has come for the Son of Man to be glorified. (John 12:23)

Offertory

Very truly, I tell you, unless a grain of wheat falls into the earth and dies, it remains just a single grain; but if it dies it bears much fruit. Whoever serves me must follow me, and where I am, there will my servant be also. Whoever serves me, the Father will honor. (John 12:24, 26)

YEAR A

Procession with Palms

Matthew 21:1–11
Entrance into the final days

Psalmody: Psalm 118:1–2, 19–29
Blessed is he who comes in the name of the LORD. (Ps. 118:26)

Hymns at the procession
23 O Lord, how shall I meet you
26 Prepare the royal highway
108 All glory, laud, and honor
121 Ride on, ride on in majesty!
631 Lift up your heads, O gates

Liturgy of the Passion

Hymn of the day
94, 661 My song is love unknown
116 O sacred head, now wounded
668 There in God's garden

Hymns related to the readings

First Reading: Isaiah 50:4–9a
The servant of the Lord submits to suffering

421 Lord Christ, when first you came to earth

Psalmody: Psalm 31:9–16
Into your hands, O Lord, I commend my spirit. (Ps. 31:5)

Second Reading: Philippians 2:5–11
Humbled to the point of death on a cross

179 At the name of Jesus

Gospel: Matthew 26:14—27:66 or Matthew 27:11–54
The passion of the Lord

92 Were you there
93 Jesus, refuge of the weary
94 My song is love unknown
97 Christ, the life of all the living
105 A lamb goes uncomplaining forth
107 Beneath the cross of Jesus
115 Jesus, I will ponder now
116, 117 O sacred head, now wounded
123 Ah, holy Jesus
489 Wide open are your hands
661 My song is love unknown
667 Stay here
668 There in God's garden

Additional hymns for the day/season
119 Nature with open volume stands
120 Of the glorious body telling

YEAR B

Procession with Palms

Mark 11:1–11 or John 12:12–16
Entrance into the final days
Psalmody: Psalm 118:1–2, 19–29
Blessed is he who comes in the name of the LORD.
(Ps. 118:26)

Hymns at the procession

23   O Lord, how shall I meet you
26   Prepare the royal highway
108   All glory, laud, and honor
121   Ride on, ride on in majesty!
631   Lift up your heads, O gates

Liturgy of the Passion

Hymn of the day

123   Ah, holy Jesus
94, 661   My song is love unknown
116, 117   O sacred head, now wounded

Hymns related to the readings

First Reading: Isaiah 50:4–9a
The servant of the Lord submits to suffering

421   Lord Christ, when first you came to earth

Psalmody: Psalm 31:9–16
Into your hands, O Lord, I commend my spirit. (Ps. 31:5)

Second Reading: Philippians 2:5–11
Humbled to the point of death on a cross

179   At the name of Jesus

Gospel: Mark 14:1—15:47 or Mark 15:1–39
[40–47]
The passion of the Lord

See Year A

Additional hymns for the day/season
See Year A

YEAR C

Procession with Palms

Luke 19:28–40
Entrance into the final days

Psalmody: Psalm 118:1–2, 19–29
Blessed is he who comes in the name of the LORD.
(Ps. 118:26)

Hymns at the procession

23   O Lord, how shall I meet you
26   Prepare the royal highway
108   All glory, laud, and honor
121   Ride on, ride on in majesty!
631   Lift up your heads, O gates

Liturgy of the Passion

Hymn of the day

105   A lamb goes uncomplaining forth
97   Christ, the life of all the living
94, 661   My song is love unknown

Hymns related to the readings

First Reading: Isaiah 50:4–9a
The servant of the Lord submits to suffering

421   Lord Christ, when first you came to earth

Psalmody: Psalm 31:9–16
Into your hands, O Lord, I commend my spirit. (Ps. 31:5)

Second Reading: Philippians 2:5–11
Humbled to the point of death on a cross

179   At the name of Jesus

Gospel: Luke 22:14—23:56 or Luke 23:1–49
The passion of the Lord

740   Jesus, remember me
See Year A

Additional hymns for the day/season
See Year A

Prayer of the day

O God, your Son chose the path which led to pain before joy and the cross before glory. Plant his cross in our hearts, so that in its power and love we may come at last to joy and glory; through your Son, Jesus Christ our Lord. (34)

Verse

May I never boast of anything except the cross of our Lord Jesus Christ. (Gal. 6:14)

Offertory

I have been crucified with Christ; and it is no longer I who live, but it is Christ who lives in me. And the life I now live in the flesh I live by faith in the Son of God, who loved me and gave himself for me. (Gal. 2:19–20)

YEARS A, B, C

Hymn of the day

326   My heart is longing

Hymns related to the readings

First Reading: Isaiah 42:1–9
The servant brings forth justice

659   O Sun of justice

Psalmody: Psalm 36:5–11
Your people take refuge under the shadow of your wings. (Ps. 36:7)

Second Reading: Hebrews 9:11–15
The redeeming blood of Christ

202   Victim Divine, your grace we claim

Gospel: John 12:1–11
Mary anoints the feet of Jesus

406   Take my life that I may be
457, 458 Jesus, priceless treasure

TUESDAY IN HOLY WEEK

Prayer of the day
Lord Jesus, you have called us to follow you. Grant that our love may not grow cold in your service, and that we may not fail or deny you in the hour of trial. (35)

Verse
May I never boast of anything except the cross of our Lord Jesus Christ. (Gal. 6:14)

Offertory
I have been crucified with Christ; and it is no longer I who live, but it is Christ who lives in me. And the life I now live in the flesh I live by faith in the Son of God, who loved me and gave himself for me. (Gal. 2:19–20)

YEARS A, B, C

Hymn of the day
104   In the cross of Christ I glory

Hymns related to the readings

First Reading: Isaiah 49:1–7
The servant brings salvation to earth's ends

377   Lift high the cross

Psalmody: Psalm 71:1–14
From my mother's womb you have been my strength.
(Ps. 71:6)

Second Reading: 1 Corinthians 1:18–31
Christ crucified, the wisdom of God

119   Nature with open volume stands
482   When I survey the wondrous cross

Gospel: John 12:20–36
The hour has come

101   O Christ, our king, creator, Lord
479   My faith looks up to thee
658   The Word of God is source and seed

WEDNESDAY IN HOLY WEEK

Prayer of the day

Almighty God, your Son our Savior suffered at human hands and endured the shame of the cross. Grant that we may walk in the way of his cross and find it the way of life and peace; through your Son, Jesus Christ our Lord. (36)

Verse

May I never boast of anything except the cross of our Lord Jesus Christ. (Gal. 6:14)

Offertory

I have been crucified with Christ; and it is no longer I who live, but it is Christ who lives in me. And the life I now live in the flesh I live by faith in the Son of God, who loved me and gave himself for me. (Gal. 2:19–20)

YEARS A, B, C

Hymn of the day

123   Ah, holy Jesus

Hymns related to the readings

First Reading: Isaiah 50:4–9a
The servant is vindicated by God

454   If God himself be for me

Psalmody: Psalm 70
Be pleased, O God, to deliver me. (Ps. 70:1)

Second Reading: Hebrews 12:1–3
Look to Jesus, who endured the cross

107   Beneath the cross of Jesus

Gospel: John 13:21–32
The departure of Jesus' betrayer

106   In the hour of trial
127   It happened on that fateful night

MAUNDY THURSDAY

Prayer of the day

Holy God, source of all love, on the night of his betrayal, Jesus gave his disciples a new commandment: To love one another as he had loved them. By your Holy Spirit write this commandment in our hearts; through your Son, Jesus Christ our Lord, who lives and reigns with you and the Holy Spirit, one God, now and forever. (37)

OR

Lord God, in a wonderful Sacrament you have left us a memorial of your suffering and death. May this Sacrament of your body and blood so work in us that the way we live will proclaim the redemption you have brought; for you live and reign with the Father and the Holy Spirit, one God, now and forever. (38)

Verse

As often as you eat this bread and drink the cup, you proclaim the Lord's death until he comes. (1 Cor. 11:26)

Offertory

The LORD, the LORD, a God merciful and gracious, slow to anger, and abounding in steadfast love and faithfulness, keeping steadfast love for the thousandth generation, forgiving iniquity and transgression and sin. (Exod. 34:6–7)

YEARS A, B, C

Hymn of the day

126 Where charity and love prevail
199 Thee we adore, O hidden Savior
663 When twilight comes

Hymns related to the readings

First Reading: Exodus 12:1–4 [5–10] 11–14
The passover of the Lord

Psalmody: Psalm 116:1, 10–17*
I will take the cup of salvation and call on the name of the LORD. (Ps. 116:11)

Second Reading: 1 Corinthians 11:23–26
Proclaim the Lord's death until he comes

120 Of the glorious body telling
127 It happened on that fateful night
198 Let all mortal flesh keep silence
496 Around you, O Lord Jesus
707 This is my body
709 Eat this bread

Gospel: John 13:1–17, 31b–35
The service of Christ: footwashing and meal

122 Love consecrates the humblest act
126 Where charity and love prevail
664 A new commandment
665 Ubi caritas et amor
666 Great God, your love has called us
765 Jesu, Jesu, fill us with your love

Additional hymns for the day/season

203 Now we join in celebration
206 Lord, who the night you were betrayed
207 We who once were dead
215 O Lord, we praise you
677 Stay here
711 You satisfy the hungry heart

*Psalm 116:1–2, 12–19 (NRSV)

GOOD FRIDAY

Prayer of the day

Almighty God, we ask you to look with mercy on your family, for whom our Lord Jesus Christ was willing to be betrayed and to be given over to the hands of sinners and to suffer death on the cross; who now lives and reigns with you and the Holy Spirit, one God, forever and ever. (39)

OR

Lord Jesus, you carried our sins in your own body on the tree so that we might have life. May we and all who remember this day find new life in you now and in the world to come, where you live and reign with the Father and the Holy Spirit, now and forever. (40)

YEARS A, B, C

Hymn of the day

92   Were you there
118   Sing, my tongue
668   There in God's garden

Hymns related to the readings

First Reading: Isaiah 52:13—53:12
The suffering servant

103   O Christ, thou Lamb of God
105   A lamb goes uncomplaining forth
116, 117 O sacred head, now wounded
385   What wondrous love is this

Psalmody: Psalm 22
My God, my God, why have you forsaken me? (Ps. 22:1)

Second Reading: Hebrews 10:16–25
The way to God is opened by Jesus' death

111   Lamb of God, pure and sinless

OR

Second Reading: Hebrews 4:14–16; 5:7–9
Jesus, the merciful high priest

101   O Christ, our king, creator, Lord

Gospel: John 18:1—19:42
The passion and death of Christ

92   Were you there
100   Deep were his wounds
101   O Christ, our king, creator, Lord
106   In the hour of trial
110   At the cross her station keeping
116, 117 O sacred head, now wounded
118   Sing, my tongue
123   Ah, holy Jesus
124, 125 The royal banners forward go
668   There in God's garden

Additional hymns for the day/season

97   Christ, the life of all the living
98   Alas! And did my Savior bleed
109   Go to dark Gethsemane
112, 113 Jesus. in thy dying woes
114   There is a green hill far away
115   Jesus, I will ponder now
119   Nature with open volume stands

THE RESURRECTION OF OUR LORD

VIGIL OF EASTER

Prayer of the day

O God, who made this most holy night to shine with the glory of the Lord's resurrection: Stir up in your Church that Spirit of adoption which is given to us in Baptism, that we, being renewed both in body and mind, may worship you in sincerity and truth; through Jesus Christ our Lord, who lives and reigns with you, in the unity of the Holy Spirit, one God, now and forever. (573)

Verse

Alleluia. Christ being raised from the dead will never die again; death has no more dominion over him. Alleluia. Let us sing to the Lord who has triumphed gloriously. Alleluia. (Rom. 6:9; Ex. 15:1)

Offertory

Alleluia, alleluia, alleluia. Clean out the old yeast so that you may be a new batch of dough. For Christ our paschal Lamb has been sacrificed. Therefore, let us celebrate the festival with the unleavened bread of sincerity and truth. Alleluia, alleluia, alleluia. (1 Cor. 5:7–8)

YEARS A, B, C

Hymn of the day

189	We know that Christ is raised
210	At the Lamb's high feast we sing
679	Our Paschal Lamb, that sets us free

Hymns related to the readings

First Reading: Genesis 1:1–2:4a
Creation

557	Let all things now living
794	Many and great, O God, are your works

Response: Psalm 136:1–9, 23–36
God's mercy endures forever. (Ps. 136:1b)

Almighty God, you wonderfully created the dignity of human nature and yet more wonderfully restored it. In your mercy, let us share the divine life of him who came to share our humanity, Jesus Christ your Son, our Lord. (51)

Second Reading: Genesis 7:1–5, 11–18, 8:6–18, 9:8–13
The flood

350	Even as we live each day
676	This joyful Eastertide
693	Baptized in water
695	O blessed spring

Response: Psalm 46
The LORD of hosts is with us; the God of Jacob is our stronghold. (Ps. 46:4)

228,229   A mighty fortress is our God (paraphrase)

Almighty God, you have placed the rainbow in the skies as a sign of your covenant with all living things. Grant that we, who are saved through water and the Spirit, may worthily offer to you our sacrifice of thanksgiving; through Jesus Christ our Lord. (578)

Third Reading: Genesis 22:1–18
The testing of Abraham

313	A multitude comes from the east and the west
660	I want Jesus to walk with me

Response: Psalm 16
You will show me the path of life. (Ps. 16:11)

God of all the faithful, you promised Abraham that he would become the father of all nations, and through this paschal mystery you increase your chosen people throughout the world. Help us to respond to your call by joyfully accepting the new life of grace; through your Son, Jesus Christ our Lord. (53)

Fourth Reading: Exodus 14:10–31; 15:20–21
Israel's deliverance at the Red Sea

132	Come, you faithful, raise the strain
141	The day of resurrection!
210	At the Lamb's high feast we sing
670	When Israel was in Egypt's land

Response: Exodus 15:1b–13, 17–18
I will sing to the LORD who has triumphed gloriously. (Exod. 15:1)

19   I will sing to the Lord

O God, whose wonderful deeds of old shine forth even to our day: By the power of your mighty arm you once delivered your people from slavery under Pharaoh, a sign for us of the salvation of all nations by the water of Baptism. Grant that all peoples of the earth may be numbered among the offspring of Abraham and may rejoice in the inheritance of Israel; through your Son, Jesus Christ our Lord. (54)

Fifth Reading: Isaiah 55:1–11
Salvation freely offered to all

Response: Isaiah 12:2–6
With joy you will draw water from the wells of salvation. (Isa. 12:3)

635   Surely it is God who saves me (paraphrase)

O God, you have created all things by the power of your Word, and you renew the earth by your Spirit. Give now the water of life to those who thirst for you, that they may bring forth abundant fruit in your glorious kingdom; through your Son, Jesus Christ our Lord. (55)

Sixth Reading: Proverbs 8:1–8, 19–21; 9:4b–6
or Baruch 3:9–15, 32–4:4
The wisdom of God

Response: Psalm 19
The statutes of the LORD are just and rejoice the heart. (Ps. 19:8)

O God, you increase your Church by continuing to call all peoples to salvation. Let the cleansing waters of Baptism flow, and by your love watch over those whom you have called; through your Son, Jesus Christ our Lord. (56)

Seventh Reading: Ezekiel 36:24–28
A new heart and a new spirit

Response: Psalm 42 and Psalm 43
My soul is athirst for the living God. (Ps. 42:2)

452   As pants the hart for cooling streams (paraphrase)

Almighty and everlasting God, in the mystery of the dying and rising of Christ you established a new covenant of reconciliation. Cleanse our hearts and give a new spirit to your people, that all those reborn in Baptism may show forth in their lives what they profess by their faith; through your Son, Jesus Christ our Lord. (579)

Eighth Reading: Ezekiel 37:1–14
The valley of the dry bones

Response: Psalm 143
Revive me, O LORD, for your name's sake. (Ps. 143:11)

O God, by the Passover of the Son you have brought us out of sin into righteousness and out of death into life. Give us such an understanding of your mercy that, in receiving the gifts of Word and Sacrament now, we may learn to hope for all your gifts to come; through your Son, Jesus Christ our Lord. (57)

Ninth Reading: Zephaniah 3:14–20
The gathering of God's people

Response: Psalm 98
Lift up your voice, rejoice and sing. (Ps. 98:5)

O God, strength of the powerless and light in all darkness: look in mercy upon your Church, that wonderful and sacred mystery. Bring to completion your work of salvation; let the whole world experience and see that what was fallen is being raised up, that what was old is being made new, and that all things are being restored to wholeness through him from whom they first took being, your Son, Jesus Christ our Lord. (580)

Tenth Reading: Jonah 3:1–10
The call of Jonah

752   I, the Lord of sea and sky

Response: Jonah 2:1–3 [4–6] 7–9
Deliverance belongs to the LORD. (Jonah 2:9)

O God, you have united all nations in the confession of your name. Now give us the will and the power to do what you command, that the faith of the people whom you call to everlasting life may direct their speech and actions; through your Son, Jesus Christ our Lord. (60)

Eleventh Reading: Deuteronomy 31:19–30
The song of Moses

Response: Deuteronomy 32:1–4, 7, 36a, 43a
The LORD will give his people justice. (Deut. 32:36)

O God, exaltation of the humble and strength of the righteous: You taught your people through Moses to sing your praise, that the law which he delivered to them might be helpful to us. Show your power among the nations that, in the forgiveness of sins, terror may turn to joy, and fear of retribution to salvation; through your Son, Jesus Christ our Lord. (61)

Twelfth Reading: Daniel 3:1–29
The fiery furnace

Response: Song of the Three Young Men 35–65
Sing praise to the LORD and highly exalt him forever. (Song of the Three Young Men 35b)

18   All you works of the Lord
527   All creatures of our God and King

New Testament Reading: Romans 6:3–11
Dying and rising with Christ

694   You have put on Christ
698   We were baptized in Christ Jesus

Response: Psalm 114
Tremble, O earth, at the presence of the LORD. (Ps. 114:7)

Gospel
A   Matthew 28:1–10
     Proclaim the resurrection

B   Mark 16:1–8
     The resurrection of Jesus is announced

C   Luke 24:1–12
     The women proclaim the resurrection

Additional hymns for the day/season
131   Christ is risen! Alleluia!
134   Christ Jesus lay in death's strong bands
135   The strife is o'er, the battle done
146   Rejoice, angelic choirs, rejoice!
207   We who once were dead
669   Come away to the skies
793   Shout for joy loud and long

THE RESURRECTION OF OUR LORD

Prayer of the day

O God, you gave your only Son to suffer death on the cross for our redemption, and by his glorious resurrection you delivered us from the power of death. Make us die every day to sin, so that we may live with him forever in the joy of the resurrection; through Jesus Christ our Lord, who lives and reigns with you and the Holy Spirit, one God, now and forever. (62)

OR

Almighty God, through your only Son you overcame death and opened for us the gate of everlasting life. Give us your continual help; put good desires into our minds and bring them to full effect; through Jesus Christ our Lord, who lives and reigns with you and the Holy Spirit, one God, now and forever. (63)

Verse

Alleluia. Christ being raised from the dead will never die again; death no longer has dominion over him. Alleluia. On this day the LORD has acted; we will rejoice and be glad in it. Alleluia. (Rom. 6:9; Ps. 118:24)
The Sequence hymn, LBW #137, may follow.

Offertory

Alleluia, alleluia, alleluia. Clean out the old yeast so that you may be a new batch of dough. For Christ our paschal Lamb has been sacrificed. Therefore, let us celebrate the festival with the unleavened bread of sincerity and truth. Alleluia, alleluia, alleluia. (1 Cor. 5:7–8)

YEAR A

Hymn of the day

134   Christ Jesus lay in death's strong bands
135   The strife is o'er, the battle done
678   Christ has arisen, alleluia

Hymns related to the readings

First Reading: Acts 10:34–43
God raised Jesus on the third day

140   With high delight let us unite
144   Good Christian friends, rejoice and sing!

OR

First Reading: Jeremiah 31:1–6
Joy at the restoration of God's people

153   Welcome, happy morning!
669   Come away to the skies

Psalmody: Psalm 118:1–2, 14–24
On this day the LORD has acted; we will rejoice and be glad in it. (Ps. 118:24)

Second Reading: Colossians 3:1–4
Raised with Christ to seek the higher things

143   Now all the vault of heaven resounds
671   Alleluia, alleluia, give thanks

OR

Second Reading: Acts 10:34–43 *(see first reading)*

Gospel: John 20:1–18
Seeing the risen Christ

129   Awake, my heart, with gladness
137   Christians, to the paschal victim
678   Christ has arisen, alleluia
692   For all the faithful women

OR

Gospel: Matthew 28:1–10
Proclaim the resurrection

130   Christ the Lord is risen today!
135   The strife is o'er, the battle done
137   Christians, to the paschal victim
678   Christ has arisen, alleluia

Additional hymns for the day/season

128   Christ the Lord is risen today; Alleluia!
141   The day of resurrection!
142   Hail thee, festival day!
151   Jesus Christ is risen today
153   Welcome, happy morning!
189   We know that Christ is raised
210   At the Lamb's high feast we sing
352   I know that my Redeemer lives!
671   Alleluia, alleluia, give thanks
677   Alleluia Canon

Year B

Hymn of the day

210   At the Lamb's high feast we sing
142   Hail thee, festival day!
679   Our Paschal Lamb, that sets us free

Hymns related to the readings

First Reading: Acts 10:34–43
God raised Jesus on the third day

140   With high delight let us unite
144   Good Christian friends, rejoice and sing!

OR

First Reading: Isaiah 25:6–9
The feast of victory

210   At the Lamb's high feast we sing
672   Christ is risen! Shout hosanna!

Psalmody: Psalm 118:1–2, 14–24
On this day the LORD has acted; we will rejoice and be glad in it. (Ps. 118:24)

Second Reading: 1 Corinthians 15:1–11
Witnesses to the risen Christ

132   Come, you faithful, raise the strain
149, 676   This joyful Eastertide

OR

Second Reading: Acts 10:34–43 *(see first reading)*

Gospel: John 20:1–18
Seeing the risen Christ (see Year A)

OR

Gospel: Mark 16:1–8
The resurrection of Jesus is announced

134   Christ Jesus lay in death's strong bands
135   The strife is o'er, the battle done
153   Welcome, happy morning!
678   Christ has arisen, alleluia

Additional hymns for the day/season
See Year A

Year C

Hymn of the day

676   This joyful Eastertide
129   Awake, my heart, with gladness
134   Christ Jesus lay in death's strong bands

Hymns related to the readings

First Reading: Acts 10:34–43
God raised Jesus on the third day

140   With high delight let us unite
144   Good Christian friends, rejoice and sing!

OR

First Reading: Isaiah 65:17–25
God promises a new heaven and a new earth

525   Blessing and honor
674   Alleluia! Jesus is risen!

Psalmody: Psalm 118:1–2, 14–24
On this day the LORD has acted; we will rejoice and be glad in it. (Ps. 118:24)

Second Reading: 1 Corinthians 15:19–26
Christ raised from the dead, the first fruits

131   Christ is risen! Alleluia!
148   Now the green blade rises
149, 676   This joyful Eastertide

OR

Second Reading: Acts 10:34–43
God raised Jesus on the third day

140   With high delight let us unite
144   Good Christian friends, rejoice and sing!

Gospel: John 20:1–18
Seeing the risen Christ (see Year A)

OR

Gospel: Luke 24:1–12
The women proclaim the resurrection

129   Awake, my heart, with gladness
134   Christ Jesus lay in death's strong bands
135   The strife is o'er, the battle done
137   Christians, to the paschal victim
142   Hail thee, festival day!
151   Jesus Christ is risen today
153   Welcome, happy morning!
678   Christ has arisen, alleluia
692   For all the faithful women

Additional hymns for the day/season
See Year A

THE RESURRECTION OF OUR LORD

EASTER EVENING

Prayer of the day

Almighty God, you give us the joy of celebrating our Lord's resurrection. Give us also the joys of life in your service, and bring us at last to the full joy of life eternal; through your Son, Jesus Christ our Lord, who lives and reigns with you and the Holy Spirit, one God, now and forever. (64)

Verse

Alleluia. Christ being raised from the dead will never die again; death no longer has dominion over him. Alleluia. Beginning with Moses and all the prophets, Jesus interpreted the things about himself in all the scriptures. Alleluia. (Rom. 6:9; Luke 24:27)

Offertory

Alleluia, alleluia, alleluia. The disciples said, The Lord has risen indeed, and he has appeared to Simon! Then they told what had happened on the road, and how Jesus had been made known to them in the breaking of bread. Alleluia, alleluia, alleluia. (Luke 24:34–35)

YEARS A, B, C

Hymn of the day

154   That Easter day with joy was bright
263   Abide with us, our Savior
743   Stay with us

Hymns related to the readings

First Reading: Isaiah 25:6–9
The feast of victory

513   Come, my way, my truth, my life
516   Arise, my soul, arise!
789   Now the feast and celebration

Psalmody: Psalm 114
Hallelujah. (Ps. 114:1)

Second Reading: 1 Corinthians 5:6b–8
Celebrating with sincerity and truth

134   Christ Jesus lay in death's strong bands
141   The day of resurrection!
679   Our Paschal Lamb, that sets us free

Gospel: Luke 24:13–49
At evening, the risen Christ is revealed

154   That Easter day with joy was bright
209   Come, risen Lord
263   Abide with us, our Savior
537   O Jesus, king most wonderful!
674   Alleluia! Jesus is risen!
743   Stay with us

SECOND SUNDAY OF EASTER

Prayer of the day

Almighty God, with joy we celebrate the festival of our Lord's resurrection. Graciously help us to show the power of the resurrection in all that we say and do; through your Son, Jesus Christ our Lord, who lives and reigns with you and the Holy Spirit, one God, now and forever. (65)

Verse

Alleluia. Christ being raised from the dead will never die again; death no longer has dominion over him. Alleluia. Blessed are those who have not seen and yet have come to believe. Alleluia. (Rom. 6:9; John 20:29)

Offertory

Alleluia, alleluia, alleluia. Rid yourselves of all malice, and all guile, insincerity, envy, and all slander. Like newborn infants, long for the pure, spiritual milk, so that by it you may grow into salvation—if indeed you have tasted that the Lord is good. Alleluia, alleluia, alleluia. (1 Peter 2:1–3)

YEAR A

Hymn of the day

139   O sons and daughters of the King
133   Jesus lives! The victory's won!
675   We walk by faith and not by sight

Hymns related to the readings

First Reading: Acts 2:14a, 22–32
Christ's resurrection: the fulfillment of God's promise to David

129   Awake, my heart, with gladness

Psalmody: Psalm 16
In your presence there is fullness of joy. (Ps. 16:11)

Second Reading: 1 Peter 1:3–9
New birth to a living hope through the resurrection

201   O God of life's great mystery
300   O Christ, our hope
514   O Savior, precious Savior

Gospel: John 20:19–31
Beholding the wounds of the risen Christ

129   Awake, my heart, with gladness
132   Come, you faithful, raise the strain
139   O sons and daughters of the King
145   Thine is the glory
154   That Easter day with joy was bright
246   The first day of the week
338   Peace, to soothe our bitter woes
675   We walk by faith and not by sight
722   Hallelujah! We sing your praises

Additional hymns for the day/season

131   Christ is risen! Alleluia!
135   The strife is o'er, the battle done
136   Christ is arisen
150   Make songs of joy
152   Look, now he stands!
315   Love divine, all loves excelling
537   O Jesus, king most wonderful!
672   Christ is risen! Shout hosanna!
721   Go, my children, with my blessing
724   Shalom
774   Dona nobis pacem

Year B

Hymn of the day

132 Come, you faithful, raise the strain
139 O sons and daughters of the King
649 I want to walk as a child of the light

Hymns related to the readings

First Reading: Acts 4:32–35
The believers' common life

189 We know that Christ is raised
703 Draw us in the Spirit's tether

Psalmody: Psalm 133
How good and pleasant it is to live together in unity.
(Ps. 133:1)

Second Reading: 1 John 1:1—2:2
Walking in the light

649 I want to walk as a child of the light
800 Each morning brings us fresh outpoured

Gospel: John 20:19–31
Beholding the wounds of the risen Christ
See Year A

Additional hymns for the day/season
See Year A

Year C

Hymn of the day

145 Thine is the glory
148 Now the green blade rises
675 We walk by faith and not by sight

Hymns related to the readings

First Reading: Acts 5:27–32
The God of our ancestors raised up Jesus

328, 329 All hail the power of Jesus' name!

Psalmody: Psalm 118:14–29
This is the LORD's doing and it is marvelous in our
eyes. (Ps. 118:23)

OR

Psalmody: Psalm 150
Let everything that has breath praise the LORD.
(Ps. 150:6)

Second Reading: Revelation 1:4–8
Jesus Christ, the firstborn of the dead, is coming

27   Lo! He comes with clouds descending
172 Lord, enthroned in heavenly splendor
173 The head that once was crowned

Gospel: John 20:19–31
Beholding the wounds of the risen Christ
See Year A

Additional hymns for the day/season
See Year A

Prayer of the day

O God, by the humiliation of your Son you lifted up this fallen world, rescuing us from the hopelessness of death. Grant your faithful people a share in the joys that are eternal; through your Son, Jesus Christ our Lord, who lives and reigns with you and the Holy Spirit, one God, now and forever. (66)

Verse

Alleluia. Christ being raised from the dead will never die again; death no longer has dominion over him. Alleluia. Our hearts burn within us while he opens to us the scriptures. (Rom. 6:9; Luke 24:32)

Offertory

Alleluia, alleluia, alleluia. Christ is the image of the invisible God, the firstborn of all creation; for in him all things were created. He is the head of the body, the Church; he is the beginning, the firstborn from the dead. For in him all the fullness of God was pleased to dwell, and through him God was pleased to reconcile to himself all things, whether on earth or in heaven, by making peace through the blood of his cross. Alleluia, alleluia, alleluia. (Col. 1:15–20)

YEAR A

Hymn of the day

140 With high delight let us unite
207 We who once were dead
743 Stay with us

Hymns related to the readings

First Reading: Acts 2:14a, 36–41
Receiving God's promise through baptism

693 Baptized in water
793 Shout for joy loud and long

Psalmody: Psalm 116:1–3, 10–17*
I will call upon the name of the LORD. (Ps. 116:11)

Second Reading: 1 Peter 1:17–23
Born anew through the living word of God

10   Sing praise to the Lord
189 We know that Christ is raised
769 Mothering God, you gave me birth

Gospel: Luke 24:13–35
Eating with the risen Christ

154 That Easter day with joy was bright
207 We who once were dead
209 Come, risen Lord
263 Abide with us, our Savior
674 Alleluia! Jesus is risen!
743 Stay with us
754 Let us talents and tongues employ

Additional hymns for the day/season

131 Christ is risen! Alleluia!
134 Christ Jesus lay in death's strong bands
149 This joyful Eastertide
200 For the bread which you have broken
214 Come, let us eat
336 Jesus, thy boundless love to me
508 Come down, O Love divine
672 Christ is risen! Shout hosanna!
676 This joyful Eastertide
711 You satisfy the hungry heart

Year B

Hymn of the day
675 We walk by faith and not by sight
135 The strife is o'er, the battle done
140 With high delight let us unite

Hymns related to the readings

First Reading: Acts 3:12–19
Health and forgiveness through the risen Jesus

142 Hail thee, festival day!
672 Christ is risen! Shout hosanna!

Psalmody: Psalm 4
The LORD does wonders for the faithful. (Ps. 4:3)

Second Reading: 1 John 3:1–7
The revealing of the children of God

10 Sing praise to the Lord
133 Jesus lives! The victory's won!
315 Love divine, all loves excelling

Gospel: Luke 24:36b–48
Eating with the risen Christ

207 We who once were dead
496 Around you, O Lord Jesus

537 O Jesus, king most wonderful!
672 Christ is risen! Shout hosanna!
674 Alleluia! Jesus is risen!
675 We walk by faith and not by sight
722 Hallelujah! We sing your praises
753 You are the seed

Additional hymns for the day/season
134 Christ Jesus lay in death's strong bands
143 Now all the vault of heaven resounds
149 This joyful Eastertide
209 Come, risen Lord
210 At the Lamb's high feast we sing
214 Come, let us eat
671 Alleluia, alleluia, give thanks
676 This joyful Eastertide
743 Stay with us
754 Let us talents and tongues employ

Year C

Hymn of the day
791 Alabaré
525 Blessing and honor
154 That Easter day with joy was bright

Hymns related to the readings

First Reading: Acts 9:1–6 [7–20]
Paul's conversion, baptism, and preaching

177 By all your saints in warfare (stanza 11)
793 Shout for joy loud and long

Psalmody: Psalm 30
You have turned my wailing into dancing. (Ps. 30:12)

Second Reading: Revelation 5:11–14
The song of the living creatures to the Lamb

252 You servants of God
254 Come, let us join our cheerful songs
516 Arise, my soul, arise!
525 Blessing and honor
669 Come away to the skies
789 Now the feast and celebration
791 Alabaré

Gospel: John 21:1–19
Jesus appears to the disciples at the Sea of Tiberias

433 The Church of Christ, in every age
696 I've just come from the fountain
793 Shout for joy loud and long

Additional hymns for the day/season
143 Now all the vault of heaven resounds
207 We who once were dead
209 Come, risen Lord
210 At the Lamb's high feast we sing
385 What wondrous love is this
672 Christ is risen! Shout hosanna!
674 Alleluia! Jesus is risen!
679 Our Paschal Lamb that sets us free
754 Let us talents and tongues employ

*Psalm 116:1–4, 12–19 (NRSV)

Prayer of the day

God of all power, you called from death our Lord Jesus, the great shepherd of the sheep. Send us as shepherds to rescue the lost, to heal the injured, and to feed one another with knowledge and understanding; through your Son, Jesus Christ our Lord, who lives and reigns with you and the Holy Spirit, one God, now and forever. (67)

OR

Almighty God, you show the light of your truth to those in darkness, to lead them into the way of righteousness. Give strength to all who are joined in the family of the Church, so that they will resolutely reject what erodes their faith and firmly follow what faith requires; through your Son, Jesus Christ our Lord, who lives and reigns with you and the Holy Spirit, one God, now and forever. (68)

Verse

Alleluia. Christ being raised from the dead will never die again; death no longer has dominion over him. Alleluia. I am the good shepherd. I know my own and my own know me. Alleluia. (Rom. 6:9; John 10:14)

Offertory

Alleluia, alleluia, alleluia. Thus says the Lord GOD: I myself will search for my sheep, and will seek them out. As shepherds seek out their flocks when they are among their scattered sheep, so I will seek out my sheep. I will bring them out from the peoples, and I will feed them on the mountains of Israel. Alleluia, alleluia, alleluia. (Ezek. 34:11–13)

YEAR A

Hymn of the day

456 The King of love my shepherd is
451 The Lord's my shepherd
679 Our Paschal Lamb, that sets us free

Hymns related to the readings

First Reading: Acts 2:42–47
The believers' common life

496 Around you, O Lord Jesus
703 Draw us in the Spirit's tether
780 What a fellowship, what a joy divine

Psalmody: Psalm 23
The LORD is my shepherd; I shall not be in want. (Ps. 23:1)

451 The Lord's my shepherd (paraphrase)
456 The King of love my shepherd is (paraphrase)

Second Reading: 1 Peter 2:19–25
Follow the shepherd, even in suffering

135 The strife is o'er, the battle done
300 O Christ, our hope
410 We give thee but thine own
499 Come, thou Fount of every blessing

Gospel: John 10:1–10
Christ the shepherd

196 Praise the Lord, rise up rejoicing
371 With God as our friend
372 In Adam we have all been one
481 Savior, like a shepherd lead us

Additional hymns for the day/season

128 Christ the Lord is risen today; Alleluia!
137 Christians, to the paschal victim
206 Lord, who the night you were betrayed
210 At the Lamb's high feast we sing
245 All people that on earth do dwell
256 Oh, sing jubilee to the Lord
352 I know that my Redeemer lives
371 With God as our friend
476 Have no fear, little flock
679 Our Paschal Lamb, that sets us free
711 You satisfy the hungry heart

YEAR B

Hymn of the day
451   The Lord's my shepherd
206   Lord, who the night you were betrayed
476   Have no fear, little flock

Hymns related to the readings

First Reading: Acts 4:5–12
Salvation in the name of Jesus

179   At the name of Jesus
345   How sweet the name of Jesus sounds
446   Whatever God ordains is right
750   Oh, praise the gracious power

Psalmody: Psalm 23
The LORD is my shepherd; I shall not be in want.
(Ps. 23:1)

451   The Lord's my shepherd (paraphrase)
456   The King of love my shepherd is (paraphrase)

Second Reading: 1 John 3:16–24
Love in truth and action

144   Good Christian friends, rejoice and sing!
551   Joyful, joyful we adore thee

745   Awake, O sleeper
800   Each morning brings us fresh outpoured

Gospel: John 10:11–18
Christ the shepherd

144   Good Christian friends, rejoice and sing!
196   Praise the Lord, rise up rejoicing
206   Lord, who the night you were betrayed

Additional hymns for the day/season
See Year A

YEAR C

Hymn of the day
371   With God as our friend
456   The King of love my shepherd is
673   I'm so glad Jesus lifted me

Hymns related to the readings

First Reading: Acts 9:36–43
Peter raises Tabitha/Dorcas from the dead

133   Jesus lives! The victory's won!
148   Now the green blade rises
207   We who once were dead
673   I'm so glad Jesus lifted me

Psalmody: Psalm 23
The LORD is my shepherd; I shall not be in want.
(Ps. 23:1)

451   The Lord's my shepherd (paraphrase)
456   The King of love my shepherd is (paraphrase)

Second Reading: Revelation 7:9–17
A white-robed multitude sings before the Lamb

175   Ye watchers and ye holy ones
252   You servants of God
254   Come, let us join our cheerful songs

313   A multitude comes from the east and the west
314   Who is this host arrayed in white
516   Arise, my soul, arise
525   Blessing and honor
669   Come away to the skies
691   Sing with all the saints in glory
789   Now the feast and celebration

Gospel: John 10:22–30
Jesus promises eternal life to his sheep

196   Praise the Lord, rise up rejoicing
361   Do not despair, O little flock
371   With God as our friend
372   In Adam we have all been one
476   Have no fear, little flock
552   In thee is gladness

Additional hymns for the day/season
See Year A

Prayer of the day

O God, form the minds of your faithful people into a single will. Make us love what you command and desire what you promise, that, amid all the changes of this world, our hearts may be fixed where true joy is found; through your Son, Jesus Christ our Lord, who lives and reigns with you and the Holy Spirit, one God, now and forever. (69)

Verse

Alleluia. Christ being raised from the dead will never die again; death no longer has dominion over him. Jesus said, I am the way, and the truth, and the life. Alleluia. (Rom. 6:9; John 14:6)

Offertory

Alleluia, alleluia, alleluia. Give thanks to the LORD, call on his name; make known his deeds among the nations; proclaim that his name is exalted. Sing praises to the LORD, for he has done gloriously; let this be known in all the earth. Shout aloud and sing for joy, O royal Zion, for great in your midst is the Holy One of Israel. Alleluia, alleluia, alleluia. (Isa. 12:4–6)

YEAR A

Hymn of the day

513 Come, my way, my truth, my life
143 Now all the vault of heaven resounds
691 Sing with all the saints in glory

Hymns related to the readings

First Reading: Acts 7:55–60
The martyrdom of Stephen

138 He is arisen! Glorious Word!
177 By all your saints in warfare (stanza 7)
183 The Son of God goes forth to war

Psalmody: Psalm 31:1–5, 15–16
Into your hands, O LORD, I commend my spirit. (Ps. 31:5)

Second Reading: 1 Peter 2:2–10
God's people chosen to proclaim God's mighty acts

367 Christ is made the sure foundation
446 Whatever God ordains is right
697 Wash, O God, our sons and daughters
747 Christ is made the sure foundation

Gospel: John 14:1–14
Christ the way, truth, and life

147 Hallelujah! Jesus lives
464 You are the way
465 Evening and morning
513 Come, my way, my truth, my life
674 Alleluia! Jesus is risen!
691 Sing with all the saints in glory
700 I received the living God

Additional hymns for the day/season

129 Awake, my heart, with gladness
210 At the Lamb's high feast we sing
267 Father, we praise you
336 Jesus, thy boundless love to me
340 Jesus Christ, my sure defense
352 I know that my Redeemer lives
671 Alleluia, alleluia, give thanks

YEAR B

Hymn of the day
695   O blessed spring
378   Amid the world's bleak wilderness
674   Alleluia! Jesus is risen!

Hymns related to the readings

First Reading: Acts 8:26–40
Philip teaches and baptizes an Ethiopian

260   On our way rejoicing
696   I've just come from the fountain

Psalmody: Psalm 22:24–30*
All the ends of the earth shall turn to the LORD. (Ps. 22:26)

Second Reading: 1 John 4:7–21
God's love perfected in love for one another

317   To God the Holy Spirit let us pray
441   Eternal Spirit of the living Christ
508   Come down, O Love divine
551   Joyful, joyful we adore thee
745   Awake, O sleeper
765   Jesu, Jesu, fill us with your love

Gospel: John 15:1–8
Christ the vine

378   Amid the world's bleak wilderness
668   There in God's garden
674   Alleluia! Jesus is risen!
685   Like the murmur of the dove's song
695   O blessed spring

Additional hymns for the day/season
148   Now the green blade rises
189   We know that Christ is raised
306   Chief of sinners though I be
363   Christ is alive! Let Christians sing
545, 546   When morning gilds the skies
662   Restore in us, O God

YEAR C

Hymn of the day
363   Christ is alive! Let Christians sing
143   Now all the vault of heaven resounds
666   Great God, your love has called us

Hymns related to the readings

First Reading: Acts 11:1–18
Peter's vision: God gives the Gentiles repentance that leads to life

140   With high delight let us unite
671   Alleluia, alleluia, give thanks
710   One bread, one body

Psalmody: Psalm 148
The splendor of the LORD is over earth and heaven. (Ps. 148:13)

540   Praise the Lord! O heavens (paraphrase)
541   Praise the Lord of heaven! (paraphrase)

Second Reading: Revelation 21:1–6
New heaven, new earth: springs of living water in the new Jerusalem

330   In heaven above
331   Jerusalem, my happy home

337   Oh, what their joy
347   Jerusalem the golden
348   Jerusalem, whose towers touch the skies
674   Alleluia! Jesus is risen!
742   Come, we that love the Lord

Gospel: John 13:31–35
Jesus gives a new commandment: Love one another as I have loved you

126   Where charity and love prevail
317   To God the Holy Spirit let us pray
664   A new commandment
745   Awake, O sleeper
765   Jesu, Jesu, fill us with your love

Additional hymns for the day/season
148   Now the green blade rises
210   At the Lamb's high feast we sing
336   Jesus, thy boundless love to me
419   Lord of all nations, grant me grace
423   Lord, whose love in humble service
520   Give to our God immortal praise
551   Joyful, joyful we adore thee
665   Ubi caritas et amor
672   Christ is risen! Shout hosanna!

*Psalm 22:25–31 (NRSV)

Prayer of the day

O God, from whom all good things come: Lead us by the inspiration of your Spirit to think those things which are right, and by your goodness help us to do them; through your Son, Jesus Christ our Lord, who lives and reigns with you and the Holy Spirit, one God, now and forever. (70)

Verse

Alleluia. Christ being raised from the dead will never die again; death no longer has dominion over him. Alleluia. Those who love me will keep my word, and my Father will love them, and we will come to them and make our home with them. Alleluia. (Rom 6:9; John 14:23)

Offertory

Alleluia, alleluia, alleluia. Very truly, I tell you, the one who believes in me will also do the works that I do and, in fact, will do greater works than these, because I am going to the Father. I will do whatever you ask in my name, so that the Father may be glorified in the Son. If in my name you ask me for anything, I will do it. Alleluia, alleluia, alleluia. (John 14:12–14)

YEAR A

Hymn of the day

299   Dear Christians, one and all
508   Come down, O Love divine
793   Shout for joy loud and long

Hymns related to the readings

First Reading: Acts 17:22–31
Paul's message to the Athenians

397   O Zion, haste
671   Alleluia, alleluia, give thanks
682   Praise the Spirit in creation
767   All things bright and beautiful
794   Many and great, O God, are your works

Psalmody: Psalm 66:7–18*
Be joyful in God, all you lands. (Ps. 66:1)

Second Reading: 1 Peter 3:13–22
The days of Noah, a sign of baptism

153   Welcome, happy morning!
189   We know that Christ is raised
741   Thy holy wings

Gospel: John 14:15–21
Christ our advocate

158   Alleluia! Sing to Jesus
354   Eternal God, before your throne
508   Come down, O Love divine
524   My God, how wonderful thou art
685   Like the murmur of the dove's song

Additional hymns for the day/season

315   Love divine, all loves excelling
474   Children of the heavenly Father
522   Come, thou almighty King
680   O Spirit of life
683   Loving Spirit
693   Baptized in water
795   Oh, sing to the Lord

Hymn of the day

143 Now all the vault of heaven resounds
189 We know that Christ is raised
789 Now the feast and celebration

Hymns related to the readings

First Reading: Acts 10:44–48
The Spirit poured out on the Gentiles

140 With high delight
397 O Zion, haste
671 Alleluia, alleluia, give thanks
710 One bread, one body

Psalmody: Psalm 98
Shout with joy to the LORD, all you lands. (Ps. 98:5)

Second Reading: 1 John 5:1–6
The victory of faith

327 Rock of Ages, cleft for me
703 Draw us in the Spirit's tether
746 Day by day

Gospel: John 15:9–17
Christ the friend and lover

144 Good Christian friends, rejoice and sing!
215 O Lord, we praise you
441 Eternal Spirit of the living Christ
551 Joyful, joyful we adore thee
662 Restore in us, O God
666 Great God, your love has called us
672 Christ is risen! Shout hosanna!

Additional hymns for the day/season

172 Lord, enthroned in heavenly splendor
222 O Bread of life from heaven
363 Christ is alive! Let Christians sing
439 What a friend we have in Jesus
524 My God, how wonderful thou art
765 Jesu, Jesu, fill us with your love

YEAR C

Hymn of the day

674 Alleluia! Jesus is risen!
166 All glory be to God on high
358 Glories of your name are spoken

Hymns related to the readings

First Reading: Acts 16:9–15
Lydia and her household are baptized by Paul

697 Wash, O God, our sons and daughters

Psalmody: Psalm 67
Let the nations be glad and sing for joy. (Ps. 67:4)

335 May God bestow on us his grace (paraphrase)

Second Reading: Revelation 21:10, 22—22:5
The Lamb is the light of the city of God

331 Jerusalem, my happy home
337 Oh, what their joy
347 Jerusalem the golden
348 Jerusalem, whose towers touch the skies
649 I want to walk as a child of the light
668 There in God's garden
669 Come away to the skies
672 Christ is risen! Shout hosanna!
674 Alleluia! Jesus is risen!
690 Shall we gather at the river

Gospel: John 14:23–29
The Father will send the Holy Spirit

338 Peace, to soothe our bitter woes
440 Christians, while on earth abiding
471 Grant peace, we pray in mercy, Lord
508 Come down, O Love divine
680 O Spirit of life
685 Like the murmur of the dove's song
724 Shalom
774 Dona nobis pacem

OR

Gospel: John 5:1–9
Jesus heals on the Sabbath

142 Hail thee, festival day!
393 Rise, shine, you people!
668 There in God's garden

Additional hymns for the day/season

129 Awake, my heart, with gladness
386 Christ is the king!
536 O God of God, O Light of light
537 O Jesus, king most wonderful!
650 We are marching in the light of God
721 Go, my children, with my blessing
742 Come, we that love the Lord
781 My life flows on in endless song
801 Thine the amen, thine the praise

*Psalm 66:8–20 (NRSV)

THE ASCENSION OF OUR LORD

Prayer of the day

Almighty God, your only Son was taken up into heaven and in power intercedes for us. May we also come into your presence and live forever in your glory; through your Son, Jesus Christ our Lord, who lives and reigns with you and the Holy Spirit, one God, now and forever. (71)

Verse

Alleluia. Christ being raised from the dead will never die again; death no longer has dominion over him. Alleluia. I am with you always, to the end of the age. Alleluia. (Rom. 6:9; Matt. 28:20)

Offertory

Alleluia, alleluia, alleluia. I saw one like a human being coming with the clouds of heaven. And he came to the Ancient One and was presented before him. To him was given dominion and glory and king-ship, that all peoples, nations, and languages should serve him. His dominion is an everlasting dominion that shall not pass away, and his kingship is one that shall never be destroyed. Alleluia, alleluia, alleluia. (Dan. 7:13–14)

YEARS A, B, C

Hymn of the day

157 A hymn of glory let us sing
159 Up through endless ranks of angels
756 Lord, you give the great commission

Hymns related to the readings

First Reading: Acts 1:1–11
Jesus sends the apostles

157 A hymn of glory let us sing!
682 Praise the Spirit in creation
756 Lord, you give the great commission

Psalmody: Psalm 47
God has gone up with a shout. (Ps. 47:5)

OR

Psalmody: Psalm 93
Ever since the world began, your throne has been established. (Ps. 93:3)

Second Reading: Ephesians 1:15–23
Eyes to see the risen and ascended Christ

179 At the name of Jesus
363 Christ is alive! Let Christians sing
518 Beautiful Savior

Gospel: Luke 24:44–53
Christ present in all times and places

159 Up through endless ranks of angels
756 Lord, you give the great commission

Additional hymns for the day/season

142 Hail thee, festival day! (Ascension)
156 Look, the sight is glorious
158 Alleluia! Sing to Jesus
170 Crown him with many crowns
171 Rejoice, the Lord is king!
172 Lord, enthroned in heavenly splendor
173 The head that once was crowned
400 O Christ, our hope
520 Give to our God immortal praise!
669 Come away to the skies

SEVENTH SUNDAY OF EASTER

Prayer of the day

Almighty and eternal God, your Son our Savior is with you in eternal glory. Give us faith to see that, true to his promise, he is among us still, and will be with us to the end of time; who lives and reigns with you and the Holy Spirit, one God, now and forever. (72)

OR

God, our creator and redeemer, your Son Jesus prayed that his followers might be one. Make all Christians one with him as he is one with you, so that in peace and concord we may carry to the world the message of your love; through Jesus Christ our Lord, who lives and reigns with you and the Holy Spirit, one God, now and forever. (73)

Verse

Alleluia. Christ being raised from the dead will never die again; death no longer has dominion over him. Alleluia. I will not leave you orphaned; I am coming to you. Alleluia. (Rom. 6:9; John 14:18)

Offertory

Alleluia, alleluia, alleluia. Ask, and it will be given you; search, and you will find; knock, and the door will be opened for you. Is there anyone among you who, if your child asks for bread, will give a stone? If you then know how to give good gifts to your children, how much more will your Father in heaven give good things to those who ask him! Alleluia, alleluia, alleluia. (Matt. 7:7, 9, 11)

YEAR A

Hymn of the day
88   Oh, love, how deep
156   Look, the sight is glorious
756   Lord, you give the great commission

Hymns related to the readings

First Reading: Acts 1:6–14
Jesus' companions at prayer after his departure

142   Hail thee, festival day!(Ascension)
157   A hymn of glory let us sing!
159   Up through endless ranks of angels
391   And have the bright immensities
719   God is here!

Psalmody: Psalm 68:1–10, 33–36*
Sing to God, who rides upon the heavens. (Ps. 68:4)

Second Reading: 1 Peter 4:12–14; 5:6–11
God will sustain and restore those who suffer

438   Lord, teach us how to pray aright
507   How firm a foundation
746   Day by day

Gospel: John 17:1–11
Christ's prayer for his disciples

206   Lord, who the night you were betrayed
225   Lord Jesus Christ, we humbly pray
704   Father, we thank you

Additional hymns for the day/season
170   Crown him with many crowns
173   The head that once was crowned
363   Christ is alive! Let Christians sing
364   Son of God, eternal Savior
369   The Church's one foundation
400   O Christ, our hope
703   Draw us in the Spirit's tether
711   You satisfy the hungry heart
748   Bind us together
801   Thine the amen, thine the praise

Hymn of the day

158 Alleluia! Sing to Jesus
88 Oh, love, how deep
367, 747 Christ is made the sure foundation

Hymns related to the readings

First Reading: Acts 1:15–17, 21–26
Matthias added to the apostles

177 By all your saints in warfare (stanza 12)
523 Holy Spirit, ever dwelling

Psalmody: Psalm 1
The LORD knows the way of the righteous. (Ps. 1:6)

Second Reading: 1 John 5:9–13
Life in the Son of God

364 Son of God, eternal Savior

Gospel: John 17:6–19
Christ's prayer for his disciples

206 Lord, who the night you were betrayed
405 Lord of light
432 We worship you, O God of might
364 Son of God, eternal Savior

704 Father, we thank you
705 As the grains of wheat

Additional hymns for the day/season
See Year A

YEAR C

Hymn of the day

801 Thine the amen, thine the praise
76 O Morning Star, how fair and bright!
364 Son of God, eternal Savior

Hymns related to the readings

First Reading: Acts 16:16–34
While in prison, Paul speaks to the jailer, who is then baptized

453 If you but trust in God to guide you
555, 802 When in our music God is glorified

Psalmody: Psalm 97
Rejoice in the LORD, you righteous. (Ps. 97:12)

Second Reading: Revelation 22:12–14, 16–17, 20–21
Blessed are those who wash their robes

33 The King shall come
76 O Morning Star, how fair and bright!
358 Glories of your name are spoken
668 There in God's garden

Gospel: John 17:20–26
Jesus prays that the disciples will be one and abide in his love

225 Lord Jesus Christ, we humbly pray
255 Lord, receive this company
364 Son of God, eternal Savior
704 Father, we thank you

Additional hymns for the day/season

88 Oh, love, how deep
158 Alleluia! Sing to Jesus
206 Lord, who the night you were betrayed
465 Evening and morning
545, 546 When morning gilds the skies
672 Christ is risen! Shout hosanna!
695 O blessed spring
750 Oh, praise the gracious power
See Year A

*Psalm 68:1–10, 32–35 (NRSV)

VIGIL OF PENTECOST

Prayer of the day

Almighty and ever-living God, you fulfilled the promise of Easter by sending your Holy Spirit to unite the races and nations on earth and thus to proclaim your glory. Look upon your people gathered in prayer, open to receive the Spirit's flame. May it come to rest in our hearts and heal the divisions of word and tongue, that with one voice and one song we may praise your name in joy and thanksgiving; through your Son, Jesus Christ our Lord, who lives and reigns with you and the Holy Spirit, one God, now and forever. (74)

Verse

Alleluia. Come, Holy Spirit, fill the hearts of your faithful people; set them on fire with your love. Alleluia.

Offertory

Be careful then how you live, not as unwise people but as wise. Be filled with the Spirit, as you sing psalms and hymns and spiritual songs among yourselves, singing and making melody to the Lord in your hearts, giving thanks to God the Father at all times and for everything in the name of our Lord Jesus Christ. (Eph. 5:15, 18–20)

YEARS A, B, C

Hymn of the day

508   Come down, O Love divine
472, 473 Come, Holy Ghost, our souls inspire
684   Spirit, Spirit of gentleness

Hymns related to the readings

First Reading: Exodus 19:1–9
The covenant at Sinai

282   Now rest beneath night's shadow
688   O Holy Spirit, root of life
779   You who dwell in the shelter of the Lord

OR

First Reading: Acts 2:1–11
Filled with the Spirit to tell God's deeds

161   O day full of grace
388   O Spirit of the living God
413   Father eternal, ruler of creation

Psalmody: Psalm 33:12–22
The LORD is our help and our shield. (Ps. 33:20)

OR

Psalmody: Psalm 130
There is forgiveness with you. (Ps. 130:3)

295   Out of the depths I cry to you (paraphrase)

Second Reading: Romans 8:14–17, 22–27
Praying with the Spirit

441   Eternal Spirit of the living Christ

682   Praise the Spirit in creation
688   O Holy Spirit, root of life

Gospel: John 7:37–39
Jesus is the true living water

497   I heard the voice of Jesus say
693   Baptized in water

Additional hymns for the day/season

160   Filled with the Spirit's power
358   Glories of your name are spoken
486   Spirit of God, descend upon my heart
681   Come, O Holy Spirit, come
685   Like the murmur of the dove's song
686   Veni Sancte Spiritus
773   Send me, Jesus

Prayer of the day

God, the Father of our Lord Jesus Christ, as you sent upon the disciples the promised gift of the Holy Spirit, look upon your Church and open our hearts to the power of the Spirit. Kindle in us the fire of your love, and strengthen our lives for service in your kingdom; through your Son, Jesus Christ our Lord, who lives and reigns with you in the unity of the Holy Spirit, one God, now and forever. (75)

OR

(Year C) God our creator, earth has many languages, but your Gospel announces your love to all nations in one heavenly speech. Make us messengers of the good news that, through the power of your Spirit, everyone everywhere may unite in one song of praise; through your Son, Jesus Christ our Lord, who lives and reigns with you in the unity of the Holy Spirit, one God, now and forever. (76)

Verse

Alleluia. Come, Holy Spirit, fill the hearts of your faithful people; set them on fire with your love. Alleluia.
The Sequence hymn, LBW #472, may follow.

Offertory

Be careful then how you live, not as unwise people but as wise. Be filled with the Spirit, as you sing psalms and hymns and spiritual songs among yourselves, singing and making melody to the Lord in your hearts, giving thanks to God the Father at all times and for everything in the name of our Lord Jesus Christ. (Eph. 5:15, 18–20)

YEAR A

Hymn of the day

161	O day full of grace
163	Come, Holy Ghost, God and Lord
682	Praise the Spirit in creation

Hymns related to the readings

First Reading: Acts 2:1–21
Filled with the Spirit to tell God's deeds

161	O day full of grace
284	Creator Spirit, heavenly dove
387	Spirit of God, unleashed on earth
388	O Spirit of the living God
396	O God, O Lord of heaven and earth
472, 473	Come, Holy Ghost, our souls inspire
681	Come, O Holy Spirit, come
686	Veni Sancte Spiritus

OR

First Reading: Numbers 11:24–30
The Spirit comes upon the elders of Israel

682	Praise the Spirit in creation
683	Loving Spirit

Psalmody: Psalm 104:25–35, 37*
Alleluia. OR Send forth your Spirit and renew the face of the earth. (Ps. 104:31)

Second Reading: 1 Corinthians 12:3b–13
Varieties of gifts from the same Spirit

204	Cup of blessing that we share
703	Draw us in the Spirit's tether
710	One bread, one body
755	We all are one in mission
758	Come to us, creative Spirit

OR

Second Reading: Acts 2:1–21 *(see first reading)*

Gospel: John 20:19–23
The Spirit poured out

685	Like the murmur of the dove's song
756	Lord, you give the great commission
773	Send me, Jesus

OR

Gospel: John 7:37–39
Jesus is the true living water

251	O day of rest and gladness
693	Baptized in water

Additional hymns for the day/season

160	Filled with the Spirit's power
162	Lord God, the Holy Ghost
164	Creator Spirit, by whose aid
317	To God the Holy Spirit let us pray
459	O Holy Spirit, enter in

472, 473 Come, Holy Ghost, our souls inspire
475 Come, gracious Spirit, heavenly dove
478 Come, oh, come, O quickening Spirit
508 Come down, O Love divine
523 Holy Spirit, ever dwelling

680 O Spirit of life
684 Spirit, Spirit of gentleness
685 Like the murmur of the dove's song
687 Gracious Spirit, heed our pleading

YEAR B

Hymn of the day
685 Like the murmur of the dove's song
161 O day full of grace
163 Come, Holy Ghost, God and Lord

Hymns related to the readings

First Reading: Acts 2:1–21
Filled with the Spirit to tell God's deeds
See Year A, first reading

OR

First Reading: Ezekiel 37:1–14
Life to dry bones

488 Breathe on me, breath of God
658 The Word of God is source and seed
686 Veni Sancte Spiritus

Psalmody: Psalm 104:25–35, 37*
Alleluia. OR *Send forth your Spirit and renew the face of the earth. (Ps. 104:31)*

Second Reading: Romans 8:22–27
Praying with the Spirit

441 Eternal Spirit of the living Christ
682 Praise the Spirit in creation
688 O Holy Spirit, root of life

OR

Second Reading: Acts 2:1–21
Filled with the Spirit to tell God's deeds
See Year A, first reading

Gospel: John 15:26–27; 16:4b–15
Christ sends the Spirit of truth

472, 473 Come, Holy Ghost, our souls inspire
680 O Spirit of life
687 Gracious Spirit, heed our pleading

Additional hymns for the day/season
See Year A

YEAR C

Hymn of the day
284 Creator Spirit, heavenly dove
523 Holy Spirit, ever dwelling
687 Gracious Spirit, heed our pleading

Hymns related to the readings

First Reading: Acts 2:1–21
Filled with the Spirit to tell God's deeds
See Year A, first reading

OR

First Reading: Genesis 11:1–9
God destroys the tower of Babel

413 Father eternal, ruler of creation
531 Before Jehovah's awesome throne

Psalmody: Psalm 104:25–35, 37*
Alleluia. OR *Send forth your Spirit and renew the face of the earth. (Ps. 104:31)*

Second Reading: Romans 8:14–17
The Spirit makes us children of God

225 Lord Jesus Christ, we humbly pray
683 Loving Spirit

OR

Second Reading: Acts 2:1–21
Filled with the Spirit to proclaim God's deeds
See Year A, first reading

Gospel: John 14:8–17 [25–27]
The Father will give you another Advocate, the Spirit of truth

475 Come, gracious Spirit, heavenly dove
508 Come down, O Love divine
537 O Jesus, king most wonderful!

Additional hymns for the day/season
See Year A

*Psalm 104:24–34, 35b (NRSV)

THE HOLY TRINITY

Prayer of the day

Almighty God our Father, dwelling in majesty and mystery, renewing and fulfilling creation by your eternal Spirit, and revealing your glory through our Lord, Jesus Christ: Cleanse us from doubt and fear, and enable us to worship you, with your Son and the Holy Spirit, one God, living and reigning, now and forever. (77)

OR

Almighty and ever-living God, you have given us grace, by the confession of the true faith, to acknowledge the glory of the eternal Trinity and, in the power of your divine majesty, to worship the unity. Keep us steadfast in this faith and worship, and bring us at last to see you in your eternal glory, one God, now and forever. (78)

Verse

Alleluia. Holy, holy, holy is the LORD of hosts; the whole earth is full of his glory. Alleluia. (Isa. 6:3)

Offertory

Great and amazing are your deeds, Lord God the Almighty! Just and true are your ways, King of the nations! Lord, who will not fear and glorify your name? For you alone are holy. All nations will come and worship you, for your judgments have been revealed. (Rev. 15:3–4)

YEAR A

Hymn of the day

535	Holy God, we praise your name
400	God, whose almighty word
799	When long before time

Hymns related to the readings

First Reading: Genesis 1:1—2:4a
The creation of the heavens and the earth

164	Creator Spirit, by whose aid
233	Thy strong Word
266	Maker of the earth and heaven
400	God, whose almighty word
467	Eternal Father, strong to save
527	All creatures of our God and King
557	Let all things now living
682	Praise the Spirit in creation
688	O Holy Spirit, root of life
726	Oh, sing to God above
727	Lord, your hands have formed
757	Creating God, your fingers trace
769	Mothering God, you gave me birth
793	Shout for joy loud and long
794	Many and great, O God, are your works
799	When long before time

Psalmody: Psalm 8
How exalted is your name in all the world! (Ps. 8:1)

Second Reading: 2 Corinthians 13:11–13
Paul's farewell to the church at Corinth

166	All glory be to God on high
440	Christians, while on earth abiding
721	Go, my children, with my blessing

Gospel: Matthew 28:16–20
Living in the community of the Trinity

140	With high delight let us unite
379	Spread, oh, spread, almighty Word
393	Rise, shine, you people!
396	O God, O Lord of heaven and earth
756	Lord, you give the great commission

Additional hymns for the day/season

165	Holy, holy, holy
167	Glory be to God the Father!
168	Kyrie, God Father
169	Father, most holy
188	I bind unto myself today
205	Now the silence

230 Lord, keep us steadfast in your Word	517 Praise to the Father
267 Father, we praise you	522 Come, thou almighty King
284 Creator Spirit, heavenly dove	533, 534 Now thank we all our God
354 Eternal God, before your throne	535 Holy God, we praise your name
374 We all believe in one true God	564, 565 Praise God from whom all blessings flow
472, 473 Come, Holy Ghost, our souls inspire	717 Come, all you people
490 Let me be yours forever	796 My Lord of light

YEAR B

Hymn of the day
165 Holy, holy, holy
166 All glory be to God on high
769 Mothering God, you gave me birth

Hymns related to the readings

First Reading: Isaiah 6:1–8
Isaiah's vision and call

247 Holy Majesty, before you
253 Lord Jesus Christ, be present now
432 We worship you, O God of might
528 Isaiah in a vision did of old
535 Holy God, we praise your name
544 The God of Abraham praise
547 Thee we adore, eternal Lord

Psalmody: Psalm 29
Worship the LORD in the beauty of holiness. (Ps. 29:2)

Second Reading: Romans 8:12–17
Living by the Spirit

472, 473 Come, Holy Ghost, our souls inspire
475 Come, gracious Spirit, heavenly dove

Gospel: John 3:1–17
Entering the reign of God through water and the Spirit

292 God loved the world
693 Baptized in water
769 Mothering God, you gave me birth

Additional hymns for the day/season
See Year A

YEAR C

Hymn of the day
169 Father, most holy
164 Creator Spirit, by whose aid
796 My Lord of light

Hymns related to the readings

First Reading: Proverbs 8:1–4, 22–31
Wisdom rejoices in the creation

526 Immortal, invisible, God only wise
688 O Holy Spirit, root of life
726 Oh, sing to God above

Psalmody: Psalm 8
Your majesty is praised above the heavens. (Ps. 8:2)

Second Reading: Romans 5:1–5
God's love poured into our hearts through the Holy Spirit

317 To God the Holy Spirit let us pray

Gospel: John 16:12–15
The Spirit will guide you into the truth

164 Creator Spirit, by whose aid
284 Creator Spirit, heavenly dove
317 To God the Holy Spirit let us pray
472, 473 Come, Holy Ghost, our souls inspire
687 Gracious Spirit, heed our pleading

Additional hymns for the day/season
See Year A

Sunday between May 24 and 28 inclusive

Proper 3 (if after Holy Trinity)

Prayer of the day

Almighty and everlasting God, ruler of heaven and earth: Hear our prayer and give us your peace now and forever; through your Son, Jesus Christ our Lord. (19)

Verse

Alleluia. The steadfast love of the LORD never ceases; his mercies never come to an end. Alleluia. (Lam. 3:22)

Offertory

I put my trust in your mercy; my heart is joyful because of your saving help. I will sing to you, O LORD, for you have dealt with me richly. (Ps. 13:5–6)

YEAR A

Hymn of the day

542 Sing praise to God, the highest good
714 The thirsty fields drink in the rain
783 Seek ye first the kingdom of God

Hymns related to the readings

First Reading: Isaiah 49:8–16a
God's motherly compassion for the people

313 A multitude comes from the east and the west
519 My soul, now praise your maker!
524 My God, how wonderful thou art
714 The thirsty fields drink in the rain
800 Each morning brings us

Psalmody: Psalm 131
Like a child upon its mother's breast, my soul is quieted within me. (Ps. 131:3)

Second Reading: 1 Corinthians 4:1–5
Servants accountable to God for their stewardship

283 O God, send heralds
405 Lord of light

Gospel: Matthew 6:24–34
The teaching of Christ: trust in God

474 Children of the heavenly Father
783 Seek ye first the kingdom of God
790 Praise to you, O God of mercy

Additional hymns for the day/season

362 We plow the fields and scatter
447 All depends on our possessing
457, 458 Jesus, priceless treasure
453 If you but trust in God to guide you
469 Lord of all hopefulness
543 Praise to the Lord, the Almighty
548 Oh, worship the King
552 In thee is gladness
769 Mothering God, you gave me birth

Hymn of the day

542 Sing praise to God, the highest good
298 One there is, above all others
790 Praise to you, O God of mercy

Hymns related to the readings

First Reading: Hosea 2:14–20
The covenant renewed by God's persistent love

369 The Church's one foundation
762 O day of peace

Psalmody: Psalm 103:1–13, 22
*The LORD is full of compassion and mercy.
(Ps. 103:8)*

519 My soul, now praise your maker! (paraphrase)
543 Praise to the Lord, the Almighty (paraphrase)
549 Praise, my soul, the King of heaven (paraphrase)
798 Bless the Lord, O my soul (Ps. 103:1)

Second Reading: 2 Corinthians 3:1–6
Equipped as ministers of God's new covenant

680 O Spirit of life

Gospel: Mark 2:13–22
Eating and drinking with tax collectors and prostitutes

290 There's a wideness in God's mercy
291 Jesus sinners will receive
360 O Christ, the healer, we have come
434 The Son of God, our Christ

Additional hymns for the day/season

297 Salvation unto us has come
375 Only-begotten, Word of God eternal
465 Evening and morning
478 Come, oh, come, O quickening Spirit

Year C

Hymn of the day

542 Sing praise to God, the highest good
293, 294 My hope is built on nothing less
781 My life flows on in endless song

Hymns related to the readings

First Reading: Isaiah 55:10–13
The word goes forth from the mouth of God

530 Jesus shall reign
695 O blessed spring
714 The thirsty fields drink in the rain

OR

First Reading: Sirach 27:4–7
Wisdom rules both heaven and earth

403 Lord, speak to us, that we may speak

Psalmody: Psalm 92:1–4, 11–14*
The righteous shall flourish like a palm tree. (Ps. 92:11)

Second Reading: 1 Corinthians 15:51–58
The mystery of the resurrection

133 Jesus lives! The victory's won!
140 With high delight let us unite

340 Jesus Christ, my sure defense
790 Praise to you, O God of mercy

Gospel: Luke 6:39–49
Take the speck from your eye; build your house on a firm foundation

293, 294 My hope is built on nothing less
413 Father eternal, ruler of creation
454 If God himself be for me
459 O Holy Spirit, enter in
552 In thee is gladness

Additional hymns for the day/season

425 O God of mercy, God of light
446 Whatever God ordains is right
507 How firm a foundation
520 Give to our God immortal praise!
793 Shout for joy loud and long

*Psalm 92:1–4, 12–15 (NRSV)

SUNDAY BETWEEN MAY 29 AND JUNE 4 INCLUSIVE

PROPER 4 (IF AFTER HOLY TRINITY)

Prayer of the day
Lord God of all nations, you have revealed your will to your people and promised your help to us all. Help us to hear and to do what you command, that the darkness may be overcome by the power of your light; through your Son, Jesus Christ our Lord. (79)

Verse
Alleluia. Your word is a lantern to my feet and a light upon my path. Alleluia. (Ps. 119:105)

Offertory
The steadfast love of the LORD never ceases, his mercies never come to an end; they are new every morning; great is your faithfulness. "The LORD is my portion," says my soul, "therefore I will hope in him." (Lam. 3:22–24)

YEAR A

Hymn of the day
293, 294 My hope is built on nothing less
465   Evening and morning
712   Listen, God is calling

Hymns related to the readings

First Reading: Deuteronomy 11:18–21, 26–28
Keeping the words of God at the center of life

257 Holy Spirit, truth divine
266 Maker of the earth and heaven
459 O Holy Spirit, enter in
480 Oh, that the Lord would guide my ways
721 Go, my children, with my blessing

Psalmody: Psalm 31:1–5, 19–24
Be my strong rock, a castle to keep me safe. (Ps. 31:3)

Alternate First Reading: Genesis 6:9–22; 7:24; 8:14–19
The great flood

324 O Love that will not let me go
465 Evening and morning
741 Thy holy wings

Alternate Psalmody: Psalm 46
The LORD of hosts is with us; the God of Jacob is our stronghold. (Ps. 46:4)

228, 229 A mighty fortress is our God (paraphrase)

Second Reading: Romans 1:16–17; 3:22b–28 [29–31]
Justified by God's grace as a gift

297 Salvation unto us has come
299 Dear Christians, one and all
448 Amazing grace, how sweet the sound
499 Come, thou Fount of every blessing
710 One bread, one body

Gospel: Matthew 7:21–29
The teaching of Christ: doing the works of God

248 Dearest Jesus, at your word
293, 294 My hope is built on nothing less
446 Whatever God ordains is right
453 If you but trust in God to guide you
454 If God himself be for me
507 How firm a foundation
552 In thee is gladness

Additional hymns for the day/season
353 May we your precepts, Lord, fulfill
369 The Church's one foundation
459 O Holy Spirit, enter in
464 You are the way
680 O Spirit of life
750 Oh, praise the gracious power

Year B

Hymn of the day

251   O day of rest and gladness
317   To God the Holy Spirit let us pray
719   God is here!

Hymns related to the readings

First Reading: Deuteronomy 5:12–15
The commandment regarding the sabbath

214   Come, let us eat
459   O Holy Spirit, enter in

Psalmody: Psalm 81:1–10
Raise a loud shout to the God of Jacob. (Ps. 81:1)

Alternate First Reading: 1 Samuel 3:1–10 [11–20]
The calling of Samuel

403   Lord, speak to us, that we may speak
503   O Jesus, I have promised
752   I, the Lord of sea and sky
768   He comes to us as one unknown

Alternate Psalmody: Psalm 139:1–6, 13–18
You have searched me out and known me. (Ps. 139:1)

311   Wondrous are your ways, O God! (paraphrase)

Second Reading: 2 Corinthians 4:5–12
Treasure in clay jars

198   Let all mortal flesh keep silence
447   All depends on our possessing
468   From God can nothing move me
478   Come, oh, come, O quickening Spirit

Gospel: Mark 2:23—3:6
Doing the work of God on the sabbath

246   The first day of the week
251   O day of rest and gladness
435   O God, whose will is life and good
718   Here in this place

Additional hymns for the day/season

233   Thy strong Word
248   Dearest Jesus, at your word
363   Christ is alive! Let Christians sing
257   Holy Spirit, truth divine
496   Around you, O Lord Jesus
504   O God, my faithful God
712   Listen, God is calling
766   We come to the hungry feast
796   My Lord of light

Year C

Hymn of the day

423   Lord, whose love in humble service
419   Lord of all nations, grant me grace
750   Oh, praise the gracious power

Hymns related to the readings

First Reading: 1 Kings 8:22–23, 41–43
God's everlasting covenant is for all people

313   A multitude comes from the east and the west
359   In Christ there is no east or west
432   We worship you, O God of might
530   Jesus shall reign

Psalmody: Psalm 96:1–9
Declare the glory of the LORD among the nations. (Ps. 96:3)

Alternate First Reading: 1 Kings 18:20–21 [22–29] 30–39
Elijah and the prophets of Baal

542   Sing praise to God, the highest good
684   Spirit, Spirit of gentleness

Alternate Psalmody: Psalm 96
Ascribe to the LORD honor and power. (Ps. 96:7b)

Second Reading: Galatians 1:1–12
Beware of contrary gospels

163   Come Holy Ghost, God and Lord
230   Lord, keep us steadfast in your Word
297   Salvation unto us has come

Gospel: Luke 7:1–10
Jesus heals the centurion's slave

359   In Christ there is no east or west
360   O Christ, the healer, we have come
435   O God, whose will is life and good

Additional hymns for the day/season

400   God, whose almighty word
431   Your hand, O Lord, in days of old
543   Praise to the Lord, the Almighty
550   From all that dwell below the skies
559   Oh, for a thousand tongues to sing
668   There in God's garden
716   Word of God, come down on earth
782   All my hope on God is founded

Sunday between June 5 and 11 inclusive

Proper 5 (if after Holy Trinity)

Prayer of the day

O God, the strength of those who hope in you: Be present and hear our prayers; and, because in the weakness of our mortal nature we can do nothing good without you, give us the help of your grace, so that in keeping your commandments we may please you in will and deed; through your Son, Jesus Christ our Lord. (80)

Verse

Alleluia. In Christ God was reconciling the world to himself, and entrusting the message of reconciliation to us. Alleluia. (2 Cor. 5:19)

Offertory

They devoted themselves to the apostles' teaching and fellowship, to the breaking of bread and the prayers. Day by day, as they spent much time together in the temple, they broke bread at home and ate their food with glad and generous hearts. (Acts 2:42, 46)

Year A

Hymn of the day

476 Have no fear, little flock
290 There's a wideness in God's mercy
736 By gracious powers

Hymns related to the readings

First Reading: Hosea 5:15—6:6
God desires steadfast love

290 There's a wideness in God's mercy
291 Jesus sinners will receive
551 Joyful, joyful we adore thee

Psalmody: Psalm 50:7–15
To those who keep in my way will I show the salvation of God. (Ps. 50:24)

Alternate First Reading: Genesis 12:1–9
Abram's journey in the promise

485 Lord, as a pilgrim
544 The God of Abraham praise
660 I want Jesus to walk with me

Alternate Psalmody: Psalm 33:1–12
Happy is the nation whose God is the LORD! (Ps. 33:12)

Second Reading: Romans 4:13–25
The promise to those who share Abraham's faith

479 My faith looks up to thee
507 How firm a foundation
544 The God of Abraham praise

Gospel: Matthew 9:9–13, 18–26
Christ heals a woman and raises a synagogue leader's daughter

290 There's a wideness in God's mercy
291 Jesus sinners will receive
298 One there is above all others
342 I know of a sleep in Jesus' name
360 O Christ, the healer, we have come
427 O Jesus Christ, may grateful hymns be rising
431 Your hand, O Lord, in days of old
455 "Come, follow me," the Savior spake
519 My soul, now praise your maker!
673 I'm so glad Jesus lifted me
703 Draw us in the Spirit's tether

Additional hymns for the day/season

267 Father, we praise you
304 Today your mercy calls us
543 Praise to the Lord, the Almighty
549 Praise, my soul, the King of heaven
731 Precious Lord, take my hand
737 There is a balm in Gilead
738 Healer of our every ill
782 All my hope on God is founded

YEAR B

Hymn of the day

228, 229 A mighty fortress is our God
393 Rise, shine, you people!
757 Creating God, your fingers trace

Hymns related to the readings

First Reading: Genesis 3:8–15
God confronts Adam and Eve in the garden

155 Praise the Savior, now and ever
372 In Adam we have all been one
393 Rise, shine, you people!
470 Praise and thanks and adoration

Psalmody: Psalm 130
With the LORD there is mercy and plenteous redemption. (Ps. 130:7)

295 Out of the depths I cry to you (paraphrase)

Alternate First Reading: 1 Samuel 8:4–11 [12–15] 16–20 [11:14–15]
Israel determined to have a king

Alternate Psalmody: Psalm 138
Your love endures forever; do not abandon the work of your hands. (Ps. 138:9)

Second Reading: 2 Corinthians 4:13—5:1
Renewed in the inner nature

189 We know that Christ is raised
260 On our way rejoicing
340 Jesus Christ, my sure defense
352 I know that my Redeemer lives!
365 Built on a rock

Gospel: Mark 3:20–35
Doing the work of God as brothers and sisters of Christ

203 Now we join in celebration
228, 229 A mighty fortress is our God
478 Come, oh, come, O quickening Spirit

Additional hymns for the day/season

210 At the Lamb's high feast we sing
233 Thy strong Word
252 You servants of God
326 My heart is longing
464 You are the way
559 Oh, for a thousand tongues to sing
718 Here in this place
721 Go, my children, with my blessing

YEAR C

Hymn of the day

673 I'm so glad Jesus lifted me
303 When in the hour of deepest need
453 If you but trust in God to guide you

Hymns related to the readings

First Reading: 1 Kings 17:17–24
Elijah revives a widow's son

340 Jesus Christ, my sure defense
350 Even as we live each day
552 In thee is gladness

Psalmody: Psalm 30
My God, I cried out to you, and you restored me to health. (Ps. 30:2)

Alternate First Reading: 1 Kings 17:8–16 [17–24]
A widow offers hospitality to Elijah

408 God, whose giving knows no ending
See First Reading

Alternate Psalmody: Psalm 146
The LORD lifts up those who are bowed down. (Ps. 96:15)

538 Oh, praise the Lord, my soul (paraphrase)
539 Praise the Almighty (paraphrase)

Second Reading: Galatians 1:11–24
The gospel is received through a revelation of Jesus Christ

177 By all your saints in warfare (stanza 11)
237 O God of light

Gospel: Luke 7:11–17
Jesus revives a widow's son

340 Jesus Christ, my sure defense
350 Even as we live each day
745 Awake, O sleeper

Additional hymns for the day/season

272 Abide with me
303 When in the hour of deepest need
319 Oh, sing, my soul, your maker's praise
468 From God can nothing move me
431 Your hand, O Lord, in days of old
493 Hope of the world
552 In thee is gladness
559 Oh, for a thousand tongues to sing

PROPER 6 (IF AFTER HOLY TRINITY)

Prayer of the day

God, our maker and redeemer, you have made us a new company of priests to bear witness to the Gospel. Enable us to be faithful to our calling to make known your promises to all the world; through your Son, Jesus Christ our Lord. (81)

Verse

Alleluia. Let your priests be clothed with righteousness; let your faithful people sing for joy. Alleluia. (Ps. 132:9)

Offertory

You are a chosen race, a royal priesthood, a holy nation, God's own people, in order that you may proclaim the mighty acts of him who called you out of darkness into his marvelous light. Once you were not a people, but now you are God's people; once you had not received mercy, but now you have received mercy. (1 Peter 2:9–10)

YEAR A

Hymn of the day

376 Your kingdom come!
396 O God, O Lord of heaven and earth
756 Lord, you give the great commission

Hymns related to the readings

First Reading: Exodus 19:2–8a
The covenant with Israel at Sinai

543 Praise to the Lord, the Almighty
652 Arise, your light has come!
688 O Holy Spirit, root of life
715 Open your ears, O faithful people
779 You who dwell in the shelter of the Lord

Psalmody: Psalm 100
We are God's people and the sheep of God's pasture.
(Ps. 100:2)

245 All people that on earth do dwell (paraphrase)
256 Oh, sing jubilee to the Lord (paraphrase)
531 Before Jehovah's awesome throne (paraphrase)

Alternate First Reading: Genesis 18:1–15 [21:1–7]
The LORD appears to Abraham and Sarah

544 The God of Abraham praise
730 My soul proclaims your greatness

Alternate Psalmody: Psalm 116:1, 10–17*
I will call upon the name of the LORD. (Ps. 116:11)

Second Reading: Romans 5:1–8
While we were sinners, Christ died for us

215 O Lord, we praise you
297 Salvation unto us has come
306 Chief of sinners though I be
385 What wondrous love is this
680 O Spirit of life

Gospel: Matthew 9:35—10:8 [9–23]
The sending of the Twelve

286 Bow down your ear, almighty Lord
379 Spread, oh, spread, almighty Word
381 Hark, the voice of Jesus calling
382 Awake, O Spirit of the watchmen
384 Your kingdom come, O Father
397 O Zion, haste
429 Where cross the crowded ways of life
434 The Son of God, our Christ
505 Forth in thy name, O Lord, I go
704 Father, we thank you
722 Hallelujah! We sing your praises

Additional hymns for the day/season

214 Come, let us eat
250 Open now thy gates of beauty
371 With God as our friend
383 Rise up, O saints of God!
393 Rise, shine, you people!
403 Lord, speak to us that we may speak
652 Arise, your light has come!
719 God is here!

Hymn of the day

189 We know that Christ is raised
232 Your word, O Lord, is gentle dew
727 Lord, your hands have formed

Hymns related to the readings

First Reading: Ezekiel 17:22–24
The sign of the cedar, planted on the mountain of Israel

15 Seek the Lord while he may be found
541 Praise the Lord of heaven
658 The Word of God is source and seed
668 There in God's garden

Psalmody: Psalm 92:1–4, 11–14**
The righteous shall spread abroad like a cedar of Lebanon. (Ps. 92:11)

Alternate First Reading: 1 Samuel 15:34—16:13
David anointed by Samuel

328, 329 All hail the power of Jesus' name

Alternate Psalmody: Psalm 20
The LORD gives victory to the anointed one. (Ps. 20:6)

Second Reading: 2 Corinthians 5:6–10 [11–13] 14–17
In Christ, a new creation

189 We know that Christ is raised

194 All who believe and are baptized
315 Love divine, all loves excelling
511 Renew me, O eternal Light
662 Restore in us, O God
669 Come away to the skies
675 We walk by faith and not by sight
698 We were baptized in Christ Jesus
781 My life flows on in endless song

Gospel: Mark 4:26–34
The parable of the mustard seed

15 Seek the Lord while he may be found
221 Sent forth by God's blessing
234 Almighty God, your Word is cast
236 When seed falls on good soil
250 Open now thy gates of beauty
563, 760 For the fruit of all creation
658 The Word of God is source and seed

Additional hymns for the day/season

261 On what has now been sown
331 Jerusalem, my happy home
532 How Great Thou Art
554 This is my Father's world
558 Earth and all stars!
695 O blessed spring
714 The thirsty fields drink in the rain
768 He comes to us as one unknown

Hymn of the day

738 Healer of our every ill
356 O Jesus, joy of loving hearts
396 O God, O Lord of heaven and earth

Hymns related to the readings

First Reading: 2 Samuel 11:26—12:10, 13–15
Nathan tells the story of the lamb to David

295 Out of the depths I cry to you
304 Today your mercy calls us
428 O God of earth and altar

Psalmody: Psalm 32
Then you forgave me the guilt of my sin. (Ps. 32:6)

Alternate First Reading: 1 Kings 21:1–10 [11–14] 15–21a
Ahab kills the owner of a vineyard

Alternate Psalmody: Psalm 5:1–8
Lead me, O LORD, in your righteousness; make your way straight before me. (Ps. 5:8)

Second Reading: Galatians 2:15–21
Crucified with Christ; justification through grace

297 Salvation unto us has come
299 Dear Christians, one and all
671 Alleluia, alleluia, give thanks
680 O Spirit of life

Gospel: Luke 7:36—8:3
The woman anointing the feet of Jesus is forgiven

304 Today your mercy calls us
406 Take my life, that I may be
460 I am trusting you, Lord Jesus
549 Praise, my soul, the King of heaven

Additional hymns for the day/season

290 There's a wideness in God's mercy
327 Rock of Ages, cleft for me
336 Jesus, thy boundless love to me
438 Lord, teach us how to pray aright
479 My faith looks up to thee
524 My God, how wonderful thou art
733 Our Father, we have wandered

*Psalm 116:1–2, 12–19 (NRSV)
**Psalm 92:1–4, 12–15 (NRSV)

Sunday between June 19 and 25 inclusive

Proper 7 (if after Holy Trinity)

Prayer of the day

O God our defender, storms rage about us and cause us to be afraid. Rescue your people from despair, deliver your sons and daughters from fear, and preserve us all from unbelief; through your Son, Jesus Christ our Lord. (82)

Verse

Alleluia. Because you are children, God has sent the Spirit of his Son into your hearts, crying, "Abba! Father!" Alleluia. (Gal. 4:6)

Offertory

The LORD is faithful in all his words and merciful in all his deeds. The LORD upholds all those who fall; he lifts up those who are bowed down. The eyes of all wait upon you, O LORD, and you give them their food in due season. You open wide your hand and satisfy the needs of every living creature. (Ps. 145:14–17)

YEAR A

Hymn of the day

507   How firm a foundation
366   Lord of our life
785   Weary of all trumpeting

Hymns related to the readings

First Reading: Jeremiah 20:7–13
The prophet must speak despite opposition

242   Let the whole creation cry
453   If you but trust in God to guide you

Psalmody: Psalm 69:8–11 [12–17] 18–20*
Answer me, O Lord, for your love is kind. (Ps. 69:18)

Alternate First Reading: Genesis 21:8–21
The rescue of Hagar and Ishmael

343   Guide me ever, great Redeemer

Alternate Psalmody: Psalm 86:1–10, 16–17
Have mercy upon me; give strength to your servant. (Ps. 86:16)

Second Reading: Romans 6:1b–11
Buried and raised with Christ by baptism

189   We know that Christ is raised
194   All who believe and are baptized
662   Restore in us, O God
693   Baptized in water
695   O blessed spring
698   We were baptized in Christ Jesus

Gospel: Matthew 10:24–39
The cost of discipleship

283   O God, send heralds
312   Once he came in blessing
384   Your kingdom come, O Father
398   "Take up your cross," the Savior said
474   Children of the heavenly Father
487   Let us ever walk with Jesus
503   O Jesus, I have promised
504   O God, my faithful God
755   We all are one in mission

Additional hymns for the day/season

192   Baptized into your name most holy
324   O Love that will not let me go
453   If you but trust in God to guide you
476   Have no fear, little flock
490   Let me be yours forever
520   Give to our God immortal praise!
554   This is my Father's world
736   By gracious powers
770   I was there to hear your borning cry

YEAR B

Hymn of the day

781   My life flows on in endless song
334   Jesus, Savior, pilot me
465   Evening and morning

Hymns related to the readings

First Reading: Job 38:1–11
The creator of earth and sea

188   I bind unto myself today
462   God the omnipotent!

Psalmody: Psalm 107:1–3, 23–32
God stilled the storm and quieted the waves of the sea. (Ps. 107:29)

Alternate First Reading: 1 Samuel 17:[1a, 4–11, 19–23] 32–49
The LORD's victory over Goliath

498   All who would valiant be

OR

Alternate First Reading: 1 Samuel 17:57—18:5, 10–16
David and Jonathan; Saul fears David's success

498   All who would valiant be

Alternate Psalmody: Psalm 9:9–20
The LORD will be a refuge in time of trouble. (Ps. 9:9)

OR

Alternate Psalmody: Psalm 133
How good and pleasant it is to live together in unity. (Ps. 133:1)

Second Reading: 2 Corinthians 6:1–13
Paul's defense of his ministry

283   O God, send heralds

Gospel: Mark 4:35–41
Christ calming the sea

333   Lord, take my hand and lead me
334   Jesus, Savior, pilot me
417   In a lowly manger born
457, 458 Jesus, priceless treasure
465   Evening and morning
467   Eternal Father, strong to save
503   O Jesus, I have promised
731   Precious Lord, take my hand
781   My life flows on in endless song

Additional hymns for the day/season

320   O God, our help in ages past
460   I am trusting you, Lord Jesus
507   How firm a foundation
741   Thy holy wings
746   Day by day
752   I, the Lord of sea and sky

YEAR C

Hymn of the day

393   Rise, shine, you people!
415   God of grace and God of glory
750   Oh, praise the gracious power

Hymns related to the readings

First Reading: Isaiah 65:1–9
The prophet sent to a rebellious people

237   O God of light
489   Wide open are your hands

Psalmody: Psalm 22:18–27**
In the midst of the congregation I will praise you. (Ps. 22:21)

Alternate First Reading: 1 Kings 19:1–4 [5–7] 8–15a
Elijah hears the word of the LORD in the midst of silence

205   Now the silence
768   He comes to us as one unknown

Alternate Psalmody: Psalm 42 and 43
Send out your light and truth that they may lead me. (Ps. 43:3)

452   As pants the hart for cooling streams (paraphrase)

Second Reading: Galatians 3:23–29
In baptism, clothed with Christ; no longer Jew or Greek

192   Baptized into your name most holy
194   All who believe and are baptized
225   Lord Jesus Christ, we humbly pray
359   In Christ there is no east or west
523   Holy Spirit, ever dwelling
680   O Spirit of life
694   You have put on Christ
710   One bread, one body

Gospel: Luke 8:26–39
Jesus casts out demons possessing a man of the Gerasenes

393   Rise, shine, you people!
435   O God, whose will is life and good
506   Dear Lord and Father of mankind

Additional hymns for the day/season

520   Give to our God immortal praise
545, 546 When morning gilds the skies
559   Oh, for a thousand tongues to sing
560   Oh, that I had a thousand voices
682   Praise the Spirit in creation

*Psalm 69:7–10 (11–15) 16–18 (NRSV)
**Psalm 22:19–28 (NRSV)

SUNDAY BETWEEN JUNE 26 AND JULY 2 INCLUSIVE

PROPER 8

Prayer of the day

O God, you have prepared for those who love you joys beyond understanding. Pour into our hearts such love for you that, loving you above all things, we may obtain your promises, which exceed all that we can desire; through your Son, Jesus Christ our Lord. (83)

Verse

Alleluia. May the God of our Lord Jesus Christ enlighten the eyes of our hearts that we may know the hope to which he has called us. Alleluia. (Eph. 1:17)

Offertory

The LORD is the strength of my life; of whom then shall I be afraid? I believe that I shall see the goodness of the LORD in the land of the living! I will offer in his dwelling an oblation with sounds of great gladness; I will sing and make music to the LORD. (Ps. 27:1, 17, 9)

YEAR A

Hymn of the day

487 Let us ever walk with Jesus
429 Where cross the crowded ways of life
750 Oh, praise the gracious power

Hymns related to the readings

First Reading: Jeremiah 28:5–9
The test of a true prophet

362 God the omnipotent!
436 All who love and serve your city

Psalmody: Psalm 89:1–4, 15–18
Your love, O LORD, forever will I sing. (Ps. 89:1)

Alternate First Reading: Genesis 22:1–14
The testing of Abraham

105 A lamb goes uncomplaining forth
438 Lord, teach us how to pray aright

Alternate Psalmody: Psalm 13
I put my trust in your mercy, O LORD. (Ps. 13:5)

Second Reading: Romans 6:12–23
No longer under law but under grace

296 Just as I am, without one plea
297 Salvation unto us has come
448 Amazing grace, how sweet the sound
520 Give to our God immortal praise!

Gospel: Matthew 10:40–42
Welcome Christ in those he sends

338 Peace, to soothe our bitter woes
410 We give thee but thine own
424 Lord of glory, you have bought us
429 Where cross the crowded ways of life

Additional hymns for the day/season

225 Lord Jesus Christ, we humbly pray
403 Lord, speak to us, that we may speak
423 Lord, whose love in humble service
425 O God of mercy, God of light
433 The Church of Christ, in every age
719 God is here!

Year B

Hymn of the day

360 O Christ, the healer, we have come
453 If you but trust in God to guide you
771 Great is thy faithfulness

Hymns related to the readings

First Reading: Lamentations 3:22–33
Great is the LORD's faithfulness

264 When all your mercies, O my God
319 Oh, sing, my soul, your maker's praise
395 I trust, O Christ, in you alone
453 If you but trust in God to guide you
771 Great is thy faithfulness

OR

First Reading: Wisdom of Solomon 1:13–15; 2:23–24
God created humankind for immortality

669 Come away to the skies

Psalmody: Psalm 30
I will exalt you, O LORD, because you have lifted me up. (Ps. 30:1)

Alternate First Reading: 2 Samuel 1:1, 17–27
Lamentation over Saul and Jonathan

735 God! When human bonds are broken

Alternate Psalmody: Psalm 130
Out of the depths have I called to you, O LORD. (Ps. 130:1)

295 Out of the depths I cry to you (paraphrase)

Second Reading: 2 Corinthians 8:7–15
Excel in generosity, following the Lord Jesus

406 Take my life, that I may be
408 God, whose giving knows no ending
411 Lord of all good

Gospel: Mark 5:21–43
Christ healing a woman and Jairus' daughter

292 God loved the world
342 I know of a sleep in Jesus' name
352 I know that my Redeemer lives!
360 O Christ, the healer, we have come
427 O Jesus Christ, may grateful hymns be rising
431 Your hand, O Lord, in days of old
435 O God, whose will is life and good
519 My soul, now praise your maker!
673 I'm so glad Jesus lifted me
716 Word of God, come down on earth
721 Go, my children, with my blessing
738 Healer of our every ill

Additional hymns for the day/season

345 How sweet the name of Jesus sounds
425 O God of mercy, God of light
551 Joyful, joyful, we adore thee
703 Draw us in the Spirit's tether
731 Precious Lord, take my hand

Year C

Hymn of the day

455 "Come, follow me," the Savior spake
503 O Jesus, I have promised
777 In the morning when I rise

Hymns related to the readings

First Reading: 1 Kings 19:15–16, 19–21
Elijah says to Elisha, Follow me and do not continue plowing

494 Jesus calls us; o'er the tumult

Psalmody: Psalm 16
I have set the LORD always before me. (Ps. 16:8)

Alternate First Reading: 2 Kings 2:1–2, 6–14
Elijah ascends into heaven in a whirlwind

651 Shine, Jesus, shine

Alternate Psalmody: Psalm 77:1–2, 11–20
By your strength you have redeemed your people. (Ps. 77:15)

Second Reading: Galatians 5:1, 13–25
Love is the whole law, gift of the Spirit

325 Lord, thee I love with all my heart
353 May we your precepts, Lord, fulfill
459 O Holy Spirit, enter in
662 Restore in us, O God
745 Awake, O sleeper

Gospel: Luke 9:51–62
Jesus says, Follow me and do not look back

325 Lord, thee I love with all my heart
384 Your kingdom come, O Father
434 The Son of God, our Christ
455 "Come, follow me," the Savior spake
503 O Jesus, I have promised
703 Draw us in the Spirit's tether

Additional hymns for the day/season

283 O God, send heralds
501 He leadeth me: oh, blessed thought!
552 In thee is gladness
782 All my hope on God is founded

Sunday between July 3 and 9 inclusive

Proper 9

Prayer of the day

God of glory and love, peace comes from you alone. Send us as peacemakers and witnesses to your kingdom, and fill our hearts with joy in your promises of salvation; through your Son, Jesus Christ our Lord. (84)

Verse

Alleluia. Happy are they who hear the word, hold it fast in an honest and good heart, and bear fruit with patient endurance. Alleluia. (Luke 8:15)

Offertory

Come to me, all you that are weary and are carrying heavy burdens, and I will give you rest. Take my yoke upon you, and learn from me; for I am gentle and humble in heart, and you will find rest for your souls. For my yoke is easy, and my burden is light. (Matt. 11:28–30)

Year A

Hymn of the day

469	Lord of all hopefulness
497	I heard the voice of Jesus say
746	Day by day

Hymns related to the readings

First Reading: Zechariah 9:9–12
The king will come in humility and peace

530	Jesus shall reign
631	Lift up your heads, O gates
762	O day of peace

Psalmody: Psalm 145:8–15*
The LORD is gracious and full of compassion. (Ps. 145:8)

Alternate First Reading: Genesis 24:34–38, 42–49, 58–67
The marriage of Isaac and Rebekah

749	When love is found

Alternate Psalmody: Psalm 45:10–17
God has anointed you with the oil of gladness. (Ps. 45:8)

OR

Alternate Psalmody: Song of Solomon 2:8–13
Arise, my love, my fair one, and come away. (Song of Sol. 2:10)

Second Reading: Romans 7:15–25a
The struggle within the self

269	Awake, my soul, and with the sun
296	Just as I am, without one plea
475	Come, gracious Spirit, heavenly dove
480	Oh, that the Lord would guide my ways
790	Praise to you, O God of mercy

Gospel: Matthew 11:16–19, 25–30
The yoke of discipleship

208	Lord Jesus Christ, you have prepared
213	I come, O Savior, to your table
324	O Love that will not let me go
497	I heard the voice of Jesus say
505	Forth in thy name, O Lord, I go
529	Praise God. Praise him

Additional hymns for the day/season

305	I lay my sins on Jesus
345	How sweet the name of Jesus sounds
401	Before you, Lord, we bow
439	What a friend we have in Jesus
464	You are the way
516	Arise, my soul, arise!
553	Rejoice, O pilgrim throng!
734	Softly and tenderly Jesus is calling

<h1>YEAR B</h1>

Hymn of the day

380   O Christ, our light, O Radiance true
396   O God, O Lord of heaven and earth
715   Open your ears, O faithful people

Hymns related to the readings

First Reading: Ezekiel 2:1–5
The call of Ezekiel

237   O God of light
238   God has spoken through his prophets
684   Spirit, Spirit of gentleness

Psalmody: Psalm 123
Our eyes look to you, O God, until you show us your mercy. (Ps. 123:3)

Alternate First Reading: 2 Samuel 5:1–5, 9–10
The reign of David

87   Hail to the Lord's anointed
328, 329   All hail the power of Jesus' name!

Alternate Psalmody: Psalm 48
God shall be our guide forevermore. (Ps. 48:13)

Second Reading: 2 Corinthians 12:2–10
God's power made perfect in weakness

341   Jesus, still lead on
439   What a friend we have in Jesus
484   God, my Lord, my strength
673   I'm so glad Jesus lifted me

Gospel: Mark 6:1–13
Sending of the Twelve to preach and heal

221   Sent forth by God's blessing
237   O God of light
238   God has spoken through his prophets
434   The Son of God, our Christ
722   Hallelujah! We sing your praises
756   Lord, you give the great commission

Additional hymns for the day/season

163   Come, Holy Ghost, God and Lord
382   Awake, O Spirit of the watchmen
712   Listen, God is calling
754   Let us talents and tongues employ

<h1>YEAR C</h1>

Hymn of the day

755   We all are one in mission
381   Hark, the voice of Jesus calling
384   Your kingdom come, O Father

Hymns related to the readings

First Reading: Isaiah 66:10–14
Jerusalem, a nursing mother giving life to her children

519   My soul, now praise your maker!
533, 534   Now thank we all our God
549   Praise, my soul, the King of heaven
683   Loving Spirit
697   Wash, O God, our sons and daughters
741   Thy holy wings
769   Mothering God, you gave me birth

Psalmody: Psalm 66:1–8**
God holds our souls in life. (Ps. 66:8)

Alternate First Reading: 2 Kings 5:1–14
Elisha heals a warrior with leprosy

431   Your hand, O Lord, in days of old
696   I've just come from the fountain

Alternate Psalmody: Psalm 30
My God, I cried out to you, and you restored me to health. (Ps. 30:2)

Second Reading: Galatians 6:[1–6] 7–16
Do what is right now and reap at the harvest time

104   In the cross of Christ I glory
194   All who believe and are baptized
315   Love divine, all loves excelling
370   Blest be the tie that binds
487   Let us ever walk with Jesus
511   Renew me, O eternal Light
669   Come away to the skies
781   My life flows on in endless song

Gospel: Luke 10:1–11, 16–20
Jesus sends out seventy disciples into the harvest

379   Spread, oh, spread, almighty Word
381   Hark, the voice of Jesus calling
382   Awake, O Spirit of the watchmen
384   Your kingdom come, O Father
436   All who love and serve your city
756   Lord, you give the great commission

Additional hymns for the day/season

221   Sent forth by God's blessing
397   O Zion, haste
434   The Son of God, our Christ
524   My God, how wonderful thou art
548   Oh, worship the King

*Psalm 145:8–14 (NRSV)
**Psalm 66:1–9 (NRSV)

Proper 10

Prayer of the day

Almighty God, we thank you for planting in us the seed of your word. By your Holy Spirit help us to receive it with joy, live according to it, and grow in faith and hope and love; through your Son, Jesus Christ our Lord. (85)

OR

(Year C) Lord God, use our lives to touch the world with your love. Stir us, by your Spirit, to be neighbor to those in need, serving them with willing hearts; through your Son, Jesus Christ our Lord. (86)

Verse

Alleluia. The word is very near to you; it is in your mouth and in your heart for you to observe. Alleluia. (Deut. 30:14)

Offertory

Jesus said, "The first commandment is: 'Hear, O Israel: the Lord our God, the Lord is one; you shall love the Lord your God with all your heart, and with all your soul, and with all your mind, and with all your strength.' The second is this: 'You shall love your neighbor as yourself.'" (Mark 12:29–31)

YEAR A

Hymn of the day

232 Your Word, O Lord, is gentle dew
234 Almighty God, your Word is cast
658 The Word of God is source and seed

Hymns related to the readings

First Reading: Isaiah 55:10–13
The growth of the word to accomplish God's purpose

221 Sent forth by God's blessing
234 Almighty God, your Word is cast
236 When seed falls on good soil
250 Open now thy gates of beauty
261 On what has now been sown

Psalmody: Psalm 65:[1–8] 9–14*
Your paths overflow with plenty. (Ps. 65:12)

Alternate First Reading: Genesis 25:19–34
Esau sells his birthright to Jacob

477 O God of Jacob

Alternate Psalmody: Psalm 119:105–112
Your word is a lantern to my feet and a light upon my path. (Ps. 119:105)

Second Reading: Romans 8:1–11
Living according to the Spirit

297 Salvation unto us has come
484 God, my Lord, my strength
508 Come down, O Love divine
680 O Spirit of life

Gospel: Matthew 13:1–9, 18–23
The parable of the sower and the seed

221 Sent forth by God's blessing
234 Almighty God, your Word is cast
236 When seed falls on good soil
250 Open now thy gates of beauty
261 On what has now been sown
563 For the fruit of all creation
714 The thirsty fields drink in the rain
715 Open your ears, O faithful people
760 For the fruit of all creation

Additional hymns for the day/season

259 Lord, dismiss us with your blessing
362 We plow the fields and scatter
412 Sing to the Lord of harvest
705 As the grains of wheat
713 Lord, let my heart be good soil
723 The Spirit sends us forth to serve
727 Lord, your hands have formed

Year B

Hymn of the day

495 Lead on, O King eternal
183 The Son of God goes forth to war
763 Let justice flow like streams

Hymns related to the readings

First Reading: Amos 7:7–15
The sign of the plumb line: God's judgment on Israel

322 The clouds of judgment gather
763 Let justice flow like streams

Psalmody: Psalm 85:8–13
I will listen to what the LORD God is saying. (Ps. 85:8)

Alternate First Reading: 2 Samuel 6:1–5, 12b–19
David and the house of Israel dance before the Lord

558 Earth and all stars!
795 Oh, sing to the Lord

Alternate Psalmody: Psalm 24
Lift up your heads, O gates, and the King of glory shall come in. (Ps. 24:7)

631 Lift up your heads, O gates (paraphrase)

Second Reading: Ephesians 1:3–14
Chosen in Christ to live to the praise of God's glory

299 Dear Christians, one and all
396 O God, O Lord of heaven and earth
468 From God can nothing move me
499 Come, thou Fount of every blessing
536 O God of God, O Light of light
693 Baptized in water

Gospel: Mark 6:14–29
The death of John the Baptist

178 By all your saints in warfare (stanza 15)
182 Rise, O children of salvation
500 Faith of our fathers

Additional hymns for the day/season

483 God moves in a mysterious way
498 All who would valiant be
549 Praise, my soul, the King of heaven
766 We come to the hungry feast
790 Praise to you, O God of mercy

Year C

Hymn of the day

765 Jesu, Jesu, fill us with your love
425 O God of mercy, God of light
505 Forth in thy name, O Lord, I go

Hymns related to the readings

First Reading: Deuteronomy 30:9–14
The LORD will take delight in your fruitfulness

250 Open now thy gates of beauty
480 Oh, that the Lord would guide my ways

Psalmody: Psalm 25:1–9**
Show me your ways, O LORD, and teach me your paths. (Ps. 25:3)

Alternate First Reading: Amos 7:7–17
A plumb line will judge the people

322 The clouds of judgment gather
763 Let justice flow like streams

Alternate Psalmody: Psalm 82
Arise, O God, and rule the earth. (Ps. 82:8)

Second Reading: Colossians 1:1–14
The gospel is growing, bearing fruit in the whole world

227 How blest are they who hear God's Word
444 With the Lord begin your task
464 You are the way
800 Each morning brings us fresh outpoured

Gospel: Luke 10:25–37
The parable of the merciful Samaritan

419 Lord of all nations, grant me grace
425 O God of mercy, God of light
493 Hope of the world
495 Lead on, O King eternal!
765 Jesu, Jesu, fill us with your love

Additional hymns for the day/season

126 Where charity and love prevail
423 Lord, whose love in humble service
504 O God, my faithful God
551 Joyful, joyful we adore thee
666 Great God, your love has called us

*Psalm 65:[1–8] 9–13 (NRSV)
**Psalm 25:1–10 (NRSV)

Proper 11

Prayer of the day

O Lord, pour out upon us the spirit to think and do what is right, that we, who cannot even exist without you, may have the strength to live according to your will; through your Son, Jesus Christ our Lord. (87)

OR

(Year C) O God, you see how busy we are with many things. Turn us to listen to your teachings and lead us to choose the one thing which will not be taken from us, Jesus Christ our Lord. (88)

Verse

Alleluia. My word shall accomplish that which I purpose, and succeed in the thing for which I sent it. Alleluia. (Isa. 55:11)

Offertory

I will wash my hands in innocence, O LORD, that I may go in procession round your altar, singing aloud a song of thanksgiving and recounting all your wonderful deeds. LORD, I love the house in which you dwell and the place where your glory abides. (Ps. 26:6–8)

YEAR A

Hymn of the day

459   O Holy Spirit, enter in
234   Almighty God, your Word is cast
760   For the fruit of all creation

Hymns related to the readings

First Reading: Isaiah 44:6–8
There is no other God than the LORD

244   Lord our God, with praise we come
453   If you but trust in God to guide you
459   O Holy Spirit, enter in

OR

First Reading: Wisdom of Solomon 12:13, 16–19
God's sovereignty: both righteous and forbearing

521   Let us with a gladsome mind

Psalmody: Psalm 86:11–17
Teach me your way, O LORD, and I will walk in your truth. (Ps. 86:11)

Alternate First Reading: Genesis 28:10–19a
Jacob's dream of the ladder to heaven

186   How blessed is this place, O Lord
375   Only-begotten, Word of God eternal
477   O God of Jacob
499   Come, thou Fount of every blessing
699   Blessed assurance

Alternate Psalmody: Psalm 139:1–12, 23–24
You have searched me out and known me. (Ps. 139:1)

311   Wondrous are your ways, O God! (paraphrase)

Second Reading: Romans 8:12–25
The revealing of the children of God

315   Love divine, all loves excelling
326   My heart is longing
441   Eternal Spirit of the living Christ
662   Restore in us, O God
688   O Holy Spirit, root of life

Gospel: Matthew 13:24–30, 36–43
The parable of the weeds

261   On what has now been sown
407   Come, you thankful people, come
412   Sing to the Lord of harvest
658   The Word of God is source and seed

Additional hymns for the day/season

362   We plow the fields and scatter
409   Praise and thanksgiving
542   Sing praise to God, the highest good
548   Oh, worship the King
704   Father, we thank thee
705   As the grains of wheat
771   Great is thy faithfulness
779   You who dwell in the shelter of the Lord

YEAR B

Hymn of the day
750   Oh, praise the gracious power
313   A multitude comes from east and west
459   O Holy Spirit, enter in

Hymns related to the readings

First Reading: Jeremiah 23:1–6
From David's line, a righteous shepherd for Israel

196   Praise the Lord, rise up rejoicing

Psalmody: Psalm 23
The LORD is my shepherd; I shall not be in want. (Ps. 23:1)

451   The Lord's my shepherd (paraphrase)
456   The King of love my shepherd is (paraphrase)

Alternate First Reading: 2 Samuel 7:1–14a
The promise of the LORD to David

87   Hail to the Lord's anointed
328, 329   All hail the power of Jesus' name!

Alternate Psalmody: Psalm 89:20–37
Your love, O LORD, forever will I sing. (Ps. 89:1)

Second Reading: Ephesians 2:11–22
Reconciled to God through Christ, our peace

296   Just as I am, without one plea
367   Christ is made the sure foundation
369   The Church's one foundation

419   Lord of all nations, grant me grace
446   Whatever God ordains is right
685   Like the murmur of the dove's song
704   Father, we thank you
710   One bread, one body
735   God! When human bonds are broken
747   Christ is made the sure foundation
750   Oh, praise the gracious power
782   All my hope on God is founded

Gospel: Mark 6:30–34, 53–56
Christ healing the multitudes

196   Praise the Lord, rise up rejoicing
206   Lord, who the night you were betrayed
313   A multitude comes from the east and the west
431   Your hand, O Lord, in days of old
497   I heard the voice of Jesus say
531   Before Jehovah's awesome throne

Additional hymns for the day/season
212   Let us break bread together
245   All people that on earth do dwell
256   Oh, sing jubilee to the Lord
292   God loved the world
371   With God as our friend
410   We give thee but thine own
485   Lord, as a pilgrim
703   Draw us in the Spirit's tether
719   God is here!

YEAR C

Hymn of the day
248   Dearest Jesus, at your word
325   Lord, thee I love with all my heart
776   Be thou my vision

Hymns related to the readings

First Reading: Genesis 18:1–10a
The hospitality of Abraham and Sarah to three visitors of the LORD

544   The God of Abraham praise
730   My soul proclaims your greatness

Psalmody: Psalm 15
Who may abide upon your holy hill? Whoever leads a blameless life and does what is right. (Ps. 15:1–2)

Alternate First Reading: Amos 8:1–12
A famine of hearing the words of the LORD

322   The clouds of judgment gather
384   Your kingdom come, O Father
428   O God of earth and altar
627   My Lord, what a morning
716   Word of God, come down on earth

Alternate Psalmody: Psalm 52
I am like a green olive tree in the house of God. (Ps. 52:8)

Second Reading: Colossians 1:15–28
Hymn to Christ, the firstborn of all creation

179   At the name of Jesus
252   You servants of God
466   Great God, our source
526   Immortal, invisible, God only wise
558   Earth and all stars!

Gospel: Luke 10:38–42
Jesus says: Martha, your sister Mary has chosen the better part

248   Dearest Jesus, at your word
325   Lord, thee I love with all my heart

Additional hymns for the day/season
214   Come, let us eat
316   Jesus, the very thought of you
545, 546   When morning gilds the skies
746   Day by day
777   In the morning when I rise
778   O Christ the same

PROPER 12

Prayer of the day

O God, your ears are open always to the prayers of your servants. Open our hearts and minds to you, that we may live in harmony with your will and receive the gifts of your Spirit; through your Son, Jesus Christ our Lord. (89)

Verse

Alleluia. Lord, to whom shall we go? You have the words of eternal life. Alleluia. (John 6:68)

Offertory

The sparrow has found her a house and the swallow a nest where she may lay her young, by the side of your altars, O LORD of hosts, my King and my God. Happy are they who dwell in your house! They will always be praising you. (Ps. 84:2–3)

YEAR A

Hymn of the day

415 God of grace and God of glory
457, 458 Jesus, priceless treasure
753 You are the seed

Hymns related to the readings

First Reading: 1 Kings 3:5–12
Solomon's prayer for wisdom

415 God of grace and God of glory
464 You are the way

Psalmody: Psalm 119:129–136
When your word goes forth, it gives light and understanding. (Ps. 119:130)

Alternate First Reading: Genesis 29:15–28
Leah and Rachel become Jacob's wives

Alternate Psalmody: Psalm 105:1–11, 45b
Make known the deeds of the LORD among the peoples. Hallelujah! (Ps. 105:1, 45)

OR

Alternate Psalmody: Psalm 128
Happy are they who follow in the ways of the LORD. (Ps. 128:1)

Second Reading: Romans 8:26–39
Nothing can separate us from God's love

326 My heart is longing
441 Eternal Spirit of the living Christ

446 Whatever God ordains is right
447 All depends on our possessing
454 If God himself be for me
474 Children of the heavenly Father
478 Come, oh, come, O quickening Spirit
558 In thee is gladness
782 All my hope on God is founded

Gospel: Matthew 13:31–33, 44–52
Parables of the reign of heaven

221 Sent forth by God's blessing
234 Almighty God, your Word is cast
250 Open now thy gates of beauty
362 We plow the fields and scatter
457, 458 Jesus, priceless treasure
753 You are the seed
778 Be thou my vision

Additional hymns for the day/season

224 Soul, adorn yourself with gladness
526 Immortal, invisible, God only wise
767 All things bright and beautiful
782 All my hope on God is founded

Hymn of the day

457, 458 Jesus, priceless treasure
235 Break now the bread of life
704 Father, we thank you

Hymns related to the readings

First Reading: 2 Kings 4:42–44
Elisha feeding a hundred people

222 O Bread of life from heaven

Psalmody: Psalm 145:10–19*
You open wide your hand and satisfy the needs of every living creature. (Ps. 145:17)

Alternate First Reading: 2 Samuel 11:1–15
Bathsheba and Uriah wronged by David

735 God! When human bonds are broken
739 In all our grief

Alternate Psalmody: Psalm 14
God is in the company of the righteous. (Ps. 14:5)

Second Reading: Ephesians 3:14–21
Prayer for wisdom, strength, and Christ's indwelling

256 Oh, sing jubilee to the Lord
745 Awake, O sleeper

Gospel: John 6:1–21
Christ feeding the five thousand

235 Break now the bread of life
333 Lord, take my hand and lead me
334 Jesus, Savior, pilot me
417 In a lowly manger born
450 Who trusts in God, a strong abode
457, 458 Jesus, priceless treasure
465 Evening and morning
467 Eternal Father, strong to save
493 Hope of the world
503 O Jesus, I have promised
701 What feast of love
731 Precious Lord, take my hand
754 Let us talents and tongues employ
781 My life flows on in endless song

Additional hymns for the day/season

197 O living Bread from heaven
200 For the bread which you have broken
409 Praise and thanksgiving
706 Eat this bread, drink this cup
711 You satisfy the hungry heart
766 We come to the hungry feast

YEAR C

Hymn of the day

438 Lord, teach us how to pray aright
442 O thou, who hast of thy pure grace
746 Day by day

Hymns related to the readings

First Reading: Genesis 18:20–32
Abraham bargains with God for the righteous of Sodom and Gomorrah

438 Lord, teach us how to pray aright

Psalmody: Psalm 138
Your love endures forever; do not abandon the works of your hands. (Ps. 138:9)

Alternate First Reading: Hosea 1:2–10
Hosea's marriage: a message to Israel

517 Praise to the Father
733 Our Father, we have wandered

Alternate Psalmody: Psalm 85
Righteousness and peace shall go before the LORD. (Ps. 85:13)

Second Reading: Colossians 2:6–15 [16–19]
Buried with Christ in baptism, raised with him through faith

189 We know that Christ is raised
207 We who once were dead
338 Peace, to soothe our bitter woes
559 Oh, for a thousand tongues to sing

Gospel: Luke 11:1–13
Jesus teaches the disciples to pray

163 Come, Holy Ghost, God and Lord
307 Forgive our sins as we forgive
319 Oh, sing, my soul, your maker's praise
357 Our Father, by whose name
376 Your kingdom come!
405 Lord of light
438 Lord, teach us how to pray aright
441 Eternal Spirit of the living Christ
442 O thou, who hast of thy pure grace
447 O God of Jacob
775 Lord, listen to your children praying

Additional hymns for the day/season

439 What a friend we have in Jesus
783 Seek ye first the kingdom of God

*Psalm 145:10–18 (NRSV)

Sunday between July 31 and August 6 inclusive

Proper 13

Prayer of the day

Gracious Father, your blessed Son came down from heaven to be the true bread which gives life to the world. Give us this bread, that he may live in us and we in him, Jesus Christ our Lord. (90)

OR

(Year C) Almighty God, judge of us all, you have placed in our hands the wealth we call our own. Give us such wisdom by your Spirit that our possessions may not be a curse in our lives, but an instrument for blessing; through your Son, Jesus Christ our Lord. (91)

Verse

Alleluia. Jesus said, Those who love me will keep my word, and my Father will love them, and we will come to them and make our home with them. Alleluia. (John 14:23)

Offertory

Honor the LORD with your substance and with the first fruits of all your produce; then your barns will be filled with plenty, and your vats will be bursting with wine. (Prov. 3:9–10)

YEAR A

Hymn of the day

423 Lord, whose love in humble service
409 Praise and thanksgiving
754 Let us talents and tongues employ

Hymns related to the readings

First Reading: Isaiah 55:1–5
Eat and drink that which truly satisfies

213 I come, O Savior, to your table
214 Come, let us eat
412 Sing to the Lord of harvest
497 I heard the voice of Jesus say
711 You satisfy the hungry heart

Psalmody: Psalm 145:8–9, 15–22*
You open wide your hand and satisfy the needs of every living creature. (Ps. 145:17)

Alternate First Reading: Genesis 32:22–31
Jacob receives a blessing from God

477 O God of Jacob
499 Come, thou Fount of every blessing
720 In the presence of your people

Alternate Psalmody: Psalm 17:1–7, 15
I shall see your face; when I awake, I shall be satisfied. (Ps. 17:16)

Second Reading: Romans 9:1–5
The glory of God's people Israel

358 Glories of your name are spoken

Gospel: Matthew 14:13–21
Christ feeding five thousand

235 Break now the bread of life
433 The Church of Christ, in every age
493 Hope of the world
701 What feast of love
711 You satisfy the hungry heart
766 We come to the hungry feast

Additional hymns for the day/season

197 O living Bread from heaven
224 Soul, adorn yourself with gladness
390 I love to tell the story
392 O Lord, send forth your Spirit
702 I am the Bread of life
722 Hallelujah! We sing your praises

YEAR B

Hymn of the day

358 Glories of your name are spoken
172 Lord, enthroned in heavenly splendor
700 I received the living God

Hymns related to the readings

First Reading: Exodus 16:2–4, 9–15
The LORD gives manna in the wilderness

172 Lord, enthroned in heavenly splendor
210 At the Lamb's high feast we sing
222 O Bread of life from heaven

343 Guide me ever, great Redeemer
345 How sweet the name of Jesus sounds
358 Glories of your name are spoken
403 Lord, speak to us, that we may speak
477 O God of Jacob

Psalmody: Psalm 78:23–29
The Lord rained down manna upon them to eat.
(Ps. 78:24)

Alternate First Reading: 2 Samuel 11:26—12:13a
David rebuked by the prophet Nathan

295 Out of the depths I cry to you
304 Today your mercy calls us

Alternate Psalmody: Psalm 51:1–12
Have mercy on me, O God, according to your lov-
ingkindness. (Ps. 51:1)

732 Create in me a clean heart

Second Reading: Ephesians 4:1–16
Maintain the unity of the faith

191 Praise and thanksgiving be to God
209 Come, risen Lord
225 Lord Jesus Christ, we humbly pray
317 To God the Holy Spirit let us pray
355 Through the night of doubt and sorrow
369 The Church's one foundation
370 Blest be the tie that binds

373 Eternal Ruler of the ceaseless round
508 Come down, O Love divine
523 Holy Spirit, ever dwelling
745 Awake, O sleeper
755 We all are one in mission

Gospel: John 6:24–35
Christ the bread of life

197 O living Bread from heaven
211 Here, O my Lord, I see thee
222 O Bread of life from heaven
224 Soul, adorn yourself with gladness
345 How sweet the name of Jesus sounds
392 O Lord, send forth your Spirit
704 Father, we thank you

Additional hymns for the day/season
199 Thee we adore, O hidden Savior
213 I come, O Savior, to your table
223 In the quiet consecration
356 O Jesus, joy of loving hearts
699 Blessed assurance
702 I am the Bread of life
703 Draw us in the Spirit's tether
707 This is my body
722 Hallelujah! We sing your praises
761 Now we offer

YEAR C

Hymn of the day
537 O Jesus, king most wonderful!
447 All depends on our possessing
782 All my hope on God is founded

Hymns related to the readings

First Reading: Ecclesiastes 1:2, 12–14; 2:18–23
Search out wisdom, for all is vanity

454 If God himself be for me
482 When I survey the wondrous cross
537 O Jesus, king most wonderful!

Psalmody: Psalm 49:1–11**
We can never ransom ourselves or deliver to God the
price of our life. (Ps. 49:6)

Alternate First Reading: Hosea 11:1–11
Like a mother, God will love Israel forever

313 A multitude comes from the east and the west
519 My soul, now praise your maker!
769 Mothering God, you gave me birth

Alternate Psalmody: Psalm 107:1–9, 43
Give thanks to the Lord, all those whom the Lord
has redeemed. (Ps. 107:1–2)

Second Reading: Colossians 3:1–11
Clothed in Christ, your life is hidden with him in God

209 Come, risen Lord
306 Chief of sinners though I be
327 Rock of Ages, cleft for me
359 In Christ there is no east or west
373 Eternal Ruler of the ceaseless round
504 O God, my faithful God
511 Renew me, O eternal Light
704 Father, we thank you
710 One bread, one body

Gospel: Luke 12:13–21
Jesus says: Be on guard against greed; be rich toward
God, your treasure

364 Son of God, eternal Savior
415 God of grace and God of glory
776 Be thou my vision

Additional hymns for the day/season
358 Glories of your name are spoken
408 God, whose giving knows no ending
457, 458 Jesus, priceless treasure

*Psalm 145:8–9, 14–21 (NRSV)
**Psalm 49:1–12 (NRSV)

Proper 14

Prayer of the day

Almighty and everlasting God, you are always more ready to hear than we are to pray, and to give more than we either desire or deserve. Pour upon us the abundance of your mercy, forgiving us those things of which our conscience is afraid, and giving us those good things for which we are not worthy to ask, except through the merit of your Son, Jesus Christ our Lord. (92)

Verse

Alleluia. Faith is the assurance of things hoped for, the conviction of things not seen. Alleluia. (Heb. 11:1)

Offertory

The earth is fully satisfied by the fruit of your works. You make grass grow for flocks and herds, and plants to serve humankind; that they may bring forth food from the earth, and wine to gladden our hearts, oil to make a cheerful countenance, and bread to strengthen the heart. (Ps. 104:13–15)

YEAR A

Hymn of the day

467   Eternal Father, strong to save
366   Lord of our life
781   My life flows on in endless song

Hymns related to the readings

First Reading: 1 Kings 19:9–18
The LORD speaks to Elijah on Mount Horeb

506   Dear Lord and Father of mankind
526   Immortal, invisible, God only wise
682   Praise the Spirit in creation
768   He comes to us as one unknown

Psalmody: Psalm 85:8–13
I will listen to what the LORD God is saying. (Ps. 85:8)

Alternate First Reading: Genesis 37:1–4, 12–28
Joseph sold by his brothers

735   God! When human bonds are broken

Alternate Psalmody: Psalm 105:1–6, 16–22, 45b
Make known the deeds of the LORD among the peoples. Hallelujah! (Ps. 105:1, 45)

Second Reading: Romans 10:5–15
Hearing and confessing the word of faith

11   Now listen, you servants of God
202   Victim Divine, your grace we claim
312   Once he came in blessing
396   O God, O Lord of heaven and earth
397   O Zion, haste
671   Alleluia, alleluia, give thanks

Gospel: Matthew 14:22–33
Jesus walking on the sea

333   Lord, take my hand and lead me
334   Jesus, Savior, pilot me
366   Lord of our life
457, 458   Jesus, priceless treasure
465   Evening and morning
467   Eternal Father, strong to save
468   From God can nothing move me
731   Precious Lord, take my hand
781   My life flows on in endless song

Additional hymns for the day/season

205   Now the silence
320   O God, our help in ages past
417   In a lowly manger born
503   O Jesus, I have promised
507   How firm a foundation
548   Oh, worship the King
780   What a fellowship, what a joy divine

Year B

Hymn of the day
224 Soul, adorn yourself with gladness
343 Guide me ever, great Redeemer
709 Eat this bread

Hymns related to the readings

First Reading: 1 Kings 19:4–8
Elijah receives bread for his journey

197 O living Bread from heaven

Psalmody: Psalm 34:1–8
Taste and see that the LORD is good. (Ps. 34:8)

706 Eat this bread, drink this cup (paraphrase)

Alternate First Reading: 2 Samuel 18:5–9, 15, 31–33
David laments his son Absalom's death

739 In all our grief

Alternate Psalmody: Psalm 130
Out of the depths have I cried to you, O LORD. (Ps. 130:1)

295 Out of the depths I cry to you (paraphrase)

Second Reading: Ephesians 4:25—5:2
Put away evil, live in love

268 Now that the daylight fills the sky
307 Forgive our sins as we forgive
504 O God, my faithful God
551 Joyful, joyful we adore thee

Gospel: John 6:35, 41–51
Christ the bread of life

197 O living Bread from heaven
207 We who once were dead
208 Lord Jesus Christ, you have prepared
224 Soul, adorn yourself with gladness
343 Guide me ever, great Redeemer
356 O Jesus, joy of loving hearts
493 Hope of the world
702 I am the Bread of life
704 Father, we thank you
722 Hallelujah! We sing your praises

Additional hymns for the day/season
199 Thee we adore, O hidden Savior
213 I come, O Savior, to your table
223 In the quiet consecration
718 Here in this place
801 Thine the amen, thine the praise

Year C

Hymn of the day
463 God, who stretched the spangled heavens
532 How Great Thou Art
794 Many and great, O God, are your works

Hymns related to the readings

First Reading: Genesis 15:1–6
God's promise of a child for Abram and Sarai

544 The God of Abraham praise
794 Many and great, O God, are your works

Psalmody: Psalm 33:12–22
Let your lovingkindness be upon us, as we have put our trust in you. (Ps. 33:22)

Alternate First Reading: Isaiah 1:1, 10–20
Learn to do good, seek justice, and rescue the oppressed

305 I lay my sins on Jesus
419 Lord of all nations, grant me grace

Alternate Psalmody: Psalm 50:1–8, 22–23
To those who keep in my way will I show the salvation of God. (Ps. 50:2–4)

Second Reading: Hebrews 11:1–3, 8–16
A model for us: Abraham's faith in a new home given by God

297 Salvation unto us has come
355 Through the night of doubt and sorrow
453 If you but trust in God to guide you
507 How firm a foundation
689 Rejoice in God's saints

Gospel: Luke 12:32–40
God will give you the treasure of the kingdom; sell all that you have

31 Wake, awake, for night is flying
224 Soul, adorn yourself with gladness
361 Do not despair, O little flock
382 Awake, O Spirit of the watchmen
443 Rise, my soul, to watch and pray
476 Have no fear, little flock

Additional hymns for the day/season
203 Now we join in celebration
457, 458 Jesus, priceless treasure
459 O Holy Spirit, enter in
477 O God of Jacob
725 Blessed be the God of Israel
771 Great is thy faithfulness

PROPER 15

Prayer of the day

Almighty and ever-living God, you have given great and precious promises to those who believe. Grant us the perfect faith which overcomes all doubts, through your Son, Jesus Christ our Lord. (93)

Verse

Alleluia. The Word of God is living and active, sharper than any two–edged sword, able to judge the thoughts and intentions of the heart. Alleluia. (Heb. 4:12)

Offertory

Ascribe to the LORD, O families of the peoples, ascribe to the LORD glory and strength! Ascribe to the LORD the glory due his name; bring an offering and come before him. Worship the LORD in holy splendor. Oh, give thanks to the LORD, for he is good; for his steadfast love endures forever. (1 Chron. 16:28–29, 34)

YEAR A

Hymn of the day

359 In Christ there is no east or west
423 Lord, whose love in humble service
757 Creating God, your fingers trace

Hymns related to the readings

First Reading: Isaiah 56:1, 6–8
A house of prayer for all peoples

313 A multitude comes from the east and the west
359 In Christ there is no east or west
432 We worship you, O God of might
530 Jesus shall reign

Psalmody: Psalm 67
Let all the peoples praise you, O God. (Ps. 67:3)

335 May God bestow on us his grace (paraphrase)

Alternate First Reading: Genesis 45:1–15
Joseph reconciles with his brothers

307 Forgive our sins as we forgive

Alternate Psalmody: Psalm 133
How good and pleasant it is to live together in unity. (Ps. 133:1)

Second Reading: Romans 11:1–2a, 29–32
God's mercy to all, Jew and Gentile

710 One bread, one body

Gospel: Matthew 15:[10–20] 21–28
The healing of the Canaanite woman's daughter

303 When in the hour of deepest need
310 To you, omniscient Lord of all
359 In Christ there is no east or west
360 O Christ, the healer, we have come
393 Rise, shine, you people!
423 Lord, whose love in humble service
435 O God, whose will is life and good

Additional hymns for the day/season

290 There's a wideness in God's mercy
400 God, whose almighty word
419 Lord of all nations, grant me grace
517 Praise to the Father
550 From all that dwell below the skies
559 Oh, for a thousand tongues to sing
668 There in God's garden
718 Here in this place
750 Oh, praise the gracious power

Year B

Hymn of the day

702   I am the Bread of life
214   Come, let us eat
409   Praise and thanksgiving

Hymns related to the readings

First Reading: Proverbs 9:1–6
Invited to dine at wisdom's feast

214   Come, let us eat
688   O Holy Spirit, root of life

Psalmody: Psalm 34:9–14
*Those who seek the LORD lack nothing that is good.
(Ps. 34:10)*

Alternate First Reading: 1 Kings 2:10–12; 3:3–14
Solomon's prayer for wisdom

415   God of grace and God of glory
464   You are the way

Alternate Psalmody: Psalm 111
*The fear of the LORD is the beginning of wisdom.
(Ps. 111:10)*

Second Reading: Ephesians 5:15–20
Filled with the Spirit, sing thanks to God

267   Father, we praise you
406   Take my life, that I may be
465   Evening and morning

545, 546   When morning gilds the skies
553   Rejoice, O pilgrim throng!
555   When in our music God is glorified
557   Let all things now living
560   Oh, that I had a thousand voices
802   When in our music God is glorified

Gospel: John 6:51–58
Christ the true food and drink

197   O living Bread from heaven
198   Let all mortal flesh keep silence
199   Thee we adore, O hidden Savior
205   Now the silence
207   We who once were dead
208   Lord Jesus Christ, you have prepared
222   O Bread of life from heaven
224   Soul, adorn yourself with gladness
356   O Jesus, joy of loving hearts
375   Only-begotten, Word of God eternal
496   Around you, O Lord Jesus

Additional hymns for the day/season

210   At the Lamb's high feast we sing
226   Draw near and take the body of the Lord
464   You are the way
513   Come, my way, my truth, my life
552   In thee is gladness
707   This is my body

Year C

Hymn of the day

454   If God himself be for me
500   Faith of our fathers
785   Weary of all trumpeting

Hymns related to the readings

First Reading: Jeremiah 23:23–29
*God's word is like fire, like a hammer that breaks
rocks*

232   Your Word, O Lord, is gentle dew
233   Thy strong Word

Psalmody: Psalm 82
Arise, O God, and rule the earth. (Ps. 82:8)

Alternate First Reading: Isaiah 5:1–7
The vineyard of the LORD is destroyed

295   Out of the depths I cry to you
421   Lord Christ, when first you came to earth

Alternate Psalmody: Psalm 80:1–2, 8–19
*Look down from heaven, O God; behold and tend
this vine. (Ps. 80:14)*

Second Reading: Hebrews 11:29—12:2
*The faith of the Hebrew people, a great cloud of wit-
nesses*

183   The Son of God goes forth to war
308   God the Father, be our stay
461   Fight the good fight
502   Thee will I love, my strength
505   Forth in thy name, O Lord, I go
649   I want to walk as a child of the light

Gospel: Luke 12:49–56
*Jesus brings fire on earth and has a baptism with
which to be baptized*

230   Lord, keep us steadfast in your Word
495   Lead on, O King eternal
529   Praise God. Praise him

Additional hymns for the day/season

174   For all the saints
418   Judge eternal, throned in splendor
507   How firm a foundation
522   Come, thou almighty King
736   By gracious powers

SUNDAY BETWEEN AUGUST 21 AND 27

PROPER 16

Prayer of the day

God of all creation, you reach out to call people of all nations to your kingdom. As you gather disciples from near and far, count us also among those who boldly confess your Son Jesus Christ as Lord. (94)

Verse

Alleluia. Our Savior Jesus Christ abolished death and brought life and immortality to light through the gospel. Alleluia. (2 Tim. 1:10)

Offertory

Do not worry, saying "What will we eat?" or "What will we drink?" or "What will we wear?" Your heavenly Father knows that you need all these things. But strive first for the kingdom of God and its righteousness, and all these things will be given to you as well. (Matt. 6:31–33)

YEAR A

Hymn of the day

365   Built on a rock
369   The Church's one foundation
367, 747   Christ is made the sure foundation

Hymns related to the readings

First Reading: Isaiah 51:1–6
The enduring foundation of God's salvation

457   O Holy Spirit, enter in
384   Your kingdom come, O Father

Psalmody: Psalm 138
O LORD, your love endures forever. (Ps. 138:9)

Alternate First Reading: Exodus 1:8—2:10
Pharaoh's daughter takes Moses as her son

533, 534   Now thank we all our God
670   When Israel was in Egypt's land
692   For all the faithful women

Alternate Psalmody: Psalm 124
We have escaped like a bird from the snare of the fowler. (Ps. 124:7)

Second Reading: Romans 12:1–8
One body in Christ, with gifts that differ

206   Lord, who the night you were betrayed
209   Come, risen Lord
360   O Christ, the healer, we have come
381   Hark, the voice of Jesus calling
411   Lord of all good
487   Let us ever walk with Jesus
705   As the grains of wheat
708   Grains of wheat
710   One bread, one body

Gospel: Matthew 16:13–20
The profession of Peter's faith

177   By all your saints in warfare (stanza 10)
293, 294   My hope is built on nothing less
365   Built on a rock

Additional hymns for the day/season

345   How sweet the name of Jesus sounds
514   O Savior, precious Savior
704   Father, we thank you
755   We all are one in mission
781   My life flows on in endless song
793   Shout for joy loud and long

YEAR B

Hymn of the day

373   Eternal Ruler of the ceaseless round
493   Hope of the world
706   Eat this bread, drink this cup

Hymns related to the readings

First Reading: Joshua 24:1–2a, 14–18
Joshua calls all Israel to serve the LORD

503   O Jesus, I have promised
512   Oh, blest the house
561   For the beauty of the earth

Psalmody: Psalm 34:15–22
The eyes of the LORD are upon the righteous. (Ps. 34:15)

Alternate First Reading: 1 Kings 8:[1, 6, 10–11] 22–30, 41–43
Solomon's prayer at the temple dedication

313 A multitude comes from the east and the west
359 In Christ there is no east or west
432 We worship you, O God of might
530 Jesus shall reign

Alternate Psalmody: Psalm 84
How dear to me is your dwelling, O LORD. (Ps. 84:1)

Second Reading: Ephesians 6:10–20
Put on the armor of God

228, 229 A mighty fortress is our God
242 Let the whole creation cry
308 God the Father, be our stay
344 We sing the praise of him who died
361 Do not despair, O little flock
373 Eternal Ruler of the ceaseless round
389 Stand up, stand up for Jesus
444 With the Lord begin your task

461 Fight the good fight
478 Come, oh, come, O quickening Spirit
509 Onward, Christian soldiers
522 Come, thou almighty King

Gospel: John 6:56–69
The bread of eternal life

197 O living Bread from heaven
222 O Bread of life from heaven
464 You are the way
490 Let me be yours forever
503 O Jesus, I have promised
493 Hope of the world
704 Father, we thank you

Additional hymns for the day/season

200 For the bread which you have broken
231 O Word of God incarnate
495 Lead on, O King eternal!
699 Blessed assurance
782 All my hope on God is founded

YEAR C

Hymn of the day

507 How firm a foundation
358 Glories of your name are spoken
742 Come, we that love the Lord

Hymns related to the readings

First Reading: Isaiah 58:9b–14
Do not trample the sabbath, but feed the hungry

212 Let us break bread together
405 Lord of light
409 Praise and thanksgiving
420 Lord, save your world
423 Lord, whose love in humble service
433 The Church of Christ, in every age

Psalmody: Psalm 103:1–8
The LORD crowns you with mercy and lovingkindness. (Ps. 103:4)

519 My soul, now praise your maker! (paraphrase)
543 Praise to the Lord, the Almighty (paraphrase)
549 Praise, my soul, the King of heaven (paraphrase)
798 Bless the Lord, O my soul (Ps. 103:1)

Alternate First Reading: Jeremiah 1:4–10
Jeremiah is called to be a prophet

510 O God of youth

Alternate Psalmody: Psalm 71:1–6
From my mother's womb you have been my strength. (Ps. 71:6)

Second Reading: Hebrews 12:18–29
You have come to the city of the living God and to Jesus

331 Jerusalem, my happy home
347 Jerusalem the golden
348 Jerusalem, whose towers touch the skies
358 Glories of your name are spoken
553 Rejoice, O pilgrim throng!
742 Come, we that love the Lord

Gospel: Luke 13:10–17
Jesus heals a crippled woman on the sabbath and is condemned

426 O Son of God, in Galilee
435 O God, whose will is life and good

Additional hymns for the day/season

251 O day of rest and gladness
360 O Christ the healer, we have come
419 Lord of all nations, grant me grace
548 Oh, worship the King
716 Word of God, come down on earth

PROPER 17

Prayer of the day

O God, we thank you for your Son who chose the path of suffering for the sake of the world. Humble us by his example, point us to the path of obedience, and give us strength to follow his commands; through your Son, Jesus Christ our Lord. (95)

Verse

Alleluia. Your words became to me a joy, and the delight of my heart. Alleluia. (Jer. 15:16)

Offertory

This is the bread that comes down from heaven, so that one may eat of it and not die. I am the living bread that came down from heaven. Whoever eats of this bread will live forever; and the bread that I will give for the life of the world is my flesh. (John 6:50–51)

YEAR A

Hymn of the day

364   Son of God, eternal Savior
398   "Take up your cross," the Savior said
736   By gracious powers

Hymns related to the readings

First Reading: Jeremiah 15:15–21
God fortifies the prophet against opposition

237   O God of light
454   If God himself be for me

Psalmody: Psalm 26:1–8
Your love is before my eyes; I have walked faithfully with you. (Ps. 26:3)

Alternate First Reading: Exodus 3:1–15
From the blazing bush God calls Moses

544   The God of Abraham praise
670   When Israel was in Egypt's land

Alternate Psalmody: Psalm 105:1–6, 23–26, 45c
Make known the deeds of the LORD among the peoples. Hallelujah! (Ps. 105:1, 45)

Second Reading: Romans 12:9–21
Live in harmony

370   Blest be the tie that binds
409   Praise and thanksgiving
420   Lord, save your world
508   Come down, O Love divine
748   Bind us together

756   Lord, you give the great commission
799   When long before time

Gospel: Matthew 16:21–28
The passion prediction and rebuke to Peter

384   Your kingdom come, O Father
398   "Take up your cross," the Savior said
455   "Come, follow me," the Savior spake
487   Let us ever walk with Jesus
504   O God, my faithful God

Additional hymns for the day/season

377   Lift high the cross
408   God, whose giving knows no ending
419   Lord of all nations, grant me grace
503   O Jesus, I have promised
793   Shout for joy loud and long

YEAR B

Hymn of the day

504 O God, my faithful God
511 Renew me, O eternal Light
713 Lord, let my heart be good soil

Hymns related to the readings

First Reading: Deuteronomy 4:1–2, 6–9
God's law: a sign of a great nation

464 You are the way
480 Oh, that the Lord would guide my ways
715 Open your ears, O faithful people

Psalmody: Psalm 15
LORD, who may dwell in your tabernacle? (Ps. 15:1)

Alternate First Reading: Song of Solomon 2:8–13
Song of two lovers

513 Come, my way, my truth, my life
518 Beautiful Savior
669 Come away to the skies

Alternate Psalmody: Psalm 45:1–2, 6–9
God has anointed you with the oil of gladness. (Ps. 45:8)

Second Reading: James 1:17–27
Be doers of the word, not hearers only

268 Now that the daylight fills the sky
362 We plow the fields and scatter
410 We give thee but thine own
504 O God, my faithful God

Gospel: Mark 7:1–8, 14–15, 21–23
Authentic religion

102 On my heart imprint your image
296 Just as I am, without one plea
504 O God, my faithful God
511 Renew me, O eternal Light
662 Restore in us, O God
732 Create in me a clean heart

Additional hymns for the day/season

248 Dearest Jesus, at your word
504 O God, my faithful God
537 O Jesus, king most wonderful!
561 For the beauty of the earth
763 Let justice flow like streams
767 All things bright and beautiful

YEAR C

Hymn of the day

718 Here in this place
211 Here, O my Lord, I see thee
428 O God of earth and altar

Hymns related to the readings

First Reading: Proverbs 25:6–7
Do not put yourself forward

718 Here in this place

OR

First Reading: Sirach 10:12–18
Judgment upon the proud

415 God of grace and God of glory
782 All my hope on God is founded

Psalmody: Psalm 112
The righteous are merciful and full of compassion. (Ps. 112:4)

Alternate First Reading: Jeremiah 2:4–13
The people of Israel forsake the LORD

499 Come, thou Fount of every blessing
542 Sing praise to God, the highest good
684 Spirit, Spirit of gentleness

Alternate Psalmody: Psalm 81:1, 10–16
I feed you with the finest wheat and satisfy you with honey from the rock. (Ps. 81:16)

Second Reading: Hebrews 13:1–8, 15–16
God is with us: let acts of mutual love continue

203 Now we join in celebration
429 Where cross the crowded ways of life
778 O Christ the same
797 O God beyond all praising

Gospel: Luke 14:1, 7–14
An image of God's reign: invite the poor, crippled to your banquet

316 Jesus, the very thought of you
718 Here in this place
750 Oh, praise the gracious power
790 Praise to you, O God of mercy

Additional hymns for the day/season

403 Lord, speak to us, that we may speak
419 Lord of all nations, grant me grace
441 Eternal Spirit of the living Christ
508 Come down, O Love divine
723 The Spirit sends us forth to serve
730 My soul proclaims your greatness
757 Creating God, your fingers trace
766 We come to the hungry feast

SUNDAY BETWEEN SEPTEMBER 4 AND 10 INCLUSIVE

PROPER 18

Prayer of the day
Almighty and eternal God, you know our problems and our weaknesses better than we ourselves. In your love and by your power help us in our confusion and, in spite of our weakness, make us firm in faith; through your Son, Jesus Christ our Lord. (96)

Verse
Alleluia. Rejoice in the Lord always; again I will say, Rejoice. Alleluia. (Phil. 4:4)

Offertory
Do not lag in zeal, be ardent in spirit, serve the Lord. Rejoice in hope, be patient in suffering, persevere in prayer. Contribute to the needs of the saints; extend hospitality to strangers. (Rom. 12:11–13)

YEAR A

Hymn of the day
419   Lord of all nations, grant me grace
126   Where charity and love prevail
739   In all our grief

Hymns related to the readings

First Reading: Ezekiel 33:7–11
The prophet's responsibility to warn the people

382   Awake, O Spirit of the watchmen

Psalmody: Psalm 119:33–40
I desire the path of your commandments. (Ps. 119:35)

Alternate First Reading: Exodus 12:1–14
The passover of the LORD

210   At the Lamb's high feast we sing

Alternate Psalmody: Psalm 149
Sing the praise of the LORD in the congregation of the faithful. (Ps. 149:1)

Second Reading: Romans 13:8–14
Live honorably as in the day

382   Awake, O Spirit of the watchmen
422   O God, empower us to stem
441   Eternal Spirit of the living Christ
443   Rise, my soul, to watch and pray
666   Great God, your love has called us
745   Awake, O sleeper
748   Bind us together
765   Jesu, Jesu, fill us with your love

Gospel: Matthew 18:15–20
Reconciliation in the community of faith

365   Built on a rock
427   O Jesus Christ, may grateful hymns be rising
703   Draw us in the Spirit's tether
783   Seek ye first the kingdom of God

Additional hymns for the day/season
126   Where charity and love prevail
307   Forgive our sins as we forgive
353   May we your precepts, Lord, fulfill
551   Joyful, joyful we adore thee
735   God! When human bonds are broken

Year B

Hymn of the day
716   Word of God, come down on earth
419   Lord of all nations, grant me grace
426   O Son of God, in Galilee

Hymns related to the readings

First Reading: Isaiah 35:4–7a
Like streams in the desert, God comes with healing

402   Look from your sphere of endless day
384   Your kingdom come, O Father
716   Word of God, come down on earth

Psalmody: Psalm 146
I will praise the LORD as long as I live. (Ps. 146:1)

538   Oh, praise the Lord, my soul (paraphrase)
539   Praise the Almighty (paraphrase)

Alternate First Reading: Proverbs 22:1–2, 8–9, 22–23
Sayings concerning a good name and generosity

409   Praise and thanksgiving
410   We give thee but thine own
776   Be thou my vision

Alternate Psalmody: Psalm 125
Those who trust in the LORD stand fast forever. (Ps. 125:1)

Second Reading: James 2:1–10 [11–13] 14–17
Faith without works is dead

317   To God the Holy Spirit let us pray
419   Lord of all nations, grant me grace
422   O God, empower us
423   Lord, whose love in humble service
425   O God of mercy, God of light
429   Where cross the crowded ways of life
433   The Church of Christ, in every age
441   Eternal Spirit of the living Christ
765   Jesu, Jesu, fill us with your love

Gospel: Mark 7:24–37
Christ healing a little girl and a deaf man

345   How sweet the name of Jesus sounds
380   O Christ, our light, O Radiance true
426   O Son of God, in Galilee
435   O God, whose will is life and good
716   Word of God, come down on earth

Additional hymns for the day/season
376   Your kingdom come!
400   God, whose almighty word
559   Oh, for a thousand tongues to sing
668   There in God's garden
737   There is a balm in Gilead
738   Healer of our every ill
755   We all are one in mission

Year C

Hymn of the day
406   Take my life, that I may be
398   Take up your cross, the Savior said
782   All my hope on God is founded

Hymns related to the readings

First Reading: Deuteronomy 30:15–20
Walk in the way of life and hold fast to God

475   Come, gracious Spirit, heavenly dove
478   Come, oh, come, O quickening Spirit
480   Oh, that the Lord would guide my ways
486   Spirit of God, descend upon my heart
746   Day by day

Psalmody: Psalm 1
Their delight is in the law of the LORD. (Ps. 1:2)

Alternate First Reading: Jeremiah 18:1–11
Like a potter, the LORD will reshape Israel

531   Before Jehovah's awesome throne

Alternate Psalmody: Psalm 139:1–6, 13–18
You have searched me out and known me. (Ps. 139:1)

311   Wondrous are your ways, O God! (paraphrase)

Second Reading: Philemon 1–21
Paul says: Receive Onesimus as a coworker

126   Where charity and love prevail

Gospel: Luke 14:25–33
Jesus says: Disciples, give up your possessions and carry the cross

384   Your kingdom come, O Father
398   "Take up your cross," the Savior said
487   Let us ever walk with Jesus
504   O God, my faithful God
510   O God of youth

Additional hymns for the day/season
377   Lift high the cross
447   All depends on our possessing
785   Weary of all trumpeting
797   O God beyond all praising

PROPER 19

Prayer of the day

O God, you declare your almighty power chiefly in showing mercy and pity. Grant us the fullness of your grace, that, pursuing what you have promised, we may share your heavenly glory; through your Son, Jesus Christ our Lord. (97)

Verse

Alleluia. Whatever was written in former days was written for our instruction, so that by steadfastness and by the encouragement of the scriptures we might have hope. Alleluia. (Rom. 15:4)

Offertory

Those who observe the day, observe it in honor of the Lord. Also those who eat, eat in honor of the Lord. We do not live to ourselves, and we do not die to ourselves. If we live, we live to the Lord, and if we die, we die to the Lord; so then, whether we live or whether we die, we are the Lord's. (Rom. 14:6–8)

YEAR A

Hymn of the day

307 Forgive our sins as we forgive
126 Where charity and love prevail
733 Our Father, we have wandered

Hymns related to the readings

First Reading: Genesis 50:15–21
Joseph reconciles with his brothers

126 Where charity and love prevail
307 Forgive our sins as we forgive

Psalmody: Psalm 103:[1–7] 8–13
The LORD is full of compassion and mercy. (Ps. 103:8)

519 My soul, now praise your maker! (paraphrase)
543 Praise to the Lord, the Almighty (paraphrase)
549 Praise, my soul, the King of heaven (paraphrase)
798 Bless the Lord, O my soul (Ps. 103:1)

Alternate First Reading: Exodus 14:19–31
Israel's deliverance at the Red Sea

132 Come, you faithful, raise the strain
343 Guide me ever, great Redeemer
557 Let all things now living
670 When Israel was in Egypt's land

Alternate Psalmody: Psalm 114
Tremble, O earth, at the presence of the LORD. (Ps. 114:7)

OR

Alternate Psalmody: Exodus 15:1b–11, 20–21
I will sing to the LORD who has triumphed gloriously. (Exod. 15:1)

19 I will sing to the Lord

Second Reading: Romans 14:1–12
Accepting diversity in the community of faith

13 Keep in mind that Jesus Christ has died for us
179 At the name of Jesus
272 Abide with me
399 We are the Lord's
552 In thee is gladness
797 O God beyond all praising

Gospel: Matthew 18:21–35
A parable of forgiveness in the community of faith

126 Where charity and love prevail
307 Forgive our sins as we forgive

Additional hymns for the day/season

196 Praise the Lord, rise up rejoicing
205 Now the silence
358 Glories of your name are spoken
419 Lord of all nations, grant me grace
527 All creatures of our God and King
530 Jesus shall reign
665 Ubi caritas et amor
721 Go, my children, with my blessing
750 Oh, praise the gracious power

Hymn of the day
377 Lift high the cross
537 O Jesus, king most wonderful!
750 Oh, praise the gracious power

Hymns related to the readings

First Reading: Isaiah 50:4–9a
The servant is vindicated by God

454 If God himself be for me

Psalmody: Psalm 116:1–8*
I will walk in the presence of the LORD. (Ps. 116:8)

Alternate First Reading: Proverbs 1:20–33
Wisdom's rebuke to the foolish

312 Once he came in blessing
380 O Christ, our Light, O Radiance true

Alternate Psalmody: Psalm 19
The statutes of the LORD are just and rejoice the heart. (Ps. 19:8)

OR

Alternate Psalmody: Wisdom of Solomon 7:26—8:1
God loves nothing so much as the person who lives with wisdom. (Wis. of Sol. 7:28)

Second Reading: James 3:1–12
Dangers of the unbridled tongue

218 Strengthen for service, Lord
268 Now that the daylight fills the sky
266 Maker of the earth and heaven
504 O God, my faithful God

Gospel: Mark 8:27–38
Peter's confession of faith

177 By all your saints in warfare (stanza 10)
312 Once he came in blessing
398 "Take up your cross," the Savior said
465 Built on a rock

Additional hymns for the day/season
221 Sent forth by God's blessing
233 Thy strong Word
503 O Jesus, I have promised
777 In the morning when I rise
785 Weary of all trumpeting

Year C

Hymn of the day
448 Amazing grace, how sweet the sound
291 Jesus sinners will receive
734 Softly and tenderly Jesus is calling

Hymns related to the readings

First Reading: Exodus 32:7–14
Moses begs the LORD to turn from anger against the Hebrews

494 Jesus calls us; o'er the tumult
670 When Israel was in Egypt's land

Psalmody: Psalm 51:1–11**
Have mercy on me, O God, according to your lovingkindness. (Ps. 51:1)

732 Create in me a clean heart

Alternate First Reading: Jeremiah 4:11–12, 22–28
Judgment is spoken against Jerusalem

418 Judge eternal, throned in splendor
462 God the omnipotent!

Alternate Psalmody: Psalm 14
The LORD looks down from heaven upon us all. (Ps. 14:2)

Second Reading: 1 Timothy 1:12–17
Christ Jesus came for sinners

306 Chief of sinners though I be
398 One there is, above all others
526 Immortal, invisible, God only wise

Gospel: Luke 15:1–10
Looking for the lost sheep, silver coin: Jesus eating with sinners

243 Lord, with glowing heart
291 Jesus sinners will receive
325 Lord, thee I love with all my heart
403 Lord, speak to us, that we may speak
424 Lord of glory, you have bought us
448 Amazing grace, how sweet the sound
496 Around you, O Lord Jesus
499 Come, thou Fount of every blessing
529 Praise God. Praise him
734 Softly and tenderly Jesus is calling

Additional hymns for the day/season
290 There's a wideness in God's mercy
456 The King of love my shepherd is
479 My faith looks up to thee
481 Savior, like a shepherd lead us
699 Blessed assurance

*Psalm 116:1–9 (NRSV)
**Psalm 51:1–10 (NRSV)

SUNDAY BETWEEN SEPTEMBER 18 AND 24 INCLUSIVE

PROPER 20

Prayer of the day

Lord God, you call us to work in your vineyard and leave no one standing idle. Set us to our tasks in the work of your kingdom, and help us to order our lives by your wisdom; through your Son, Jesus Christ our Lord. (98)

Verse

Alleluia. Live your life in a manner worthy of the gospel of Christ; strive side by side for the faith of the Gospel. Alleluia. (Phil. 1:27)

Offertory

I am the true vine, and my Father is the vinegrower. Abide in me as I abide in you. Just as the branch cannot bear fruit by itself unless it abides in the vine, neither can you unless you abide in me. I am the vine, you are the branches. Those who abide in me and I in them bear much fruit. (John 15:1, 4–5)

YEAR A

Hymn of the day

297 Salvation unto us has come
405 Lord of light
666 Great God, your love has called us

Hymns related to the readings

First Reading: Jonah 3:10—4:11
God's concern for the city of Nineveh

427 O Jesus Christ, may grateful hymns be rising
436 All who love and serve your city

Psalmody: Psalm 145:1–8
The LORD is slow to anger and of great kindness. (Ps. 145:8)

Alternate First Reading: Exodus 16:2–15
Manna and quails feed the Israelites in the wilderness

172 Lord, enthroned in heavenly splendor
210 At the Lamb's high feast we sing
345 How sweet the name of Jesus sounds
358 Glories of your name are spoken
403 Lord, speak to us, that we may speak
477 O God of Jacob

Alternate Psalmody: Psalm 105:1–6, 37–45
Make known the deeds of the LORD among the peoples. Hallelujah! (Ps. 105:1, 45)

Second Reading: Philippians 1:21–30
Standing firm in the gospel

176 For all your saints, O Lord
389 Stand up, stand up for Jesus
399 We are the Lord's

484 God, my Lord, my strength
785 Weary of all trumpeting
797 O God beyond all praising

Gospel: Matthew 20:1–16
The parable of the vineyard workers

405 Lord of light
436 All who love and serve your city
469 Lord of all hopefulness
505 Forth in thy name, O Lord, I go

Additional hymns for the day/season

290 There's a wideness in God's mercy
373 Eternal Ruler of the ceaseless round
378 Amid the world's bleak wilderness
383 Rise up, O saints of God!
406 Take my life, that I may be
759 Accept, O Lord, the gifts we bring
777 In the morning when I rise
801 Thine the amen, thine the praise

Year B

Hymn of the day

474   Children of the heavenly Father
423   Lord, whose love in humble service
683   Loving Spirit

Hymns related to the readings

First Reading: Jeremiah 11:18–20
The prophet led like a lamb to slaughter

105   A lamb goes uncomplaining forth
118   Sing, my tongue

OR

First Reading: Wisdom of Solomon 1:16—2:1, 12–22
The righteous shall live

421   Lord Christ, when first you came to earth

Psalmody: Psalm 54
God is my helper; it is the LORD who sustains my life.
(Ps. 54:4)

Alternate First Reading: Proverbs 31:10–31
Poem celebrating the capable wife

692   For all the faithful women
769   Mothering God, you gave me birth

Alternate Psalmody: Psalm 1
Their delight is in the law of the LORD. (Ps. 1:2)

Second Reading: James 3:13—4:3, 7–8a
The wisdom from above

126   Where charity and love prevail
363   Christ is alive! Let Christians sing
416   O God of every nation
776   Be thou my vision

Gospel: Mark 9:30–37
Prediction of the passion

119   Nature with open volume stands
193   Cradling children in his arm
421   Lord Christ, when first you came to earth
474   Children of the heavenly Father

Additional hymns for the day/season

226   Draw near and take the body of the Lord
536   O God of God, O Light of light
649   I want to walk as a child of the light
719   God is here!
741   Thy holy wings

Year C

Hymn of the day

408   God, whose giving knows no ending
413   Father eternal, ruler of creation
763   Let justice flow like streams

Hymns related to the readings

First Reading: Amos 8:4–7
Warnings to those who trample on the needy and
poor

428   O God of earth and altar
763   Let justice flow like streams

Psalmody: Psalm 113
The LORD lifts up the poor from the ashes. (Ps. 113:6)

Alternate First Reading: Jeremiah 8:18—9:1
The LORD laments over Judah

96   Your heart, O God, is grieved
542   Sing praise to God, the highest good
737   There is a balm in Gilead

Alternate Psalmody: Psalm 79:1–9
Deliver us and forgive us our sins, for your name's
sake. (Ps. 79:9)

Second Reading: 1 Timothy 2:1–7
One God, one mediator—Christ Jesus—who gave
himself for all people

168   Kyrie, God Father
568   God save our gracious Queen!
569   God bless our native land

Gospel: Luke 16:1–13
A shrewd manager: faithful in little, faithful in much;
serving God/wealth

428   O God of earth and altar
447   All depends on our possessing
776   Be thou my vision

Additional hymns for the day/season

364   Son of God, eternal Savior
383   Rise up, O saints of God!
406   Take my life, that I may be
410   We give thee but thine own
413   Father eternal, ruler of creation
416   O God of every nation

Sunday between September 25 and October 1

Proper 21

Prayer of the day

God of love, you know our frailties and failings. Give us your grace to overcome them; keep us from those things that harm us; and guide us in the way of salvation; through your Son, Jesus Christ our Lord. (99)

Verse

Alleluia. At the name of Jesus every knee should bend, and every tongue should confess that Jesus Christ is Lord, to the glory of God the Father. Alleluia. (Phil. 2:10–11)

Offertory

Listen! I am standing at the door, knocking; if you hear my voice and open the door, I will come in to you and eat with you and you with me. To the one who conquers, I will give a place with me on my throne, just as I myself conquered and sat down with my Father on his throne. (Rev. 3:20–21)

Year A

Hymn of the day

179   At the name of Jesus
230   Lord, keep us steadfast in your Word
695   O blessed spring

Hymns related to the readings

First Reading: Ezekiel 18:1–4, 25–32
The fairness of God's way

311   Wondrous are your ways, O God!
446   What God ordains is always right
732   Create in me a clean heart

Psalmody: Psalm 25:1–8*
Remember, O LORD, your compassion and love.
(Ps. 25:5)

Alternate First Reading: Exodus 17:1–7
Water from the rock in the wilderness

172   Lord, enthroned in heavenly splendor
327   Rock of Ages, cleft for me
358   Glories of your name are spoken
497   I heard the voice of Jesus say
635   Surely it is God who saves me
772   The Lord is my song

Alternate Psalmody: Psalm 78:1–4, 12–16
We will recount to generations to come the power of the LORD. (Ps. 78:4)

Second Reading: Philippians 2:1–13
Christ humbled to the point of death on a cross

156   Look, the sight is glorious
179   At the name of Jesus
254   Come, let us join our cheerful songs
328,329   All hail the power of Jesus' name!
703   Draw us in the Spirit's tether

Gospel: Matthew 21:23–32
A parable of doing God's will

504   O God, my faithful God
505   Forth in thy name, O Lord, I go

Additional hymns for the day/season

378   Amid the world's bleak wilderness
423   Lord, whose love in humble service
459   O Holy Spirit, enter in
492   O Master, let me walk with you
719   God is here!
761   Now we offer

Year B

Hymn of the day
429   Where cross the crowded ways of life
508   Come down, O Love divine
684   Spirit, Spirit of gentleness

Hymns related to the readings

First Reading: Numbers 11:4–6, 10–16, 24–29
The LORD's spirit comes upon seventy elders

388   O Spirit of the living God
684   Spirit, Spirit of gentleness

Psalmody: Psalm 19:7–14
The commandment of the LORD gives light to the eyes. (Ps. 19:8)

Alternate First Reading: Esther 7:1–6, 9–10; 9:20–22
Esther's intercession spares the lives of her people

692   For all the faithful women

Alternate Psalmody: Psalm 124
We have escaped like a bird from the snare of the fowler. (Ps. 124:7)

Second Reading: James 5:13–20
Prayer and anointing in the community

360   O Christ the healer, we have come
380   O Christ, our Light, O Radiance true
423   Lord, whose love in humble service
737   There is a balm in Gilead

Gospel: Mark 9:38–50
Warnings to those who obstruct faith

415   God of grace and God of glory
423   Lord, whose love in humble service
429   Where cross the crowded ways of life
493   Hope of the world
753   You are the seed

Additional hymns for the day/season
218   Strengthen for service, Lord
259   Lord, dismiss us with your blessing
270   God of our life, all-glorious Lord
338   Peace, to soothe our bitter woes
719   God is here!
723   The Spirit sends us forth to serve

Year C

Hymn of the day
325   Lord, thee I love with all my heart
538   Oh, praise the Lord, my soul!
730   My soul proclaims your greatness

Hymns related to the readings

First Reading: Amos 6:1a, 4–7
Warnings to those who are comfortable or wealthy

430   Where restless crowds are thronging
763   Let justice flow like streams

Psalmody: Psalm 146
The LORD gives justice to those who are oppressed. (Ps. 146:6)

538   Oh, praise the Lord, my soul (paraphrase)
539   Praise the Almighty (paraphrase)

Alternate First Reading: Jeremiah 32:1–3a, 6–15
Jeremiah buys a field

Alternate Psalmody: Psalm 91:1–6, 14–16
You are my refuge and my stronghold, my God in whom I put my trust. (Ps. 91:2)

779   You who dwell in the shelter of the Lord (paraphrase)

*Psalm 25:1–9 (NRSV)

Second Reading: 1 Timothy 6:6–19
Eager to be rich or eager to pursue richness of God's justice?

308   God the Father, be our stay
461   Fight the good fight
498   All who would valiant be
516   Arise, my soul, arise
526   Immortal, invisible, God only wise
687   Gracious Spirit, heed our pleading

Gospel: Luke 16:19–31
Story of poor Lazarus and the wealthy man

423   Lord, whose love in humble service
429   Where cross the crowded ways of life
718   Here in this place

Additional hymns for the day/season
383   Rise up, O saints of God!
408   God, whose giving knows no ending
415   God of grace and God of glory
419   Lord of all nations, grant me grace
766   We come to the hungry feast

Sunday between October 2 and 8 inclusive

Proper 22

Prayer of the day
Our Lord Jesus, you have endured the doubts and foolish questions of every generation. Forgive us for trying to be judge over you, and grant us the confident faith to acknowledge you as Lord. (100)

Verse
Alleluia. I will proclaim your name to my brothers and sisters; in the midst of the congregation I will praise you. Alleluia. (Heb. 2:12)

Offertory
Taste and see that the LORD is good; happy are they who trust in him! Fear the LORD, you that are his saints, for those who fear him lack nothing. The young lions lack and suffer hunger, but those who seek the LORD lack nothing that is good. (Ps. 34:8–10)

Year A

Hymn of the day
378 Amid the world's bleak wilderness
421 Lord Christ, when first you came to earth
668 There in God's garden

Hymns related to the readings

First Reading: Isaiah 5:1–7
The song of the vineyard

295 Out of the depths I cry to you
421 Lord Christ, when first you came to earth

Psalmody: Psalm 80:7–14*
Look down from heaven, O God; behold and tend this vine. (Ps. 80:14)

Alternate First Reading: Exodus 20:1–4, 7–9, 12–20
The commandments given at Sinai

480 Oh, that the Lord would guide my ways
504 O God, my faithful God
715 Open your ears, O faithful people
796 My Lord of light

Alternate Psalmody: Psalm 19
The statutes of the LORD are just and rejoice the heart. (Ps. 19:8)

Second Reading: Philippians 3:4b–14
Nothing surpasses the value of knowing Christ

11 Now listen, you servants of God
207 We who once were dead

344 We sing the praise of him who died
408 God, whose giving knows no ending
482 When I survey the wondrous cross

Gospel: Matthew 21:33–46
The parable of the vineyard owner's son

421 Lord Christ, when first you came to earth
436 All who love and serve your city

Additional hymns for the day/season
88 Oh, love, how deep
292 God loved the world
433 The Church of Christ, in every age
446 Whatever God ordains is right
796 My Lord of light
801 Thine the amen, thine the praise

YEAR B

Hymn of the day

357 Our Father, by whose name
735 God! When human bonds are broken
749 When love is found

Hymns related to the readings

First Reading: Genesis 2:18–24
Created for relationship

749 When love is found
751 As man and woman we were made

Psalmody: Psalm 8
You adorn us with glory and honor. (Ps. 8:6)

Alternate First Reading: Job 1:1; 2:1–10
Job's integrity in the face of suffering

450 Who trusts in God, a strong abode

Alternate Psalmody: Psalm 26
Your love is before my eyes; I have walked faithfully with you. (Ps. 26:3)

Second Reading: Hebrews 1:1–4; 2:5–12
God has spoken by a Son

88 Oh, love, how deep
156 Look, the sight is glorious
170 Crown him with many crowns
179 At the name of Jesus

252 You servants of God
328, 329 All hail the power of Jesus' name!
516 Arise, my soul, arise!
518 Beautiful Savior
520 Give to our God immortal praise!
525 Blessing and honor

Gospel: Mark 10:2–16
Teaching on marriage

187 Dearest Jesus, we are here
193 Cradling children in his arm
357 Our Father, by whose name
512 Oh, blest the house
561 For the beauty of the earth
683 Loving Spirit
749 When love is found and hope comes home
751 As man and woman we were made

Additional hymns for the day/season

259 Lord, dismiss us with your blessing
465 Evening and morning
514 O Savior, precious Savior
533, 534 Now thank we all our God
547 Thee we adore, eternal Lord
703 Draw us in the Spirit's tether
735 God! When human bonds are broken
767 All things bright and beautiful
797 O God beyond all praising

YEAR C

Hymn of the day

503 O Jesus, I have promised
524 My God, how wonderful thou art
680 O Spirit of life

Hymns related to the readings

First Reading: Habakkuk 1:1–4; 2:1–4
Wicked surround the righteous; wait for the LORD

7 Climb to the top of the highest mountain
318 The Lord will come and not be slow

Psalmody: Psalm 37:1–10**
Commit your way to the LORD; put your trust in the LORD. (Ps. 37:5)

Alternate First Reading: Lamentations 1:1–6
Jerusalem is empty and destroyed

436 All who love and serve your city

Alternate Psalmody: Lamentations 3:19–26
Great is your faithfulness, O LORD. (Lam. 3:23b)

OR

Alternate Psalmody: Psalm 137
Remember the day of Jerusalem, O LORD. (Ps. 137:7)

656 By the Babylonian rivers (paraphrase)

Second Reading: 2 Timothy 1:1–14
Guard the treasure entrusted to you: faith and love in Christ

230 Lord, keep us steadfast in your Word
257 Holy Spirit, truth divine
395 I trust, O Christ, in you alone
533, 534 Now thank we all our God

Gospel: Luke 17:5–10
Faith the size of a mustard seed

253 Lord Jesus Christ, be present now
433 The Church of Christ, in every age
680 O Spirit of life

Additional hymns for the day/season

447 All depends on our possessing
492 O Master, let me walk with you
500 Faith of our fathers
563 For the fruit of all creation
719 God is here!
760 For the fruit of all creation

*Psalm 80:7–15 (NRSV)
**Psalm 37:1–9 (NRSV)

Proper 23

Prayer of the day

Almighty God, source of every blessing, your generous goodness comes to us anew every day. By the work of your Spirit lead us to acknowledge your goodness, give thanks for your benefits, and serve you in willing obedience; through your Son, Jesus Christ our Lord. (101)

Verse

Alleluia. This is the LORD for whom we have waited; let us be glad and rejoice in his salvation. Alleluia. (Isa. 25:9)

Offertory

If anyone does sin, we have an advocate with the Father, Jesus Christ the righteous; and he is the atoning sacrifice for our sins, and not for ours only but also for the sins of the whole world. See what love the Father has given us, that we should be called children of God: and that is what we are. (1 John 2:1–2; 3:1)

Year A

Hymn of the day

203 Now we join in celebration
210 At the Lamb's high feast we sing
789 Now the feast and celebration

Hymns related to the readings

First Reading: Isaiah 25:1–9
The feast of victory

210 At the Lamb's high feast we sing
314 Who is this host arrayed in white
320 O God, our help in ages past
516 Arise, my soul, arise!
701 What feast of love
789 Now the feast and celebration

Psalmody: Psalm 23
You spread a table before me, and my cup is running over. (Ps. 23:5)

451 The Lord's my shepherd (paraphrase)
456 The King of love my shepherd is (paraphrase)

Alternate First Reading: Exodus 32:1–14
The Israelites forge a golden calf

428 O God of earth and altar
494 Jesus calls us; o'er the tumult
542 Sing praise to God, the highest good
684 Spirit, Spirit of gentleness

Alternate Psalmody: Psalm 106:1–6, 19–23
Remember, O LORD, the favor you have for your people. (Ps. 106:4)

Second Reading: Philippians 4:1–9
Rejoice in the Lord always

171 Rejoice, the Lord is king!
516 Arise, my soul, arise!
553 Rejoice, O pilgrim throng!

Gospel: Matthew 22:1–14
The parable of the unwelcome guest at the wedding feast

203 Now we join in celebration
214 Come, let us eat
313 A multitude comes from the east and the west
516 Arise, my soul, arise!

Additional hymns for the day/season

211 Here, O my Lord, I see thee
371 With God as our friend
496 Around you, O Lord Jesus
514 O Savior, precious Savior
708 Grains of wheat
719 God is here!
801 Thine the amen, thine the praise

Year B

Hymn of the day
364 Son of God, eternal Savior
408 God, whose giving knows no ending
783 Seek ye first the kingdom of God

Hymns related to the readings

First Reading: Amos 5:6–7, 10–15
Turn from injustice to the poor, that you may live

428 O God of earth and altar
430 Where restless crowds are thronging
763 Let justice flow like streams

Psalmody: Psalm 90:12–17
So teach us to number our days that we may apply
our hearts to wisdom. (Ps. 90:12)

320 O God, our help in ages past (paraphrase)

Alternate First Reading: Job 23:1–9, 16–17
The Almighty hidden from Job's searching

738 Healer of our every ill

Alternate Psalmody: Psalm 22:1–15
My God, my God, why have you forsaken me? (Ps. 22:1)

Second Reading: Hebrews 4:12–16
Approach the throne of grace with boldness

232 Your Word, O Lord, is gentle dew
522 Come, thou almighty King
739 In all our grief

Gospel: Mark 10:17–31
Teaching on wealth and reward

364 Son of God, eternal Savior
406 Take my life, that I may be
408 God, whose giving knows no ending

Additional hymns for the day/season
383 Rise up, O saints of God!
403 Lord, speak to us that we may speak
409 Praise and thanksgiving
410 We give thee but thine own
415 God of grace and God of glory
433 The Church of Christ in every age
493 Hope of the world
776 Be thou my vision
782 All my hope on God is founded

Year C

Hymn of the day
696 I've just come from the fountain
431 Your hand, O Lord, in days of old
693 Baptized in water

Hymns related to the readings

First Reading: 2 Kings 5:1–3, 7–15c
Naaman washes in the Jordan and is cleansed

431 Your hand, O Lord, in days of old
696 I've just come from the fountain

Psalmody: Psalm 111
I will give thanks to the LORD with my whole heart.
(Ps. 111:1)

Alternate First Reading: Jeremiah 29:1, 4–7
Israel builds houses and plants gardens in Babylon

Alternate Psalmody: Psalm 66:1–12
God holds our souls in life. (Ps. 66:8)

Second Reading: 2 Timothy 2:8–15
If we die with Christ, we will live with Christ

13 Keep in mind that Jesus Christ has died for us

484 God, my Lord, my strength
502 Thee will I love, my strength

Gospel: Luke 17:11–19
One leper made clean by Jesus gives thanks to God

264 When all your mercies, O my God
431 Your hand, O Lord, in days of old
533, 534 Now thank we all our God
543 Praise to the Lord, the Almighty
559 Oh, for a thousand tongues to sing
790 Praise to you, O God of mercy

Additional hymns for the day/season
336 Jesus, thy boundless love to me
520 Give to our God immortal praise!
542 Sing praise to God, the highest good
668 There in God's garden

SUNDAY BETWEEN OCTOBER 16 AND 22 INCLUSIVE

PROPER 24

Prayer of the day

Almighty and everlasting God, in Christ you have revealed your glory among the nations. Preserve the works of your mercy, that your Church throughout the world may persevere with steadfast faith in the confession of your name; through your Son, Jesus Christ our Lord. (102)

Verse

Alleluia. In fulfillment of his own purpose God gave us birth by the word of truth, so that we would become a kind of first fruits of his creatures. Alleluia. (James 1:18)

Offertory

The cup of blessing that we bless, is it not a sharing in the blood of Christ? The bread that we break, is it not a sharing in the body of Christ? Because there is one bread, we who are many are one body, for we all partake of the one bread. (1 Cor. 10:16–17)

YEAR A

Hymn of the day

562   Lift every voice and sing
542   Sing praise to God, the highest good
719   God is here!

Hymns related to the readings

First Reading: Isaiah 45:1–7
An earthly ruler as the instrument of God's will

465   Evening and morning
542   Sing praise to God, the highest good

Psalmody: Psalm 96:1–9 [10–13]
Ascribe to the LORD honor and power. (Ps. 96:7)

Alternate First Reading: Exodus 33:12–23
The glory of God revealed to Moses

165   Holy, holy, holy
199   Thee we adore, O hidden Savior
222   O Bread of life from heaven
516   Arise, my soul, arise!
524   My God, how wonderful thou art
526   Immortal, invisible, God only wise

Alternate Psalmody: Psalm 99
Proclaim the greatness of the LORD our God. (Ps. 99:5)

Second Reading: 1 Thessalonians 1:1–10
Thanksgiving for the church at Thessalonica

284   Creator Spirit, heavenly dove
373   Eternal Ruler of the ceaseless round
800   Each morning brings us fresh outpoured

Gospel: Matthew 22:15–22
A teaching on giving to the emperor and to God

415   God of grace and God of glory
437   Not alone for mighty empire

Additional hymns for the day/season

217   We place upon your table, Lord
252   You servants of God
396   O God, O Lord of heaven and earth
406   Take my life, that I may be
408   God, whose giving knows no ending
410   We give thee but thine own
428   O God of earth and altar
545, 546   When morning gilds the skies
558   Earth and all stars!
754   Let us talents and tongues employ
761   Now we offer
782   All my hope on God is founded
795   Oh, sing to the Lord

Year B

Hymn of the day
433   The Church of Christ, in every age
529   Praise God. Praise him
785   Weary of all trumpeting

Hymns related to the readings

First Reading: Isaiah 53:4–12
The suffering servant

300   O Christ, our hope
354   Eternal God, before your throne

Psalmody: Psalm 91:9–16
You have made the LORD your refuge, and the Most High your habitation. (Ps. 91:9)

779   You who dwell in the shelter of the Lord (paraphrase)

Alternate First Reading: Job 38:1–7 [34–41]
Challenge to Job from God, the creator

188   I bind unto myself today
450   Who trusts in God, a strong abode
462   God, the omnipotent!
515   How marvelous God's greatness
557   Let all things now living
794   Many and great, O God, are your works

Alternate Psalmody: Psalm 104:1–9, 24, 35c
O LORD, how manifold are your works! In wisdom you have made them all. (Ps. 104:25)

548   Oh, worship the King (paraphrase)

Second Reading: Hebrews 5:1–10
Through suffering Christ becomes the source of salvation

202   Victim divine, your grace we claim
739   In all our grief

Gospel: Mark 10:35–45
Warnings to ambitious disciples

122   Love consecrates the humblest act
300   O Christ, our hope
423   Lord, whose love in humble service
460   I am trusting you, Lord Jesus
492   O Master, let me walk with you
514   O Savior, precious Savior
529   Praise God. Praise him
736   By gracious powers
765   Jesu, Jesu, fill us with your love

Additional hymns for the day/season
311   Wondrous are your ways, O God
363   Christ is alive! Let Christians sing
756   Lord, you give the great commission

Year C

Hymn of the day
746   Day by day
439   What a friend we have in Jesus
440   Christians, while on earth abiding

Hymns related to the readings

First Reading: Genesis 32:22–31
Jacob's struggle with the angel: I'll not let go until you bless me

259   Lord, dismiss us with your blessing
477   O God of Jacob
499   Come, thou Fount of every blessing
720   In the presence of your people

Psalmody: Psalm 121
My help comes from the LORD, the maker of heaven and earth. (Ps. 121:2)

445   Unto the hills (paraphrase)

Alternate First Reading: Jeremiah 31:27–34
The LORD promises a new covenant

484   God, my Lord, my strength
701   What feast of love
768   He comes to us as one unknown
790   Praise to you, O God of mercy

Alternate Psalmody: Psalm 119:97–104
Your words are sweeter than honey to my mouth. (Ps. 119:103)

Second Reading: 2 Timothy 3:14—4:5
In the presence of Christ the judge, proclaim the message

227   How blest are they who hear God's Word
231   O Word of God incarnate
237   O God of light
403   Lord, speak to us that we may speak
493   Hope of the world
716   Word of God, come down on earth

Gospel: Luke 18:1–8
The widow begs for justice; God grants justice to those who cry to him

440   Christians, while on earth abiding
441   Eternal Spirit of the living Christ
444   With the Lord begin your task

Additional hymns for the day/season
295   Out of the depths I cry to you
438   Lord, teach us how to pray aright
736   By gracious powers
775   Lord, listen to your children praying

PROPER 25

Prayer of the day

Almighty and everlasting God, increase in us the gifts of faith, hope, and charity; and, that we may obtain what you promise, make us love what you command; through your Son, Jesus Christ our Lord. (103)

Verse

Alleluia. The Lord will rescue me from every evil attack and save me for his heavenly kingdom. Alleluia. (2 Tim. 4:18)

Offertory

Worthy is the Lamb that was slain to receive power and wealth and wisdom and might and honor and glory and blessing! To the one seated on the throne and to the Lamb be blessing and honor and glory and might forever and ever! Amen! (Rev. 5:12–14)

YEAR A

Hymn of the day

666   Great God, your love has called us
490   Let me be yours forever
513   Come, my way, my truth, my life

Hymns related to the readings

First Reading: Leviticus 19:1–2, 15–18
Holiness revealed in acts of justice

441   Eternal Spirit of the living Christ
551   Joyful, joyful we adore thee

Psalmody: Psalm 1
Their delight is in the law of the LORD. (Ps. 1:2)

Alternate First Reading: Deuteronomy 34:1–12
The death of Moses

337   Oh, what their joy

Alternate Psalmody: Psalm 90:1–6, 13–17
Show your servants your works, and your splendor to their children. (Ps. 90:16)

320   O God, our help in ages past (paraphrase)

Second Reading: 1 Thessalonians 2:1–8
The apostle's tender care for the Thessalonians

352   I know that my Redeemer lives!

Gospel: Matthew 22:34–46
Two great commandments: love for God and neighbor

126   Where charity and love prevail
270   God of our life, all-glorious Lord
325   Lord, thee I love with all my heart

336   Jesus, thy boundless love to me
419   Lord of all nations, grant me grace
441   Eternal Spirit of the living Christ
486   Spirit of God, descend upon my heart
491   O God, I love thee
494   Jesus calls us; o'er the tumult
502   Thee will I love, my strength
524   My God, how wonderful thou art
537   O Jesus, king most wonderful!
551   Joyful, joyful we adore thee
765   Jesu, Jesu, fill us with your love

Additional hymns for the day/season

315   Love divine, all loves excelling
328, 329   All hail the power of Jesus' name!
549   Praise, my soul, the King of heaven
703   Draw us in the Spirit's tether
797   O God beyond all praising

Year B

Hymn of the day

400	God, whose almighty word
296	Just as I am, without one plea
718	Here in this place

Hymns related to the readings

First Reading: Jeremiah 31:7–9
The LORD gathers the remnant of Israel

538	Oh, praise the Lord, my soul!
718	Here in this place

Psalmody: Psalm 126
Those who sowed with tears will reap with songs of joy. (Ps. 126:6)

Alternate First Reading: Job 42:1–6, 10–17
Job's restoration

468	From God can nothing move me

Alternate Psalmody: Psalm 34:1–8 [19–22]
Taste and see that the LORD is good. (Ps. 34:8)

706	Eat this bread, drink this cup (paraphrase)

Second Reading: Hebrews 7:23–28
Christ the merciful high priest

254	Come, let us join our cheerful songs
364	Son of God, eternal Savior

Gospel: Mark 10:46–52
Christ healing the blind man Bartimaeus

400	God, whose almighty word
426	O Son of God, in Galilee
431	Your hand, O Lord, in days of old
435	O God, whose will is life and good
448	Amazing grace, how sweet the sound
538	Oh, praise the Lord, my soul!

Additional hymns for the day/season

376	Your kingdom come!
453	If you but trust in God to guide you
542	Sing praise to God, the highest good
559	Oh, for a thousand tongues to sing
673	I'm so glad Jesus lifted me
716	Word of God, come down on earth

Year C

Hymn of the day

310	To you, omniscient Lord of all
417	In a lowly manger born
739	In all our grief

Hymns related to the readings

First Reading: Jeremiah 14:7–10, 19–22
Jerusalem will be defeated

295	Out of the depths I cry to you
303	When in the hour of deepest need
327	Rock of Ages, cleft for me
782	All my hope on God is founded

OR

First Reading: Sirach 35:12–17
God is impartial in justice and hears the powerless.

410	We give thee but thine own

Psalmody: Psalm 84:1–6*
Happy are the people whose strength is in you. (Ps. 84:4)

Alternate First Reading: Joel 2:23–32
The LORD promises to restore Israel

412	Sing to the Lord of harvest
507	How firm a foundation
563	For the fruit of all creation
684	Spirit, Spirit of gentleness
711	You satisfy the hungry heart
760	For the fruit of all creation

Alternate Psalmody: Psalm 65
Your paths overflow with plenty. (Ps. 65:12)

Second Reading: 2 Timothy 4:6–8, 16–18
The good fight of faith

340	Jesus Christ, my sure defense
461	Fight the good fight

Gospel: Luke 18:9–14
A Pharisee and tax collector pray together

91	Savior, when in dust to you
295	Out of the depths I cry to you
303	When in the hour of deepest need
310	To you, omniscient Lord of all
417	In a lowly manger born
438	Lord, teach us how to pray aright
790	Praise to you, O God of mercy

Additional hymns for the day/season

309	Lord Jesus, think on me
401	Before you, Lord, we bow
507	How firm a foundation

*Psalm 84:1–7 (NRSV)

Sunday between October 30 and November 5 inclusive

Proper 26

Prayer of the day

Stir up, O Lord, the wills of your faithful people to seek more eagerly the help you offer, that, at the last, they may enjoy the fruit of salvation; through our Lord Jesus Christ. (105)

Verse

Alleluia. Let the word of the Lord spread rapidly and be glorified everywhere, for the Lord is faithful and will strengthen you. Alleluia. (2 Thess. 3:1, 3)

Offertory

Hallelujah! For the Lord our God the Almighty reigns. Let us rejoice and exult and give him the glory, for the marriage of the Lamb has come, and his bride has made herself ready. Blessed are those who are invited to the marriage supper of the Lamb. (Rev. 19:6–7, 9)

Year A

Hymn of the day

428	O God of earth and altar
539	Praise the Almighty
750	Oh, praise the gracious power

309	Lord Jesus, think on me
508	Come down, O Love divine
718	Here in this place
790	Praise to you, O God of mercy

Hymns related to the readings

First Reading: Micah 3:5–12
Judgment upon corrupt rulers

427	O Jesus Christ, may grateful hymns be rising
428	O God of earth and altar

Psalmody: Psalm 43
Send out your light and truth that they may lead me. (Ps. 43:3)

Alternate First Reading: Joshua 3:7–17
Israel crosses the Jordan into the land of promise

343	Guide me ever, great Redeemer
501	He leadeth me; oh, blessed thought!

Alternate Psalmody: Psalm 107:1–7, 33–37
Give thanks to the LORD, all those whom the LORD has redeemed. (Ps. 107:1–2)

Second Reading: 1 Thessalonians 2:9–13
The apostle's teaching accepted as God's word

408	God, whose giving knows no ending

Gospel: Matthew 23:1–12
All who humble themselves will be exalted

122	Love consecrates the humblest act
308	God the Father, be our stay

Additional hymns for the day/season

423	Lord, whose love in humble service
538	Oh, praise the Lord, my soul!
730	My soul proclaims your greatness
782	All my hope on God is founded

YEAR B

Hymn of the day
315 Love divine, all loves excelling
502 Thee will I love, my strength
797 O God beyond all praising

Hymns related to the readings

First Reading: Deuteronomy 6:1–9
The blessing of keeping the words of God

480 Oh, that the Lord would guide my ways
486 Spirit of God, descend upon my heart
524 My God, how wonderful thou art

Psalmody: Psalm 119:1–8
Happy are they who seek the LORD with all their hearts. (Ps. 119:2)

Alternate First Reading: Ruth 1:1–18
Ruth's dedication to her mother-in-law

692 For all the faithful women
748 Bind us together

Alternate Psalmody: Psalm 146
The LORD lifts up those who are bowed down. (Ps. 146:7)

538 Oh, praise the Lord, my soul! (paraphrase)
539 Praise the Almighty (paraphrase)

Second Reading: Hebrews 9:11–14
Redeemed through the blood of Christ

202 Victim Divine, your grace we claim
302 Jesus, your blood and righteousness
707 This is my body

Gospel: Mark 12:28–34
Two great commandments: loving God and neighbor

270 God of our life, all-glorious Lord
325 Lord, thee I love with all my heart
336 Jesus, thy boundless love to me
441 Eternal Spirit of the living Christ
486 Spirit of God, descend upon my heart
494 Jesus calls us; o'er the tumult
502 Thee will I love, my strength
524 My God, how wonderful thou art
537 O Jesus, king most wonderful!
551 Joyful, joyful we adore thee
703 Draw us in the Spirit's tether
765 Jesu, Jesu, fill us with your love

Additional hymns for the day/season
126 Where charity and love prevail
317 To God the Holy Spirit let us pray

YEAR C

Hymn of the day
297 Salvation unto us has come
312 Once he came in blessing
793 Shout for joy loud and long

Hymns related to the readings

First Reading: Isaiah 1:10–18
Learn to do good, seek justice, and rescue the oppressed

305 I lay my sins on Jesus
739 In all our grief

Psalmody: Psalm 32:1–8*
All the faithful will make their prayers to you in time of trouble. (Ps. 32:7)

Alternate First Reading: Habakkuk 1:1–4; 2:1–4
The righteous live by their faith

7 Climb to the top of the highest mountain
322 The clouds of judgment gather
382 Awake, O Spirit of the watchmen
436 All who love and serve your city
443 Rise, my soul, to watch and pray

Alternate Psalmody: Psalm 119:137–144
Grant me understanding, that I may live. (Ps. 119:144)

Second Reading: 2 Thessalonians 1:1–4, 11–12
Faith and love amid persecution and adversity

507 How firm a foundation

Gospel: Luke 19:1–10
Zacchaeus climbs into a tree to see Jesus

291 Jesus sinners will receive
298 One there is, above all others
304 Today your mercy calls us
306 Chief of sinners though I be
499 Come, thou Fount of every blessing

Additional hymns for the day/season
203 Now we join in celebration
290 There's a wideness in God's mercy
327 Rock of Ages, cleft for me
406 Take my life, that I may be
460 I am trusting you, Lord Jesus
778 O Christ the same

*Psalm 32:1–7 (NRSV)

PROPER 27

Prayer of the day

Lord, when the day of wrath comes we have no hope except in your grace. Make us so to watch for the last days that the consummation of our hope may be the joy of the marriage feast of your Son, Jesus Christ our Lord. (104)

Verse

Alleluia. Keep awake therefore, for you do not know on what day your Lord is coming. Alleluia. (Matt. 24:42)

Offertory

Hallelujah! For the Lord our God the Almighty reigns. Let us rejoice and exult and give him the glory, for the marriage of the Lamb has come, and his bride has made herself ready. Blessed are those who are invited to the marriage supper of the Lamb. (Rev. 19:6–7, 9)

YEAR A

Hymn of the day

25	Rejoice, rejoice, believers
31	Wake, awake, for night is flying
799	When long before time

Hymns related to the readings

First Reading: Amos 5:18–24
Let justice roll down like waters

318	The Lord will come and not be slow
526	Immortal, invisible, God only wise
763	Let justice flow like streams

OR

First Reading: Wisdom of Solomon 6:12–16
Wisdom makes herself known

526	Immortal, invisible, God only wise

Psalmody: Psalm 70
You are my helper and my deliverer; O LORD, do not tarry. (Ps. 70:6)

OR

Psalmody: Wisdom of Solomon 6:17–20
The beginning of wisdom is the most sincere desire for instruction. (Wis. of Sol. 6:17)

Alternate First Reading: Joshua 24:1–3a, 14–25
Joshua calls Israel to serve the LORD

503	O Jesus, I have promised
512	Oh, blest the house
542	Sing praise to God, the highest good

Alternate Psalmody: Psalm 78:1–7
We will recount to generations to come the power of the LORD. (Ps. 78:4)

Second Reading: 1 Thessalonians 4:13–18
The promise of the resurrection

281	God, who made the earth and heaven
342	I know of a sleep in Jesus' name
346	When peace, like a river
351	Oh, happy day when we shall stand

Gospel: Matthew 25:1–13
The story of the wise and foolish bridesmaids

25	Rejoice, rejoice, believers
31	Wake, awake, for night is flying
224	Soul, adorn yourself with gladness

Additional hymns for the day/season

321	The day is surely drawing near
351	Oh, happy day when we shall stand
355	Through the night of doubt and sorrow
383	Rise up, O saints of God!
436	All who love and serve your city
524	Praise God. Praise him
556	Herald, sound the note of judgment
669	Come away to the skies
699	Blessed assurance

Hymn of the day
336   Jesus, thy boundless love to me
406   Take my life, that I may be
746   Day by day

Hymns related to the readings

First Reading: 1 Kings 17:8–16
God feeds Elijah and the widow at Zarephath

408   God, whose giving knows no ending

Psalmody: Psalm 146
*The LORD lifts up those who are bowed down.
(Ps. 146:7)*

538   Oh, praise the Lord, my soul! (paraphrase)
539   Praise the Almighty (paraphrase)

Alternate First Reading: Ruth 3:1–5; 4:13–17
Ruth wins the favor of Boaz

692   For all the faithful women

Alternate Psalmody: Psalm 127
Children are a heritage from the LORD. (Ps. 127:4)

Second Reading: Hebrews 9:24–28
The once for all sacrifice of Christ

172   Lord, enthroned in heavenly splendor
179   At the name of Jesus
202   Victim Divine, your grace we claim
244   Lord our God, with praise we come
312   Once he came in blessing
490   Let me be yours forever

Gospel: Mark 12:38–44
A widow's generosity reveals the hypocrisy of the scribes

406   Take my life, that I may be
408   God, whose giving knows no ending
563,760   For the fruit of all creation

Additional hymns for the day/season
249   God himself is present
404   As saints of old
409   Praise and thanksgiving
447   All depends on our possessing
758   Come to us, creative Spirit

Hymn of the day
340   Jesus Christ, my sure defense
352   I know that my Redeemer lives!
691   Sing with all the saints in glory

Hymns related to the readings

First Reading: Job 19:23–27a
I know that my Redeemer lives and I shall see God

340   Jesus Christ, my sure defense
352   I know that my Redeemer lives!

Psalmody: Psalm 17:1–9
Keep me as the apple of your eye; hide me under the shadow of your wings. (Ps. 17:8)

Alternate First Reading: Haggai 1:15b—2:9
The LORD promises to restore Judah to prosperity

321   The day is surely drawing near
457, 458   Jesus, priceless treasure

Alternate Psalmody: Psalm 145:1–5, 17–21
Great is the LORD and greatly to be praised. (Ps. 145:3)

OR

Alternate Psalmody: Psalm 98
In righteousness shall the LORD judge the world. (Ps. 98:10)

Second Reading: 2 Thessalonians 2:1–5, 13–17
The coming of the Lord Jesus

230   Lord, keep us steadfast in your Word

Gospel: Luke 20:27–38
Jesus speaks of the resurrection; the God of the living

340   Jesus Christ, my sure defense
352   I know that my Redeemer lives!

Additional hymns for the day/season
200   For the bread which you have broken
325   Lord, thee I love with all my heart
330   In heaven above
331   Jerusalem, my happy home
337   Oh, what their joy
347   Jerusalem the golden
742   Come, we that love the Lord
801   Thine the amen, thine the praise

PROPER 28

Prayer of the day

Lord God, so rule and govern our hearts and minds by your Holy Spirit that, always keeping in mind the end of all things and the day of judgment, we may be stirred up to holiness of life here and may live with you forever in the world to come, through your Son, Jesus Christ our Lord. (106)

OR

Almighty and ever-living God, before the earth was formed and even after it ceases to be, you are God. Break into our short span of life and let us see the signs of your final will and purpose, through your Son, Jesus Christ our Lord. (107)

Verse

Alleluia. The Lord says, "Surely I am coming soon." Amen. Come, Lord Jesus! Alleluia. (Rev. 22:20)

Offertory

We give you thanks, Lord God Almighty, who are and who were, for you have taken your great power and begun to reign. Fear God and give him glory, for the hour of his judgment has come; and worship him who made heaven and earth, the sea and the springs of water. (Rev. 11:17; 14:7)

YEAR A

Hymn of the day

408   God, whose giving knows no ending
405   Lord of light
778   O Christ the same

Hymns related to the readings

First Reading: Zephaniah 1:7, 12–18
The day of the LORD

321   The day is surely drawing near

Psalmody: Psalm 90:1–8 [9–11] 12
So teach us to number our days that we may apply our hearts to wisdom. (Ps. 90:12)

320   O God, our help in ages past (paraphrase)

Alternate First Reading: Judges 4:1–7
The judgeship of Deborah

418   Judge eternal, throned in splendor
692   For all the faithful women

Alternate Psalmody: Psalm 123
Our eyes look to you, O God, until you show us your mercy. (Ps. 123:3)

Second Reading: 1 Thessalonians 5:1–11
Be alert for the day of the Lord

399   We are the Lord's
389   Stand up, stand up for Jesus
443   Rise, my soul, to watch and pray

Gospel: Matthew 25:14–30
The story of the slaves entrusted with talents

405   Lord of light
408   God, whose giving knows no ending
505   Forth in thy name, O Lord, I go

Additional hymns for the day/season

31   Wake, awake, for night is flying
312   Once he came in blessing
322   The clouds of judgment gather
332   Battle Hymn of the Republic
382   Awake, O Spirit of the watchmen
498   All who would valiant be
754   Let us talents and tongues employ

YEAR B

Hymn of the day
355 Through the night of doubt and sorrow
323 O Lord of light, who made the stars
691 Sing with all the saints in glory

Hymns related to the readings

First Reading: Daniel 12:1–3
The deliverance of God's people at the end

415 God of grace and God of glory
779 You who dwell in the shelter of the Lord

Psalmody: Psalm 16
My heart is glad and my spirit rejoices; my body shall rest in hope. (Ps. 16:9)

Alternate First Reading: 1 Samuel 1:4–20
Hannah's prayers for a child answered

6   My soul proclaims the greatness of the Lord
180 My soul now magnifies the Lord (paraphrase)
730 My soul proclaims your greatness (paraphrase)
692 For all the faithful women

Alternate Psalmody: 1 Samuel 2:1–10
My heart exults in the LORD; my strength is exalted in my God. (1 Sam. 2:2)

Second Reading: Hebrews 10:11–14 [15–18] 19–25
The way to God opened through Christ's death

27   Lo! He comes with clouds descending
300 O Christ, our hope
302 Jesus, your blood and righteousness
436 All who love and serve your city
495 Lead on, O King eternal

Gospel: Mark 13:1–8
The end and the coming of the Son

230 Lord, keep us steadfast in your Word
418 Judge eternal, throned in splendor
421 Lord Christ, when first you came to earth

Additional hymns for the day/season
312 Once he came in blessing
318 The Lord will come and not be slow
322 The clouds of judgment gather
354 Eternal God, before your throne
371 With God as our friend
443 Rise, my soul, to watch and pray
483 God moves in a mysterious way

YEAR C

Hymn of the day
418 Judge eternal, throned in splendor
321 The day is surely drawing near
736 By gracious powers

Hymns related to the readings

First Reading: Malachi 4:1–2a
A day of blistering heat for the arrogant; a day of healing sun for the righteous

265 Christ, whose glory fills the skies
418 Judge eternal, throned in splendor
762 O day of peace

Psalmody: Psalm 98
In righteousness shall the LORD judge the world. (Ps. 98:10)

Alternate First Reading: Isaiah 65:17–25
God promises a new heaven and a new earth

254 Come, let us join our cheerful songs
742 Come, we that love the Lord
762 O day of peace

Alternate Psalmody: Isaiah 12
In your midst is the Holy One of Israel. (Is. 12:6)

635 Surely it is God who saves me (paraphrase)

Second Reading: 2 Thessalonians 3:6–13
Do not be idle, but do what is right for the sake of Christ

436 All who love and serve your city
505 Forth in thy name, O Lord, I go

Gospel: Luke 21:5–19
Jesus speaks of wars, endurance, betrayal, and suffering for his sake

230 Lord, keep us steadfast in your Word
312 Once he came in blessing
355 Through the night of dark and sorrow
421 Lord Christ, when first you came to earth
460 I am trusting you, Lord Jesus
478 Come, oh, come, O quickening Spirit
507 How firm a foundation

Additional hymns for the day/season
453 If you but trust in God to guide you
785 Weary of all trumpeting

CHRIST THE KING

LAST SUNDAY AFTER PENTECOST
PROPER 29

Prayer of the day

Almighty and everlasting God, whose will it is to restore all things to your beloved Son, whom you anointed priest forever and king of all creation: Grant that all the people of the earth, now divided by the power of sin, may be united under the glorious and gentle rule of your Son, our Lord Jesus Christ, who lives and reigns with you and the Holy Spirit, one God, now and forever. (108)

Verse

Alleluia. I am the Alpha and the Omega, the first and the last, the beginning and the end. Alleluia. (Rev. 22:13)

Offertory

Beloved, we are God's children now; what we will be has not yet been revealed. What we do know is this: when he is revealed we will be like him, for we will see him as he is. And all who have this hope in him purify themselves, just as he is pure. (1 John 3:2–3)

YEAR A

Hymn of the day

363 Christ is alive! Let Christians sing
173 The head that once was crowned
801 Thine the amen, thine the praise

Hymns related to the readings

First Reading: Ezekiel 34:11–16, 20–24
God will shepherd Israel

196 Praise the Lord, rise up rejoicing
456 The King of love my shepherd is

Psalmody: Psalm 95:1–7a
We are the people of God's pasture and the sheep of God's hand. (Ps. 95:7)

Alternate First Reading: Ezekiel 34:11–16, 20–24
God will shepherd Israel

196 Praise the Lord, rise up rejoicing
456 The King of love my shepherd is

Alternate Psalmody: Psalm 100
We are God's people and the sheep of God's pasture. (Ps. 100:2)

245 All people that on earth do dwell (paraphrase)
256 Oh, sing jubilee to the Lord (paraphrase)
531 Before Jehovah's awesome throne (paraphrase)

Second Reading: Ephesians 1:15–23
The reign of Christ

254 Come, let us join our cheerful songs
525 Blessing and honor
669 Come away to the skies

Gospel: Matthew 25:31–46
The coming of the Son of Man; the separation of sheep and goats

316 Jesus, the very thought of you
363 Christ is alive! Let Christians sing
409 Praise and thanksgiving
423 Lord, whose love in humble service
424 Lord of glory, you have bought us
425 O God of mercy, God of light
433 The Church of Christ, in every age
563, 760 For the fruit of all creation

Additional hymns for the day/season

76   O Morning Star, how fair and bright!
119 Nature with open volume stands
170 Crown him with many crowns
171 Rejoice, the Lord is king!
172 Lord, enthroned in heavenly splendor
173 The head that once was crowned
179 At the name of Jesus
214 Come, let us eat
321 The day is surely drawing near
323 O Lord of light, who made the stars
328, 329 All hail the power of Jesus' name!
377 Lift high the cross
386 Christ is the king!
495 Lead on, O King eternal
514 O Savior, precious Savior
516 Arise, my soul, arise!
518 Beautiful Savior
520 Give to our God immortal praise!
525 Blessing and honor

530	Jesus shall reign		669	Come away to the skies
536	O God of God, O Light of light		740	Jesus, remember me
553	Rejoice, O pilgrim throng!		744	Soon and very soon
556	Herald, sound the note of judgment		787	Glory to God, we give you thanks
631	Lift up your heads, O gates		796	My Lord of light

YEAR B

Hymn of the day
179 At the name of Jesus
27 Lo! He comes with clouds descending
744 Soon and very soon

Hymns related to the readings

First Reading: Daniel 7:9–10, 13–14
The one coming with the clouds rules over all

198 Let all mortal flesh keep silence
432 We worship you, O God of might
518 Beautiful Savior
522 Come, thou almighty King

Psalmody: Psalm 93
Ever since the world began, your throne has been established. (Ps. 93:3)

Alternate First Reading: 2 Samuel 23:1–7
The just ruler is like the light of morning

518 Beautiful Savior
526 Immortal, invisible, God only wise

Alternate Psalmody: Psalm 132:1–12 [13–18]
Let your faithful people sing with joy. (Ps. 132:9)

Second Reading: Revelation 1:4b–8
Glory to the one who made us a kingdom

27 Lo! He comes with clouds descending
167 Glory be to God the Father
172 Lord, enthroned in heavenly splendor
530 Jesus shall reign

Gospel: John 18:33–37
The kingdom of Christ

101 O Christ, our king, creator, Lord
118 Sing, my tongue
173 The head that once was crowned
377 Lift high the cross

Additional hymns for the day/season
See Year A

YEAR C

Hymn of the day
328, 329 All hail the power of Jesus' name!
172 Lord, enthroned in heavenly splendor
778 O Christ the same

Hymns related to the readings

First Reading: Jeremiah 23:1–6
Coming of the shepherd and righteous Branch who will execute justice

172 Lord, enthroned in heavenly splendor
456 The King of love my shepherd is

Psalmody: Psalm 46
I will be exalted among the nations. (Ps. 46:11)

228, 229 A mighty fortress is our God (paraphrase)

Alternate First Reading: Jeremiah 23:1–6
Coming of the shepherd and righteous Branch who will execute justice

172 Lord, enthroned in heavenly splendor
456 The King of love my shepherd is

Alternate Psalmody: Luke 1:68–79
God has raised up for us a mighty savior. (Luke 1:69)

725 Blessed be the God of Israel (paraphrase)

Second Reading: Colossians 1:11–20
Hymn to Christ, firstborn of all creation; peace through his blood

179 At the name of Jesus
252 You servants of God
254 Come, let us join our cheerful songs
526 Immortal, invisible, God only wise

Gospel: Luke 23:33–43
Jesus is crucified between two thieves: you will be with me in Paradise

94, 661 My song is love unknown
101 O Christ, our king, creator, Lord
173 The head that once was crowned
377 Lift high the cross
421 Lord Christ, when first you came to earth
740 Jesus, remember me

Additional hymns for the day/season
See Year A

LESSER FESTIVALS AND OCCASIONS

ST. ANDREW, APOSTLE

NOVEMBER 30

Prayer of the day

Almighty God, as the apostle Andrew readily obeyed the call of Christ and followed him without delay, grant that we, called by your holy Word, may in glad obedience offer ourselves to your service; through your Son, Jesus Christ our Lord, who lives and reigns with you and the Holy Spirit, one God, now and forever. (109)

Verse

Alleluia. You will be my witnesses in Jerusalem, in all Judea and Samaria, and to the ends of the earth. Alleluia. (Acts 1:8)

Offertory

Sing to the LORD and bless his name; proclaim the good news of his salvation from day to day. Declare his glory among the nations and his wonders among all peoples. For great is the LORD and greatly to be praised. Oh, the majesty and magnificence of his presence! Oh, the power and the splendor of his sanctuary! (Ps. 96:2–4, 6)

YEARS A, B, C

Hymn of the day

494   Jesus calls us; o'er the tumult
177   By all your saints in warfare (stanza 5)

Hymns related to the readings

First Reading: Ezekiel 3:16–21
A sentinel for the house of Israel

31   Wake, awake, for night is flying
322   The clouds of judgment gather
382   Awake, O Spirit of the watchmen
556   Herald, sound the note of judgment

Psalmody: Psalm 19:1–6
Their sound has gone out into all lands. (Ps. 19:4)

Second Reading: Romans 10:10–18
Faith comes from what is heard through the word of Christ

379   Spread, oh, spread, almighty Word
396   O God, O Lord of heaven and earth
397   O Zion, haste

Gospel: John 1:35–42
Jesus calls Andrew

177   By all your saints in warfare (stanza 5)
494   Jesus calls us; o'er the tumult
506   Dear Lord and Father of mankind

Additional hymns for the day/season

174   For all the saints
175   Ye watchers and ye holy ones
176   For all your saints, O Lord
182   Rise, O children of salvation
183   The Son of God goes forth to war
200   For the bread which you have broken
337   Oh, what their joy
434   The Son of God, our Christ
535   Holy God, we praise your name
689   Rejoice in God's saints
690   Shall we gather at the river
691   Sing with all the saints in glory
706   Eat this bread, drink this cup

St. Thomas, Apostle

December 21

Prayer of the day
Almighty and ever-living God, you have given great and precious promises to those who believe. Grant us that perfect faith which overcomes all doubts; through your Son, Jesus Christ our Lord, who lives and reigns with you and the Holy Spirit, one God, now and forever. (110)

Verse
Alleluia. You will be my witnesses in Jerusalem, in all Judea and Samaria, and to the ends of the earth. Alleluia. (Acts 1:8)

Offertory
Sing to the LORD and bless his name; proclaim the good news of his salvation from day to day. Declare his glory among the nations and his wonders among all peoples. For great is the LORD and greatly to be praised. Oh, the majesty and magnificence of his presence! Oh, the power and the splendor of his sanctuary! (Ps. 96:2–4, 6)

Years A, B, C

Hymn of the day
675 We walk by faith and not by sight
177 By all your saints in warfare (stanza 6)

Hymns related to the readings

First Reading: Judges 6:36–40
God affirms Gideon's calling

87 Hail to the Lord's anointed

Psalmody: Psalm 136:1–4, 23–26
God's mercy endures forever. (Ps. 136:1b)

520 Give to our God immortal praise (paraphrase)
521 Let us with a gladsome mind (paraphrase)

Second Reading: Ephesians 4:11–16
The body of Christ has various gifts

206 Lord, who the night you were betrayed
209 Come, risen Lord
523 Holy Spirit, ever dwelling
703 Draw us in the Spirit's tether

Gospel: John 14:1–7
Jesus is the way, and the truth, and the life

177 By all your saints in warfare (stanza 6)
464 You are the way
475 Come, gracious Spirit, heavenly dove
513 Come, my way, my truth, my life
768 He comes to us as one unknown

Additional hymns for the day/season
25 Rejoice, rejoice, believers
26 Prepare the royal highway
63 From shepherding of stars
628 Each winter as the year grows older
641 Peace came to earth
See St. Andrew

St. Stephen, Deacon and Martyr

December 26

Prayer of the day

Grant us grace, O Lord, that like Stephen we may learn to love even our enemies and seek forgiveness for those who desire our hurt; through your Son, Jesus Christ our Lord, who lives and reigns with you and the Holy Spirit, one God, now and forever. (111)

Verse

Alleluia. Blessed are those who are persecuted for righteousness' sake, for theirs is the kingdom of heaven. Alleluia. (Matt. 5:10)

Offertory

I put my trust in the LORD. I will rejoice and be glad because of your mercy. Make your face to shine upon your servant, and in your lovingkindness save me. You hide in the covert of your presence those who trust in you; you keep them in your shelter from the strife of tongues. (Ps. 31:6–7, 16, 20)

Years A, B, C

Hymn of the day

54   It came upon the midnight clear
177   By all your saints in warfare (stanza 7)

Hymns related to the readings

First Reading: 2 Chronicles 24:17–22
Zechariah is stoned to death

Psalmody: Psalm 17:1–9, 16*
I call upon you, O God, for you will answer me.
(Ps. 17:6)

Second Reading: Acts 6:8—7:2a, 51–60
Stephen is stoned to death

55   Good Christian friends, rejoice
177   By all your saints in warfare (stanza 7)
183   The Son of God goes forth to war

Gospel: Matthew 23:34–39
Jesus laments that Jerusalem kills her prophets

663   When twilight comes

Additional hymns for the day/season

40   What child is this
73   All hail to you, O blessed morn!
74   A stable lamp is lighted
See St. Andrew

*Psalm 17:1–9, 15 (NRSV)

St. John, Apostle and Evangelist

Prayer of the day

Merciful Lord, let the brightness of your light shine on your Church, so that all of us, instructed by the teachings of John, your apostle and evangelist, may walk in the light of your truth and attain eternal life; through your Son, Jesus Christ our Lord, who lives and reigns with you and the Holy Spirit, one God, now and forever. (112)

Verse

Alleluia. For the message about the cross is the power of God to us who are being saved. Alleluia. (1 Cor. 1:18)

Offertory

The gifts Christ gave were that some would be apostles, some prophets, some evangelists, some pastors and teachers, to equip the saints for the work of ministry, for building up the body of Christ, until all of us come to the unity of the faith and of the knowledge of the Son of God. (Eph. 4:11–13)

Years A, B, C

Hymn of the day

48	All praise to you, eternal Lord
177	By all your saints in warfare (stanza 8)

Hymns related to the readings

First Reading: Genesis 1:1–5, 26–31
Humankind is created by God

233	Thy strong Word
400	God, whose almighty word
540	Praise the Lord! O heavens
799	When long before time

Psalmody: Psalm 116:10–17*
Precious in your sight, O LORD, is the death of your servants. (Ps. 116:13)

Second Reading: 1 John 1:1—2:2
The word of life is Jesus

649	I want to walk as a child of the light
793	Shout for joy loud and long

Gospel: John 21:20–25
The beloved disciple will remain with Jesus

177	By all your saints in warfare (stanza 8)
449	They cast their nets
470	Praise and thanks and adoration

Additional hymns for the day/season

42	Of the Father's love begotten
45	Oh, come, all ye faithful
57	Let our gladness have no end

See St. Andrew

*Psalm 116:12–19 (NRSV)

THE HOLY INNOCENTS, MARTYRS

DECEMBER 28

Prayer of the day
We remember today, O God, the slaughter of the holy innocents of Bethlehem by order of King Herod. Receive, we pray, into the arms of your mercy all innocent victims, and by your great might frustrate the designs of evil tyrants and establish your rule of justice, love, and peace; through Jesus Christ our Lord, who lives and reigns with you and the Holy Spirit, one God, now and forever. (113)

Verse
Alleluia. Blessed are those who are persecuted for righteousness' sake, for theirs is the kingdom of heaven. Alleluia. (Matt. 5:10)

Offertory
I put my trust in the LORD. I will rejoice and be glad because of your mercy. Make your face to shine upon your servant, and in your lovingkindness save me. You hide in the covert of your presence those who trust in you; you keep them in your shelter from the strife of tongues. (Ps. 31:6–7, 16, 20)

YEARS A, B, C

Hymn of the day
74   A stable lamp is lighted
177   By all your saints in warfare (stanza 9)

Hymns related to the readings

First Reading: Jeremiah 31:15–17
Rachel weeps for her children

474   Children of the heavenly Father

Psalmody: Psalm 124
We have escaped like a bird from the snare of the fowler. (Ps. 124:7)

Second Reading: 1 Peter 4:12–19
Continue to do good while suffering

58   Lo, how a rose is growing
320   O God, our help in ages past

Gospel: Matthew 2:13–18
Herod kills the innocent children in Bethlehem

85   When Christ's appearing was made known
177   By all your saints in warfare (stanza 9)
639   Oh, sleep now, holy baby

Additional hymns for the day/season
40   What child is this
48   All praise to you, eternal Lord
52   Your little ones, dear Lord
53   Cold December flies away
54   It came upon the midnight clear
61   The hills are bare at Bethlehem
63   From shepherding of stars
72   'Twas in the moon of wintertime
642   I wonder as I wander
643   Once in royal David's city
779   You who dwell in the shelter of the Lord

THE NAME OF JESUS

Prayer of the day

Eternal Father, you gave your Son the name of Jesus to be a sign of our salvation. Plant in every heart the love of the Savior of the world, Jesus Christ our Lord, who lives and reigns with you and the Holy Spirit, one God, now and forever. (114)

Verse

Alleluia. At the name of Jesus every knee should bend, in heaven and on earth and under the earth. Alleluia. (Phil. 2:10)

Offertory

Offer to God a sacrifice of thanksgiving, and make good your vows to the Most High. Whoever offers me the sacrifice of thanksgiving honors me; but to those who keep in my way will I show the salvation of God. (Ps. 50:14, 23)

YEARS A, B, C

Hymn of the day

181   Greet now the swiftly changing year
328, 329   All hail the power of Jesus' name!

Hymns related to the readings

First Reading: Numbers 6:22–27
The Aaronic blessing

256   Oh, sing jubilee to the Lord
259   Lord, dismiss us with your blessing
440   Christians, while on earth abiding
721   Go, my children, with my blessing

Psalmody: Psalm 8
How exalted is your name in all the world. (Ps. 8:1)

Second Reading: Galatians 4:4–7
We are no longer slaves, but children

48   All praise to you, eternal Lord
357   Our Father, by whose name

OR

Second Reading: Philippians 2:5–11
God takes on human form

47   Let all together praise our God
179   At the name of Jesus
328, 329   All hail the power of Jesus' name!
643   Once in royal David's city

Gospel: Luke 2:15–21
The child is circumcised and named Jesus

181   Greet now the swiftly changing year
316   Jesus, the very thought of you

Additional hymns for the day/season

51   From heaven above
345   How sweet the name of Jesus sounds
514   O Savior, precious Savior
552   In thee is gladness
559   Oh, for a thousand tongues to sing

THE CONFESSION OF ST. PETER

Prayer of the day

Almighty God, you inspired Simon Peter to confess Jesus as the Messiah and Son of the living God. Keep your Church firm on the rock of this faith, that in unity and peace it may proclaim one truth and follow one Lord, your Son, our Savior Jesus Christ, who lives and reigns with you and the Holy Spirit, one God, now and forever. (115)

Verse

Alleluia. You will be my witnesses in Jerusalem, in all Judea and Samaria, and to the ends of the earth. Alleluia. (Acts 1:8)

Offertory

Sing to the LORD and bless his name; proclaim the good news of his salvation from day to day. Declare his glory among the nations and his wonders among all peoples. For great is the LORD and greatly to be praised. Oh, the majesty and magnificence of his presence! Oh, the power and the splendor of his sanctuary! (Ps. 96:2–4, 6)3

YEARS A, B, C

Hymn of the day

367, 747 Christ is made the sure foundation
177   By all your saints in warfare (stanza 10)

Hymns related to the readings

First Reading: Acts 4:8–13
Salvation is in no one other than Jesus

179   At the name of Jesus
367   Christ is made the sure foundation
446   Whatever God ordains is right
747   Christ is made the sure foundation

Psalmody: Psalm 18:1–7, 17–20*
My God, my rock, you are worthy of praise. (Ps. 18:2)

Second Reading: 1 Corinthians 10:1–5
The ancestors drank from the spiritual rock of Christ

358   Glories of your name are spoken

Gospel: Matthew 16:13–19
Peter confesses: You are the Messiah

177   By all your saints in warfare (stanza 10)
449   They cast their nets
365   Built on a rock

Additional hymns for the day/season

237   O God of light
See Proper 16A; St. Andrew

*Psalm 18:1–6, 16–19 (NRSV)

THE CONVERSION OF ST. PAUL

Prayer of the day
Lord God, through the preaching of your apostle Paul, you established one Church from among the nations. As we celebrate his conversion, we pray that we may follow his example and be witnesses to the truth in your Son, Jesus Christ our Lord, who lives and reigns with you and the Holy Spirit, one God, now and forever. (116)

Verse
Alleluia. This Jesus God raised up, and of that all of us are witnesses. Alleluia. (Acts 2:32)

Offertory
Sing to the LORD and bless his name; proclaim the good news of his salvation from day to day. Declare his glory among the nations and his wonders among all peoples. For great is the LORD and greatly to be praised. Oh, the majesty and magnificence of his presence! Oh, the power and the splendor of his sanctuary! (Ps. 96:2–4, 6)

YEARS A, B, C

Hymn of the day
388   O Spirit of the living God
177   By all your saints in warfare (stanza 11)

Hymns related to the readings

First Reading: Acts 9:1–22
Saul is converted to Christ

177   By all your saints in warfare (stanza 11)

Psalmody: Psalm 67
Let all the peoples praise you, O God. (Ps. 67:3)

335   May God bestow on us his grace (paraphrase)

Second Reading: Galatians 1:11–24
Paul received the gospel from a revelation of Christ

793   Shout for joy loud and long

Gospel: Luke 21:10–19
The end times will require endurance

230   Lord, keep us steadfast in your Word
361   Do not despair, O little flock

Additional hymns for the day/season
237   O God of light
See St. Andrew

THE PRESENTATION OF OUR LORD

Prayer of the day

Blessed are you, O Lord our God, for you have sent us your salvation. Inspire us by your Holy Spirit to see with our own eyes him who is the glory of Israel and the light for all nations, your Son, Jesus Christ our Lord. (117)

Verse

Alleluia. My eyes have seen your salvation. Alleluia. (Luke 2:30)

Offertory

Offer to God a sacrifice of thanksgiving, and make good your vows to the Most High. Whoever offers me the sacrifice of thanksgiving honors me; but to those who keep in my way will I show the salvation of God. (Ps. 50:14, 23)

YEARS A, B, C

Hymn of the day

184   In his temple now behold him
339   O Lord, now let your servant

Hymns related to the readings

First Reading: Malachi 3:1–4
My messenger is a refiner and purifier

318   The Lord will come and not be slow

Psalmody: Psalm 84
How dear to me is your dwelling, O LORD. (Ps. 84:1)

OR

Psalmody: Psalm 24:7–10
Lift up your heads, O gates, and the King of glory shall come in. (Ps. 24:7)

631   Lift up your heads, O gates (paraphrase)

Second Reading: Hebrews 2:14–18
Jesus shares human flesh and sufferings

88   Oh, love, how deep

Gospel: Luke 2:22–40
The child is brought to the temple

184   In his temple now behold him
259   Lord, dismiss us with your blessing
339   O Lord, now let your servant
349   I leave, as you have promised, Lord
357   Our Father, by whose name
417   In a lowly manger born
634   Sing of Mary, pure and lowly

Additional hymns for the day/season

40   What child is this
42   Of the Father's love begotten
561   For the beauty of the earth
649   I want to walk as a child of the light
See 1 Christmas B

St. Matthias, Apostle

Prayer of the day

Almighty God, you chose your faithful servant Matthias to be numbered among the Twelve. Grant that your Church, being delivered from false apostles, may always be taught and guided by faithful and true pastors; through your Son, Jesus Christ our Lord, who lives and reigns with you and the Holy Spirit, one God, now and forever. (118)

Verse

Alleluia. Whoever serves me, the Father will honor. Alleluia. (John 12:26)

Offertory

LORD, you guide me along right pathways for your name's sake. You spread a table before me in the presence of those who trouble me; you have anointed my head with oil, and my cup is running over. Surely your goodness and mercy shall follow me all the days of my life, and I will dwell in the house of the LORD forever. (Ps. 23:3–6)

Years A, B, C

Hymn of the day

283   O God, send heralds
177   By all your saints in warfare (stanza 12)

Hymns related to the readings

First Reading: Isaiah 66:1–2
Heaven is the throne and earth is the footstool of God

Psalmody: Psalm 56
I am bound by the vow I made to you, O God. (Ps. 56:11)
228, 229   A mighty fortress is our God (paraphrase)

Second Reading: Acts 1:15–26
The apostles cast lots for Matthias
177   By all your saints in warfare (stanza 12)
475   Come, gracious Spirit, heavenly dove

Gospel: Luke 6:12–16
Jesus calls the twelve disciples
283   O God, send heralds

Additional hymns for the day/season

See St. Andrew

MARCH 25

Prayer of the day

Pour your grace into our hearts, O Lord, that we, who have known the incarnation of your Son, Jesus Christ, announced by an angel, may by his cross and Passion be brought to the glory of his resurrection; who lives and reigns with you and the Holy Spirit, one God, now and forever. (119)

Verse

Alleluia. Greetings, O favored one! The Lord is with you. The Holy Spirit will come upon you. Alleluia. (Luke 1:28, 35)

OR

Alleluia. From this day all generations will call me blessed: the Almighty has done great things for me, and holy is his name. Alleluia. (Luke 1:48–49)

Offertory

Who is like the LORD our God, who sits enthroned on high, but stoops to behold the heavens and the earth? He takes up the weak out of the dust, and lifts up the poor from the ashes. He sets them with the princes, with the princes of his people. (Ps. 113:5–8)

YEARS A, B, C

Hymn of the day

632   The angel Gabriel from heaven came
28   Savior of the nations, come

Hymns related to the readings

First Reading: Isaiah 7:10–14
A young woman will bear a son

641   Peace came to earth

Psalmody: Psalm 45
I will make your name to be remembered from one generation to another. (Ps. 45:18)

OR

Psalmody: Psalm 40:5–11*
I love to do your will, O my God. (Ps. 40:9)

Second Reading: Hebrews 10:4–10
The offering of Jesus' body sanctifies us

490   Let me be yours forever

Gospel: Luke 1:26–38
The angel greets Mary

6   My soul proclaims the greatness of the Lord
42   Of the Father's love begotten
64   From east to west
180   My soul now magnifies the Lord
632   The angel Gabriel from heaven came
635   Surely it is God who saves me
730   My soul proclaims your greatness

Additional hymns for the day/season

94   My song is love unknown
105   A lamb goes uncomplaining forth
224   Soul, adorn yourself with gladness
661   My song is love unknown
See 4 Advent A, B, C

*Psalm 40:5–10 (NRSV)

St. Mark, Evangelist

Prayer of the day

Almighty God, you have enriched your Church with Mark's proclamation of the Gospel. Give us grace to believe firmly in the good news of salvation and to walk daily in accord with it; through your Son, Jesus Christ our Lord, who lives and reigns with you and the Holy Spirit, one God, now and forever. (120)

Verse

Alleluia. This Jesus God raised up, and of that all of us are witnesses. Alleluia. (Acts 2:32)

Offertory

Sing to the LORD and bless his name; proclaim the good news of his salvation from day to day. Declare his glory among the nations and his wonders among all peoples. For great is the LORD and greatly to be praised. Oh, the majesty and magnificence of his presence! Oh, the power and the splendor of his sanctuary! (Ps. 96:2–4, 6)

YEARS A, B, C

Hymn of the day

237   O God of light
178   By all your saints in warfare (stanza 13)

Hymns related to the readings

First Reading: Isaiah 52:7–10
The messenger announces peace, good news, and salvation

382   Awake, O Spirit of the watchmen
396   O God, O Lord of heaven and earth
397   O Zion, haste

Psalmody: Psalm 57
I will confess you among the peoples, O LORD. (Ps. 57:9)

Second Reading: 2 Timothy 4:6–11, 18
The good fight of faith

340   Jesus Christ, my sure defense
461   Fight the good fight
495   Lead on, O King eternal!

Gospel: Mark 1:1–15
The beginning of the gospel of Jesus Christ

188   I bind unto myself today

Additional hymns for the day/season

140   With high delight let us unite
144   Good Christian friends, rejoice and sing!
671   Alleluia, alleluia, give thanks
See St. Andrew

ST. PHILIP AND ST. JAMES, APOSTLES

MAY 1

Prayer of the day

Almighty God, to know you is to have eternal life. Grant us to know your Son as the way, the truth, and the life; and guide our footsteps along the way of Jesus Christ our Lord, who lives and reigns with you and the Holy Spirit, one God, now and forever. (121)

Verse

Alleluia. You will be my witnesses in Jerusalem, in all Judea and Samaria, and to the ends of the earth. Alleluia. (Acts 1:8)

Offertory

Sing to the LORD and bless his name; proclaim the good news of his salvation from day to day. Declare his glory among the nations and his wonders among all peoples. For great is the LORD and greatly to be praised. Oh, the majesty and magnificence of his presence! Oh, the power and the splendor of his sanctuary! (Ps. 96:2–4, 6)

YEARS A, B, C

Hymn of the day

464   You are the way
178   By all your saints in warfare (stanza 14)

Hymns related to the readings

First Reading: Isaiah 30:18–21
The LORD will show mercy and justice

403   Lord, speak to us, that we may speak
492   O Master, let me walk with you

Psalmody: Psalm 44:1–3, 20–26
Save us for the sake of your steadfast love. (Ps. 44:26)

Second Reading: 2 Corinthians 4:1–6
Proclaim Jesus Christ as Lord

317   To God the Holy Spirit let us pray
380   O Christ, our light, O Radiance true
400   God, whose almighty word
402   Look from your sphere of endless day
478   Come, oh, come, O quickening Spirit
523   Holy Spirit, ever dwelling

Gospel: John 14:8–14
Jesus and the Father are one

178   By all your saints in warfare (stanza 14)
464   You are the way
514   O Savior, precious Savior

Additional hymns for the day/season

132   Come, you faithful, raise the strain
154   That Easter day with joy was bright
671   Alleluia, alleluia, give thanks
See St. Andrew

MAY 31

Prayer of the day

Almighty God, in choosing the virgin Mary to be the mother of your Son, you made known your gracious regard for the poor and the lowly and the despised. Grant us grace to receive your Word in humility, and so to be made one with your Son, Jesus Christ our Lord, who lives and reigns with you and the Holy Spirit, one God, now and forever. (122)

Verse

Alleluia. My eyes have seen your salvation. Alleluia. (Luke 2:30)

Offertory

Offer to God a sacrifice of thanksgiving, and make good your vows to the Most High. Whoever offers me the sacrifice of thanksgiving honors me; but to those who keep in my way will I show the salvation of God. (Ps. 50:14, 23)

YEARS A, B, C

Hymn of the day

386 Christ is the king!
730 My soul proclaims your greatness

Hymns related to the readings

First Reading: 1 Samuel 2:1–10
Hannah prays and exults in the LORD

6 My soul proclaims the greatness of the Lord
180 My soul now magnifies the Lord (paraphrase)
730 My soul proclaims your greatness (paraphrase)

Psalmody: Psalm 113
Let the name of the LORD be blessed from this time forth forevermore. (Ps. 113:2)

Second Reading: Romans 12:9–16b
Rejoice with those who rejoice, weep with those who weep

508 Come down, O Love divine

Gospel: Luke 1:39–57
Mary greets Elizabeth and exults in the Lord

6 My soul proclaims the greatness of the Lord (paraphrase)
64 From east to west
180 My soul now magnifies the Lord (paraphrase)
632 The angel Gabriel from heaven came
635 Surely it is God who saves me
730 My soul proclaims your greatness (paraphrase)

Additional hymns for the day/season

86 The only Son from heaven
175 Ye watchers and ye holy ones
386 Christ is the king!
692 For all the faithful women
See 4 Advent A, B, C; Annunciation

St. Barnabas, Apostle

June 11

Prayer of the day

Grant, almighty God, that we may follow the example of your faithful servant Barnabas, who, seeking not his own renown but the well-being of your Church, gave generously of his life and substance for the relief of the poor and the spread of the Gospel; through Jesus Christ our Lord, who lives and reigns with you and the Holy Spirit, one God, now and forever. (123)

Verse

Alleluia. This Jesus God raised up, and of that all of us are witnesses. Alleluia. (Acts 2:32)

Offertory

Sing to the LORD and bless his name; proclaim the good news of his salvation from day to day. Declare his glory among the nations and his wonders among all peoples. For great is the LORD and greatly to be praised. Oh, the majesty and magnificence of his presence! Oh, the power and the splendor of his sanctuary! (Ps. 96:2–4, 6)

Years A, B, C

Hymn of the day

397　O Zion, haste
381　Hark, the voice of Jesus calling

Hymns related to the readings

First Reading: Isaiah 42:5–12
The LORD calls us in righteousness

237　O God of light
400　God, whose almighty word
527　All creatures of our God and King
542　Sing praise to God, the highest good
550　From all that dwell below the skies
652　Arise, your light has come!
799　When long before time

Psalmody: Psalm 112
Happy are they who fear the LORD. (Ps. 112:1)

Second Reading: Acts 11:19–30; 13:1–3
Barnabas and Saul are set apart

160　Filled with the Spirit's power
284　Creator Spirit, heavenly dove
363　Christ is alive! Let Christians sing
377　Lift high the cross

Gospel: Matthew 10:7–16
Jesus sends out the twelve

376　Your kingdom come!
435　O God, whose will is life and good
756　Lord, you give the great commission

Additional hymns for the day/season

140　With high delight let us unite
373　Eternal Ruler of the ceaseless round
See St. Andrew

The Nativity of St. John the Baptist

June 24

Prayer of the day

Almighty God, you called John the Baptist to give witness to the coming of your Son and to prepare his way. Grant to your people the wisdom to see your purpose and the openness to hear your will, that we too may witness to Christ's coming and so prepare his way; through your Son, Jesus Christ our Lord, who lives and reigns with you and the Holy Spirit, one God, now and forever. (124)

Verse

Alleluia. Blessed are those who are persecuted for righteousness' sake, for theirs is the kingdom of heaven. Alleluia. (Matt. 5:10)

Offertory

I put my trust in the LORD. I will rejoice and be glad because of your mercy. Make your face to shine upon your servant, and in your lovingkindness save me. You hide in the covert of your presence those who trust in you; you keep them in your shelter from the strife of tongues. (Ps. 31:6–7, 16, 20)

Years A, B, C

Hymn of the day

725   Blessed be the God of Israel
178   By all your saints in warfare (stanza 15)

Hymns related to the readings

First Reading: Malachi 3:1–4
My messenger is a refiner and purifier

507   How firm a foundation
556   Herald, sound the note of judgment

Psalmody: Psalm 141
My eyes are turned to you, Lord GOD. (Ps. 141:8)

Second Reading: Acts 13:13–26
The message of the gospel is for the descendants of Abraham's family

Gospel: Luke 1:57–67 [68–80]
The birth and naming of John

2   Blessed be the Lord
725   Blessed be the God of Israel

Additional hymns for the day/season

29   Comfort, comfort now my people
36   On Jordan's banks the Baptist's cry
265   Christ, whose glory fills the skies
See 2 Advent, 3 Advent; St. Andrew

St. Peter and St. Paul, Apostles

June 29

Prayer of the day

Almighty God, whose blessed apostles Peter and Paul glorified you by their martyrdom: Grant that your Church, instructed by their teaching and example, and knit together in unity by your Spirit, may ever stand firm upon the one foundation, which is Jesus Christ our Lord, who lives and reigns with you and the Holy Spirit, one God, now and forever. (125)

Verse

Alleluia. This Jesus God raised up, and of that all of us are witnesses. Alleluia. (Acts 2:32)

Offertory

Sing to the LORD and bless his name; proclaim the good news of his salvation from day to day. Declare his glory among the nations and his wonders among all peoples. For great is the LORD and greatly to be praised. Oh, the majesty and magnificence of his presence! Oh, the power and the splendor of his sanctuary! (Ps. 96:2–4, 6)

Years A, B, C

Hymn of the day

377 Lift high the cross
367, 747 Christ is made the sure foundation

Hymns related to the readings

First Reading: Ezekiel 34:11–16
The LORD will be a shepherd for the sheep

286 Bow down your ear, almighty Lord
291 Jesus sinners will receive
402 Look from your sphere of endless day
531 Before Jehovah's awesome throne

Psalmody: Psalm 87:1–2, 4–6*
Glorious things are spoken of you, O city of our God. (Ps. 87:2)

Second Reading: 1 Corinthians 3:16–23
All belongs to Christ

164 Creator Spirit, by whose aid
177 By all your saints in warfare (stanzas 10, 11)
459 O Holy Spirit, enter in
464 You are the way
782 All my hope on God is founded

Gospel: Mark 8:27–35
Peter confesses: You are the Messiah

173 The head that once was crowned
365 Built on a rock
384 Your kingdom come, O Father
398 "Take up your cross," the Savior said
487 Let us ever walk with Jesus

Additional hymns for the day/season

358 Glories of your name are spoken
537 O Jesus, king most wonderful!
737 There is a balm in Gilead
See Proper 19B; St. Andrew

*Psalm 87:1–3, 5–7 (NRSV)

St. Mary Magdalene

Prayer of the day

Almighty God, your Son Jesus Christ restored Mary Magdalene to health of body and mind, and called her to be a witness of his resurrection. Heal us now in body and mind, and call us to serve you in the power of the resurrection of Jesus Christ, who lives and reigns with you and the Holy Spirit, one God, now and forever. (126)

Verse

Alleluia. Whoever serves me, the Father will honor. Alleluia. (John 12:26)

Offertory

LORD, you guide me along right pathways for your name's sake. You spread a table before me in the presence of those who trouble me; you have anointed my head with oil, and my cup is running over. Surely your goodness and mercy shall follow me all the days of my life, and I will dwell in the house of the LORD forever. (Ps. 23:3–6)

Years A, B, C

Hymn of the day

692   For all the faithful women
147   Hallelujah! Jesus lives!

Hymns related to the readings

First Reading: Ruth 1:6–18
Ruth stays with Naomi

692   For all the faithful women

OR

First Reading: Exodus 2:1–10
A child is saved by the daughter of Pharaoh and is named Moses

533, 534 Now thank we all our God

Psalmody: Psalm 73:23–29*
I will speak of all your works in the gates of the city of Zion. (Ps. 73:29)

Second Reading: Acts 13:26–33a
The raising of Jesus fulfills God's promise

140   With high delight let us unite

Gospel: John 20:1–2, 11–18
Mary Magdalene meets Jesus in the garden

137   Christians, to the paschal victim
147   Hallelujah! Jesus lives!
148   Now the green blade rises
692   For all the faithful women

Additional hymns for the day/season

560   Oh, that I had a thousand voices
706   Eat this bread, drink this cup
See St. Andrew

*Psalm 73:23–28 (NRSV)

St. James the Elder, Apostle

July 25

Prayer of the day

O gracious God, we remember before you today your servant and apostle James, first among the Twelve to suffer martyrdom for the name of Jesus Christ. Pour out upon the leaders of your Church that spirit of self-denying service which is the true mark of authority among your people; through Jesus Christ our Lord, who lives and reigns with you and the Holy Spirit, one God, now and forever. (127)

Verse

Alleluia. Blessed are those who are persecuted for righteousness' sake, for theirs is the kingdom of heaven. Alleluia. (Matt. 5:10)

Offertory

I put my trust in the LORD. I will rejoice and be glad because of your mercy. Make your face to shine upon your servant, and in your lovingkindness save me. You hide in the covert of your presence those who trust in you; you keep them in your shelter from the strife of tongues. (Ps. 31:6–7, 16, 20)

Years A, B, C

Hymn of the day

176   For all your saints, O Lord
178   By all your saints in warfare (stanza 16)

Additional hymns for the day/season

210   At the Lamb's high feast
529   Praise God. Praise him
See St. Andrew

Hymns related to the readings

First Reading: 1 Kings 19:9–18
Elijah hears God in the midst of silence

205   Now the silence
506   Dear Lord and Father of mankind
682   Praise the Spirit in creation
768   He comes to us as one unknown

Psalmody: Psalm 7:1–11*
God is my shield and defense. (Ps. 7:11)

Second Reading: Acts 11:27—12:3a
James is killed by Herod

178   By all your saints in warfare (stanza 16)
183   The Son of God goes forth to war
230   Lord, keep us steadfast in your Word
500   Faith of our fathers

Gospel: Mark 10:35–45
Whoever wishes to be great must become a servant

178   By all your saints in warfare (stanza 16)
183   The Son of God goes forth to war
736   By gracious powers
765   Jesu, Jesu, fill us with your love

*Psalm 7:1–10 (NRSV)

Mary, Mother of our Lord

August 15

Prayer of the day
Almighty God, you chose the virgin Mary to be the mother of your only Son. Grant that we, who have been redeemed by his blood, may share with her in the glory of your eternal kingdom; through your Son, Jesus Christ our Lord, who lives and reigns with you and the Holy Spirit, one God, now and forever. (128)

Verse
Alleluia. Greetings, O favored one! The Lord is with you. The Holy Spirit will come upon you. Alleluia. (Luke 1:28, 35)
or
Alleluia. From this day all generations will call me blessed: the Almighty has done great things for me, and holy is his name. Alleluia. (Luke 1:48–49)

Offertory
Who is like the LORD our God, who sits enthroned on high, but stoops to behold the heavens and the earth? He takes up the weak out of the dust, and lifts up the poor from the ashes. He sets them with the princes, with the princes of his people. (Ps. 113:5–8)

Years A, B, C

Hymn of the day
634 Sing of Mary, pure and lowly
180 My soul now magnifies the Lord

Hymns related to the readings

First Reading: Isaiah 61:7–11
God will cause righteousness and praise to spring up before all nations

35   Hark, the glad sound!
224 Soul, adorn yourself with gladness
652 Arise, your light has come!

Psalmody: Psalm 45:11–16*
I will make your name to be remembered from one generation to another. (Ps. 45:18)

Second Reading: Galatians 4:4–7
We are no longer slaves, but children

357 Our Father, by whose name
417 In a lowly manger born
683 Loving Spirit

Gospel: Luke 1:46–55
Mary exults in the Lord

6   My soul proclaims the greatness of the Lord
42   Of the Father's love begotten
64   From east to west
180 My soul now magnifies the Lord
632 The angel Gabriel from heaven came
730 My soul proclaims your greatness

Additional hymns for the day/season
110 At the cross, her station keeping
175 Ye watchers and ye holy ones
215 O Lord, we praise you
533, 534 Now thank we all our God
635 Surely it is God who saves me
See 4 Advent A, B, C; St. Andrew

*Psalm 45:10–15 (NRSV)

St. Bartholomew, Apostle

August 24

Prayer of the day

Almighty and everlasting God, who gave to your apostle Bartholomew grace truly to believe and to preach your Word: Grant that your Church may love what he believed and preach what he taught; through your Son, Jesus Christ our Lord, who lives and reigns with you and the Holy Spirit, one God, now and forever. (129)

Verse

Alleluia. How beautiful upon the mountains are the feet of the messenger who announces peace, who brings good news, who announces salvation. Alleluia. (Isa. 52:7)

Offertory

Sing to the LORD and bless his name; proclaim the good news of his salvation from day to day. Declare his glory among the nations and his wonders among all peoples. For great is the LORD and greatly to be praised. Oh, the majesty and magnificence of his presence! Oh, the power and the splendor of his sanctuary! (Ps. 96:2–4, 6)

Years A, B, C

Hymn of the day
689   Rejoice in God's saints
178   By all your saints in warfare (stanza 17)

Hymns related to the readings

First Reading: Exodus 19:1–6
Israel is called to be God's priestly kingdom and holy nation

543   Praise to the Lord, the Almighty
652   Arise, your light has come!
715   Open your ears, O faithful people

Psalmody: Psalm 12
The words of the LORD are pure. (Ps. 12:6)

Second Reading: 1 Corinthians 12:27–31a
The body of Christ has many gifts and callings

381   Hark, the voice of Jesus calling
737   There is a balm in Gilead

Gospel: John 1:43–51
Jesus says: Follow me

178   By all your saints in warfare (stanza 17)
455   "Come, follow me," the Savior spake
712   Listen, God is calling

Additional hymns for the day/season
703   Draw us in the Spirit's tether
See St. Andrew

HOLY CROSS DAY

Prayer of the day

Almighty God, your Son Jesus Christ was lifted high upon the cross so that he might draw the whole world to himself. Grant that we who glory in his death for our salvation may also glory in his call to take up our cross and follow him; through your Son, Jesus Christ our Lord, who lives and reigns with you and the Holy Spirit, one God, now and forever. (130)

Verse

Alleluia. May I never boast of anything except the cross of our Lord Jesus Christ. Alleluia. (Gal. 6:14)

Offertory

Christ Jesus emptied himself and became obedient to the point of death—even death on a cross. Therefore God also highly exalted him and gave him the name that is above every name, so that at the name of Jesus every knee should bend, and every tongue should confess that Jesus Christ is Lord, to the glory of God the Father. (Phil. 2:7–11)

YEARS A, B, C

Hymn of the day

118   Sing, my tongue
377   Lift high the cross

Hymns related to the readings

First Reading: Numbers 21:4b–9
Moses lifts up a bronze serpent in the wilderness

377   Lift high the cross

Psalmody: Psalm 98:1–5*
The LORD has done marvelous things. (Ps. 98:1)

OR

Psalmody: Psalm 78:1–2, 34–38
God was their rock and the Most High God their redeemer. (Ps. 78:35)

Second Reading: 1 Corinthians 1:18–24
The cross is the power of God to those who are being saved

119   Nature with open volume stands
464   You are the way

Gospel: John 3:13–17
The Son of Man will be lifted up

118   Sing, my tongue
344   We sing the praise of him who died
377   Lift high the cross
382   When I survey the wondrous cross
668   There in God's garden

Additional hymns for the day/season

104   In the cross of Christ I glory
750   Oh, praise the gracious power
785   Weary of all trumpeting
793   Shout for joy loud and long
795   Oh, sing to the Lord

*Psalm 98:1–4 (NRSV)

St. Matthew, Apostle and Evangelist

September 21

Prayer of the day

Almighty God, your Son our Savior called a despised collector of taxes to become one of his apostles. Help us, like Matthew, to respond to the transforming call of your Son, Jesus Christ our Lord, who lives and reigns with you and the Holy Spirit, one God, now and forever. (131)

Verse

Alleluia. You will be my witnesses in Jerusalem, in all Judea and Samaria, and to the ends of the earth. Alleluia. (Acts 1:8)

Offertory

Sing to the LORD and bless his name; proclaim the good news of his salvation from day to day. Declare his glory among the nations and his wonders among all peoples. For great is the LORD and greatly to be praised. Oh, the majesty and magnificence of his presence! Oh, the power and the splendor of his sanctuary! (Ps. 96:2–4, 6)

Years A, B, C

Hymn of the day

227 How blest are they who hear God's Word
178 By all your saints in warfare (stanza 18)

Hymns related to the readings

First Reading: Ezekiel 2:8—3:11
A prophet to the house of Israel

239 God's Word is our great heritage
402 Look from your sphere of endless day

Psalmody: Psalm 119:33–40
Teach me, O LORD, the way of your statutes.
(Ps. 119:33)

Second Reading: Ephesians 2:4–10
By grace you have been saved through faith

297 Salvation unto us has come
513 Come, my way, my truth, my life
680 O Spirit of life

Gospel: Matthew 9:9–13
Jesus calls to Matthew: Follow me

178 By all your saints in warfare (stanza 18)
298 One there is, above all others
455 "Come, follow me," the Savior spake

Additional hymns for the day/season

221 Sent forth by God's blessing
403 Lord, speak to us that we may speak
687 Gracious Spirit, heed our pleading
See St. Andrew

St. Michael and All Angels

Prayer of the day

Everlasting God, you have ordained and constituted in a wonderful order the ministries of angels and mortals. Mercifully grant that, as your holy angels always serve and worship you in heaven, so by your appointment they may help and defend us here on earth; through your Son, Jesus Christ our Lord, who lives and reigns with you and the Holy Spirit, one God, now and forever. (132)

Verse

Alleluia. Bless the LORD, you angels of the LORD, you mighty ones who do his bidding. Alleluia. (Ps. 103:20)

Offertory

Then I looked, and I heard the voice of many angels surrounding the throne and the living creatures and the elders; they numbered myriads of myriads and thousands of thousands, singing with full voice, "Worthy is the Lamb that was slain to receive power and wealth and wisdom and might and honor and glory and blessing!" (Rev. 5:11–12)

Years A, B, C

Hymn of the day

175 Ye watchers and ye holy ones
484 God, my Lord, my strength

Hymns related to the readings

First Reading: Daniel 10:10–14; 12:1–3
All who are dead shall arise on the day of the LORD

325 Lord, thee I love with all my heart
627 My Lord, what a morning
779 You who dwell in the shelter of the Lord

Psalmody: Psalm 103:1–5, 20–22
Bless the LORD, you angels of the LORD. (Ps. 103:20)

519 My soul, now praise your maker! (paraphrase)
543 Praise to the Lord, the Almighty (paraphrase)
549 Praise, my soul, the King of heaven (paraphrase)
798 Bless the Lord, O my soul

Second Reading: Revelation 12:7–12
Michael defeats Satan in a cosmic battle

134 Christ Jesus lay in death's strong bands
179 At the name of Jesus

Gospel: Luke 10:17–20
Jesus gives his followers authority over the enemy

382 Awake, O Spirit of the watchmen
457, 458 Jesus, priceless treasure

Additional hymns for the day/season

198 Let all mortal flesh keep silence
249 God himself is present
273 O Christ, you are the light and day
281 God, who made the earth and heaven
432 We worship you, O God of might
526 Immortal, invisible, God only wise
528 Isaiah in a vision did of old
535 Holy God, we praise your name
536 O God of God, O Light of light
547 Thee we adore, eternal Lord!
549 Praise, my soul, the King of heaven
553 Rejoice, O pilgrim throng!
699 Blessed assurance
706 Eat this bread, drink this cup
801 Thine the amen, thine the praise

ST. LUKE, EVANGELIST

Prayer of the day

Almighty God, you inspired your servant Luke the physician to reveal in his Gospel the love and healing power of your Son. Give your Church the same love and power to heal, to the glory of your name; through your Son, Jesus Christ our Lord, who lives and reigns with you and the Holy Spirit, one God, now and forever. (133)

Verse

Alleluia. How beautiful upon the mountains are the feet of the messenger who announces peace, who brings good news, who announces salvation. Alleluia. (Isa. 52:7)

Offertory

Sing to the LORD and bless his name; proclaim the good news of his salvation from day to day. Declare his glory among the nations and his wonders among all peoples. For great is the LORD and greatly to be praised. Oh, the majesty and magnificence of his presence! Oh, the power and the splendor of his sanctuary! (Ps. 96:2–4, 6)

YEARS A, B, C

Hymn of the day

431 Your hand, O Lord, in days of old
178 By all your saints in warfare (stanza 19)

Hymns related to the readings

First Reading: Isaiah 43:8–13
The LORD will heal the blind and deaf

360 O Christ, the healer, we have come
400 God, whose almighty word
435 O God, whose will is life and good
668 There in God's garden
716 Word of God, come down on earth

OR

First Reading: Isaiah 35:5–8
The LORD will heal the blind and deaf

360 O Christ, the healer, we have come
426 O Son of God, in Galilee
435 O God, whose will is life and good
716 Word of God, come down on earth

Psalmody: Psalm 124
Our help is in the name of the LORD. (Ps. 124:8)

Second Reading: 2 Timothy 4:5–11
The good fight of faith

308 God the Father, be our stay
340 Jesus Christ, my sure defense
461 Fight the good fight
502 Thee will I love, my strength

Gospel: Luke 1:1–4; 24:44–53
Luke witnesses to the ministry of Jesus

363 Christ is alive! Let Christians sing
537 O Jesus, king most wonderful!
753 You are the seed
756 Lord, you give the great commission

Additional hymns for the day/season

559 Oh, for a thousand tongues to sing
737 There is a balm in Gilead
738 Healer of our every ill
See St. Andrew

St. Simon and St. Jude, Apostles

Prayer of the day

O God, we thank you for the glorious company of the apostles and, especially on this day, for Simon and Jude. We pray that, as they were faithful and zealous in their mission, so we may with ardent devotion make known the love and mercy of our Lord and Savior Jesus Christ, who lives and reigns with you and the Holy Spirit, one God, now and forever. (134)

Verse

Alleluia. You will be my witnesses in Jerusalem, in all Judea and Samaria, and to the ends of the earth. Alleluia. (Acts 1:8)

Offertory

Sing to the LORD and bless his name; proclaim the good news of his salvation from day to day. Declare his glory among the nations and his wonders among all peoples. For great is the LORD and greatly to be praised. Oh, the majesty and magnificence of his presence! Oh, the power and the splendor of his sanctuary! (Ps. 96:2–4, 6)

Years A, B, C

Hymn of the day

689 Rejoice in God's saints
178 By all your saints in warfare (stanza 20)

Hymns related to the readings

First Reading: Jeremiah 26:[1–6] 7–16
Jeremiah promises the judgment of God

230 Lord, keep us steadfast in your Word
510 O God of youth

Psalmody: Psalm 11
In the LORD have I taken refuge. (Ps. 11:1)

Second Reading: 1 John 4:1–6
Do not believe every spirit of this world

433 The Church of Christ, in every age

Gospel: John 14:21–27
Those who love Jesus will keep his word

338 Peace, to soothe our bitter woes
471 Grant peace, we pray, in mercy, Lord
496 Around you, O Lord Jesus
524 My God, how wonderful thou art
537 O Jesus, king most wonderful!
687 Gracious Spirit, heed our pleading
719 God is here!
721 Go, my children, with my blessing

Additional hymns for the day/season

383 Rise up, O saints of God!
405 Lord of light
542 Sing praise to God, the highest good
See St. Andrew

REFORMATION DAY

Prayer of the day
Almighty God, gracious Lord, pour out your Holy Spirit upon your faithful people. Keep them steadfast in your Word, protect and comfort them in all temptations, defend them against all their enemies, and bestow on the Church your saving peace; through your Son, Jesus Christ our Lord, who lives and reigns with you and the Holy Spirit, one God, now and forever. (135)

Verse
Alleluia. If you continue in my word, you are truly my disciples, and you will know the truth, and the truth will make you free. Alleluia. (John 8:31–32)

Offertory
I appeal to you, therefore, by the mercies of God, to present your bodies as a living sacrifice, holy and acceptable to God, which is your spiritual worship. Do not be conformed to this world, but be transformed by the renewing of your minds, so that you may discern what is the will of God—what is good and acceptable and perfect. (Rom. 12:1–2)

YEARS A, B, C

Hymn of the day
230   Lord, keep us steadfast in your Word
365   Built on a rock
712   Listen, God is calling

Hymns related to the readings

First Reading: Jeremiah 31:31–34
I will write my law in their hearts, says the LORD

16   I will sing the story of your love
680   O Spirit of life
701   What feast of love
790   Praise to you, O God of mercy

Psalmody: Psalm 46
The LORD of hosts is with us; the God of Jacob is our stronghold. (Ps. 46:4)

228, 229   A mighty fortress is our God (paraphrase)

Second Reading: Romans 3:19–28
Justified by God's grace as a gift

297   Salvation unto us has come
299   Dear Christians, one and all
239   God's Word is our great heritage
680   O Spirit of life

Gospel: John 8:31–36
Jesus says, Continue in my word and you will know the truth

484   God, my Lord, my strength
679   Our Paschal Lamb that sets us free

Additional hymns for the day/season
355   Through the night of doubt and sorrow
361   Do not despair, O little flock
367   Christ is made the sure foundation
369   The Church's one foundation
374   We all believe in one true God
386   Christ is the king!
393   Rise, shine, you people!
396   O God, O Lord of heaven and earth
478   Come, oh, come, O quickening Spirit
747   Christ is made the sure foundation
750   Oh, praise the gracious power
755   We all are one in mission

All Saints' Day

Prayer of the day

Almighty God, whose people are knit together in one holy Church, the body of Christ our Lord: Grant us grace to follow your blessed saints in lives of faith and commitment, and to know the inexpressible joys you have prepared for those who love you; through your Son, Jesus Christ our Lord, who lives and reigns with you and the Holy Spirit, one God, now and forever. (136)

Verse

Alleluia. They are before the throne of God, and the one seated on the throne will shelter them. Alleluia. (Rev. 7:15)

Offertory

Let us rejoice and exult and give God the glory, for the marriage of the Lamb has come, and his Bride has made herself ready; to her it has been granted to be clothed with fine linen, bright and pure—for the fine linen is the righteous deeds of the saints. (Rev. 19:7–8)

Year A

Hymn of the day

174	For all the saints
314	Who is this host arrayed in white
691	Sing with all the saints in glory

Hymns related to the readings

First Reading: Revelation 7:9–17
The multitudes of heaven worship the Lamb

211	Here, O my Lord, I see thee
252	You servants of God
254	Come, let us join our cheerful songs
314	Who is this host arrayed in white
331	Jerusalem, my happy home
337	Oh, what their joy
347	Jerusalem, the golden
348	Jerusalem, whose towers touch the skies
385	What wondrous love is this!
516	Arise, my soul, arise!
525	Blessing and honor
536	O God of God, O Light of light
669	Come away to the skies

Psalmody: Psalm 34:1–10, 22
Fear the LORD, you saints of the LORD. (Ps. 34:9)

706	Eat this bread, drink this cup (paraphrase)

Second Reading: 1 John 3:1–3
We are God's children

315	Love divine, all loves excelling
649	I want to walk as a child of the light

Gospel: Matthew 5:1–12
Blessed are the poor in spirit

17	How blest are those who know their need of God
316	Jesus, the very thought of you
689	Rejoice in God's saints
764	Blest are they

Additional hymns for the day/season

175	Ye watchers and ye holy ones
177	By all your saints in warfare (stanza 4)
200	For the bread which you have broken
206	Lord, who the night you were betrayed
320	O God, our help in ages past
325	Lord, thee I love with all my heart
330	In heaven above
351	Oh, happy day when we shall stand
369	The Church's one foundation
513	Come, my way, my truth, my life
553	Rejoice, O pilgrim throng!
674	Alleluia! Jesus is risen!
690	Shall we gather at the river
742	Come, we that love the Lord
787	Glory to God, we give you thanks
791	Alabaré
801	Thine the amen, thine the praise

Year B

Hymn of the day
331   Jerusalem, my happy home
174   For all the saints
764   Blest are they

Hymns related to the readings

First Reading: Isaiah 25:6–9
The banquet of the LORD

210   At the Lamb's high feast we sing
516   Arise, my soul, arise!
701   What feast of love
708   Grains of wheat
766   We come to the hungry feast
789   Now the feast and celebration

OR

First Reading: Wisdom of Solomon 3:1–9
The righteous are with God

337   Oh, what their joy

Psalmody: Psalm 24
They shall receive a blessing from the God of their salvation. (Ps. 24:5)

631   Lift up your heads, O gates (paraphrase)

Second Reading: Revelation 21:1–6a
A new heaven and a new earth

330   In heaven above
337   Oh, what their joy
668   There in God's garden
674   Alleluia! Jesus is risen!
690   Shall we gather at the river

Gospel: John 11:32–44
The raising of Lazarus

340   Jesus Christ, my sure defense
352   I know that my Redeemer lives!
702   I am the Bread of life

Additional hymns for the day/season
272   Abide with me
342   I know of a sleep in Jesus' name
See Year A

Year C

Hymn of the day
764   Blest are they
175   Ye watchers and ye holy ones
369   The Church's one foundation

Hymns related to the readings

First Reading: Daniel 7:1–3, 15–18
The holy ones of the Most High shall receive the kingdom

175   Ye watchers and ye holy ones
313   A multitude comes from the east and the west

Psalmody: Psalm 149
Sing the praise of the LORD in the congregation of the faithful. (Ps. 149:1)

Second Reading: Ephesians 1:11–23
God raised Christ from the dead and made him head over all the church

76   O Morning Star, how fair and bright!
172   Lord, enthroned in heavenly splendor
179   At the name of Jesus
252   You servants of God

Gospel: Luke 6:20–31
Jesus speaks blessings and woes

17   How blest are those who know their need of God
316   Jesus, the very thought of you
689   Rejoice in God's saints
764   Blest are they

Additional hymns for the day/season
See Year A

NEW YEAR'S EVE

DECEMBER 31

Prayer of the day
Eternal Father, you have placed us in a world of space and time, and through the events of our lives you bless us with your love. Grant that in this new year we may know your presence, see your love at work, and live in the light of the event which gives us joy forever—the coming of your Son, Jesus Christ our Lord. (159)

Verse
Alleluia. Your word is a lantern to my feet and a light upon my path. Alleluia. (Ps. 119:105)

Offertory
Be careful then how you live, not as unwise people but as wise. Be filled with the Spirit, addressing one another in psalms and hymns and spiritual songs, singing and making melody to the Lord with all your heart, always and for everything giving thanks in the name of our Lord Jesus Christ to God the Father. (Eph. 5:15, 18–20)

YEARS A, B, C

Hymn of the day
54 It came upon the midnight clear
320 O God, our help in ages past
736 By gracious powers

Hymns related to the readings

First Reading: Ecclesiastes 3:1–13
For everything there is a season

736 By gracious powers
767 All things bright and beautiful
778 O Christ the same

Psalmody: Psalm 8
How exalted is your name in all the world. (Ps. 8:1)

Second Reading: Revelation 21:1–6a
A new heaven and a new earth

42 Of the Father's love begotten
61 The hills are bare at Bethlehem
315 Love divine, all loves excelling
628 Each winter as the year grows older

Gospel: Matthew 25:31–46
The Son of Man will separate the sheep and the goats

424 Lord of glory, you have bought us
433 The Church of Christ, in every age

Additional hymns for the day/season
49 O Savior of our fallen race
53 Cold December flies away
62 The bells of Christmas
181 Greet now the swiftly changing year
262 Savior, again to your dear name
276 Now all the woods are sleeping
447 All depends on our possessing
465 Evening and morning
468 From God can nothing move me
497 I heard the voice of Jesus say
533, 534 Now thank we all our God
557 Let all things now living
558 In thee is gladness
746 Day by day
771 Great is thy faithfulness
797 O God beyond all praising

Prayer of the day

Almighty God our Father, your generous goodness comes to us new every day. By the work of your Spirit lead us to acknowledge your goodness, give thanks for your benefits, and serve you in willing obedience; through your Son, Jesus Christ our Lord. (155)

Verse

Alleluia. God is able to provide you with every blessing in abundance, so that by always having enough of everything, you may share abundantly in every good work. Alleluia. (2 Cor. 9:8)

Offertory

Mountains and hills, fruit trees and all cedars; wild beasts and all cattle, creeping things and winged birds; kings of the earth and all peoples, princes and all rulers of the world; young men and maidens, old and young together: let them praise the name of the LORD, for his name only is exalted, his splendor is over earth and heaven. (Ps. 148:9–13)

YEAR A

Hymn of the day

533   Now thank we all our God
557   Let all things now living
771   Great is thy faithfulness

Hymns related to the readings

First Reading: Deuteronomy 8:7–18
God will lead you into a land of flowing streams

172   Lord, enthroned in heavenly splendor
358   Glories of your name are spoken
532   How Great Thou Art

Psalmody: Psalm 65
You crown the year with your goodness, and your paths overflow with plenty. (Ps. 65:12)

Second Reading: 2 Corinthians 9:6–15
God provides every blessing in abundance

409   Praise and thanksgiving

Gospel: Luke 17:11–19
The healed leper returns to give thanks to Jesus

527   All creatures of our God and King
533, 534 Now thank we all our God
767   All things bright and beautiful
771   Great is thy faithfulness
778   O Christ the same

Additional hymns for the day/season

217   We place upon your table, Lord
241   We praise you, O God
407   Come, you thankful people, come
408   God, whose giving knows no ending
411   Lord of all good
412   Sing to the Lord of harvest
437   Not alone for mighty empire
527   All creatures of our God and King
540   Praise the Lord! O heavens adore him
541   Praise the Lord of heaven!
759   Accept, O Lord, the gifts we bring
778   O Christ the same
790   Praise to you, O God of mercy
797   O God beyond all praising

YEAR B

Hymn of the day
760   For the fruit of all creation
241   We praise you, O God
407   Come, you thankful people, come

Hymns related to the readings

First Reading: Joel 2:21–27
The LORD promises to restore Jerusalem

412   Sing to the Lord of harvest

Psalmody: Psalm 126
The LORD has done great things for us, and we are glad indeed. (Ps. 126:4)

Second Reading: 1 Timothy 2:1–7
Make supplications, prayers, intercessions, and thanksgivings

274   The day you gave us, Lord, has ended
437   Not alone for mighty empire

Gospel: Matthew 6:25–33
God will care for all our needs

362   We plow the fields and scatter
527   All creatures of our God and King

533, 534 Now thank we all our God
543   Praise to the Lord, the Almighty
552   In thee is gladness
767   All things bright and beautiful
771   Great is thy faithfulness
778   O Christ the same

Additional hymns for the day/season
See Year A

YEAR C

Hymn of the day
754   Let us talents and tongues employ
409   Praise and thanksgiving
527   All creatures of our God and King

Hymns related to the readings

First Reading: Deuteronomy 26:1–11
The offering of the first fruits

401   Before you, Lord, we bow
404   As saints of old

Psalmody: Psalm 100
Enter the gates of the LORD with thanksgiving. (Ps. 100:3)

245   All people that on earth do dwell (paraphrase)
256   Oh, sing jubilee to the Lord (paraphrase)
531   Before Jehovah's awesome throne (paraphrase)

Second Reading: Philippians 4:4–9
Do not worry about anything

171   Rejoice, the Lord is king!
516   Arise, my soul, arise!
553   Rejoice, O pilgrim throng!

Gospel: John 6:25–35
Jesus is the bread of life

197   O living Bread from heaven
211   Here, O my Lord, I see thee
222   O Bread of life from heaven
224   Soul, adorn yourself with gladness
343   Guide me ever, great Redeemer
702   I am the Bread of life
704   Father, we thank you
722   Hallelujah! We sing your praises

Additional hymns for the day/season
See Year A

INDEX TO THE
REVISED COMMON LECTIONARY

During the Season after Pentecost, Old Testament selections without an asterisk are thematically related to the Gospel; the alternate selections, marked with an an asterisk (*), form a semi-continuous pattern of readings. Either series is designed to be read in its entirety.

Genesis

1:1–2:4a	Holy Trinity		A
1:1–2:4a	Vigil of Easter		A, B, C
1:1–5	Baptism of Our Lord		B
1:1–5, 26–31	St. John		A, B, C
2:15–17; 3:1–7	1 Lent		A
2:18–24	S. btwn. Oct. 2 and 8	Pr. 22	B
3:8–15	S. btwn. June 5 and 11	Pr. 5	B
6:9–22; 7:24; 8:14–19	S. btwn. May 29 and June 4*	Pr. 4	A
7:1–5, 11–18; 8:6–18; 9:8–13	Vigil of Easter		A, B, C
9:8–17	1 Lent		B
11:1–9	Day of Pentecost		C
12:1–4a	2 Lent		A
12:1–9	S. btwn. June 5 and 11*	Pr. 5	A
15:1–6	S. btwn. Aug. 7 and 13	Pr. 14	C
15:1–12, 17–18	2 Lent		C
17:1–7, 15–16	2 Lent		B
18:1–10a	S. btwn. July 17 and 23	Pr. 11	C
18:1–15 [21:1–7]	S. btwn. June 12 and 18*	Pr. 6	A
18:20–32	S. btwn. July 24 and 30	Pr. 12	C
21:8–21	S. btwn. June 19 and 25*	Pr. 7	A
22:1–14	S. btwn. June 26 and July 2*	Pr. 8	A
22:1–18	Vigil of Easter		A, B, C
24:34–38, 42–49, 58–67	S. btwn. July 3 and 9*	Pr. 9	A
25:19–34	S. btwn. July 10 and 16*	Pr. 10	A
28:10–19a	S. btwn. July 17 and 23*	Pr. 11	A
29:15–28	S. btwn. July 24 and 30*	Pr. 12	A
32:22–31	S. btwn. July 31 and Aug. 6*	Pr. 13	A
32:22–31	S. btwn. Oct. 16 and 22	Pr. 24	C
37:1–4, 12–28	S. btwn. Aug. 7 and 13*	Pr. 14	A
45:1–15	S. btwn. Aug. 14 and 20*	Pr. 15	A
45:3–11, 15	7 Epiphany		C
50:15–21	S. btwn. Sept. 11 and 17	Pr. 19	A

Exodus

1:8–2:10	S. btwn. Aug. 21 and 27*	Pr. 16	A
2:1–10	St. Mary Magdalene		A, B, C
3:1–15	S. btwn. Aug. 28 and Sept. 3*	Pr. 17	A
12:1–14	S. btwn. Sept. 4 and 10*	Pr. 18	A
12:1–4 [5–10] 11–14	Maundy Thursday		A, B, C
14:10–31; 15:20–21	Vigil of Easter		A, B, C
14:19–31	S. btwn. Sept. 11 and 17*	Pr. 19	A
15:1b–11, 20–21	S. btwn. Sept. 11 and 17*	Pr. 19	A
15:1b–13, 17–18	Vigil of Easter		A, B, C
16:2–4, 9–15	S. btwn. July 31 and Aug. 6	Pr. 13	B
16:2–15	S. btwn. Sept. 18 and 24*	Pr. 20	A
17:1–7	3 Lent		A
17:1–7	S. btwn. Sept. 25 and Oct. 1*	Pr. 21	A
19:1–6	St. Bartholomew		A, B, C
19:1–9	Vigil of Pentecost		A, B, C
19:2–8a	S. btwn. June 12 and 18	Pr. 6	A
20:1–4, 7–9, 12–20	S. btwn. Oct. 2 and 8*	Pr. 22	A
20:1–17	3 Lent		B
24:12–18	Transfiguration of Our Lord		A

32:1–14	S. btwn. Oct. 9 and 15*	Pr. 23	A
32:7–14	S. btwn. Sept. 11 and 17	Pr. 19	C
33:12–23	S. btwn. Oct. 16 and 22*	Pr. 24	A
34:29–35	Transfiguration of Our Lord		C

Leviticus

19:1–2, 9–18	7 Epiphany		A
19:1–2, 15–18	S. btwn. Oct. 23 and 29	Pr. 25	A

Numbers

6:22–27	Name of Jesus		A, B, C
11:4–6, 10–16, 24–29	S. btwn. Sept. 25 and Oct. 1	Pr. 21	B
11:24–30	Day of Pentecost		A
21:4–9	4 Lent		B
21:4b–9	Holy Cross Day		A, B, C

Deuteronomy

4:1–2, 6–9	S. btwn. Aug. 28 and Sept. 3	Pr. 17	B
5:12–15	S. btwn. May 29 and June 4	Pr. 4	B
6:1–9	S. btwn. Oct. 30 and Nov. 5	Pr. 26	B
8:7–18	Thanksgiving		A
11:18–21, 26–28	S. btwn. May 29 and June 4	Pr. 4	A
18:15–20	4 Epiphany		B
26:1–11	1 Lent		C
26:1–11	Thanksgiving		C
30:9–14	S. btwn. July 10 and 16	Pr. 10	C
30:15–20	6 Epiphany		A
30:15–20	S. btwn. Sept. 4 and 10	Pr. 18	C
31:19–30	Vigil of Easter		A, B, C
32:1–4, 7, 36a, 43a	Vigil of Easter		A, B, C
34:1–12	S. btwn. Oct. 23 and 29*	Pr. 25	A

Joshua

3:7–17	S. btwn. Oct. 30 and Nov. 5*	Pr. 26	A
5:9–12	4 Lent		C
24:1–2a, 14–18	S. btwn. Aug. 21 and 27	Pr. 16	B
24:1–3a, 14–25	S. btwn. Nov. 6 and 12*	Pr. 27	A

Judges

4:1–7	S. btwn. Nov. 13 and 19*	Pr. 28	A
6:36–40	St. Thomas		A, B, C

Ruth

1:1–18	S. btwn. Oct. 30 and Nov. 5*	Pr. 26	B
1:6–18	St. Mary Magdalene		A, B, C
3:1–5; 4:13–17	S. btwn. Nov. 6 and 12*	Pr. 27	B

1 Samuel

1:4–20	S. btwn. Nov. 13 and 19*	Pr. 28	B
2:1–10	S. btwn. Nov. 13 and 19*	Pr. 28	B
2:1–10	Visitation		A, B, C
2:18–20, 26	1 Christmas		C
3:1–10 [11–20]	2 Epiphany		B
3:1–10 [11–20]	S. btwn. May 29 and June 4*	Pr. 4	B
8:4–11 [12–15] 16–20; [11:14–15]	S. btwn. June 5 and 11*	Pr. 5	B
15:34–16:13	S. btwn. June 12 and 18*	Pr. 6	B
16:1–13	4 Lent		A
17:[1a, 4–11, 19–23] 32–49	S. btwn. June 19 and 25*	Pr. 7	B
17:57–18:5, 10–16	S. btwn. June 19 and 25*	Pr. 7	B

2 Samuel

1:1, 17–27	S. btwn. June 26 and July 2*	Pr. 8	B
5:1–5, 9–10	S. btwn. July 3 and 9*	Pr. 9	B

(2 Samuel)

6:1–5, 12b–19	S. btwn. July 10 and 16*	Pr. 10	B
7:1–11, 16	4 Advent		B
7:1–14a	S. btwn. July 17 and 23*	Pr. 11	B
11:1–15	S. btwn. July 24 and 30*	Pr. 12	B
11:26–12:10, 13–15	S. btwn. June 12 and 18	Pr. 6	C
11:26–12:13a	S. btwn. July 31 and Aug. 6*	Pr. 13	B
18:5–9, 15, 31–33	S. btwn. Aug. 7 and 13*	Pr. 14	B
23:1–7	Christ the King*		B

1 Kings

2:10–12; 3:3–14	S. btwn. Aug. 14 and 20*	Pr. 15	B
3:5–12	S. btwn. July 24 and 30	Pr. 12	A
8:[1, 6, 10–11] 22–30, 41–43	S. btwn. Aug. 21 and 27*	Pr. 16	B
8:22–23, 41–43	S. btwn. May 29 and June 4	Pr. 4	C
17:8–16	S. btwn. Nov. 6 and 12	Pr. 27	B
17:8–16 [17–24]	S. btwn. June 5 and 11*	Pr. 5	C
17:17–24	S. btwn. June 5 and 11	Pr. 5	C
18:20–21 [22–29] 30–39	S. btwn. May 29 and June 4*	Pr. 4	C
19:1–4 [5–7] 8–15a	S. btwn. June 19 and 25*	Pr. 7	C
19:4–8	S. btwn. Aug. 7 and 13	Pr. 14	B
19:9–18	S. btwn. Aug. 7 and 13	Pr. 14	A
19:9–18	St. James the Elder		A, B, C
19:15–16, 19–21	S. btwn. June 26 and July 2	Pr. 8	C
21:1–10 [11–14] 15–21a	S. btwn. June 12 and 18*	Pr. 6	C

2 Kings

2:1–12	Transfiguration of Our Lord		B
2:1–2, 6–14	S. btwn. June 26 and July 2*	Pr. 8	C
4:42–44	S. btwn. July 24 and 30	Pr. 12	B
5:1–3, 7–15c	S. btwn. Oct. 9 and 15	Pr. 23	C
5:1–14	6 Epiphany		B
5:1–14	S. btwn. July 3 and 9*	Pr. 9	C

2 Chronicles

24:17–22	St. Stephen		A, B, C

Nehemiah

8:1–3, 5–6, 8–10	3 Epiphany		C

Esther

7:1–6, 9–10; 9:20–22	S. btwn. Sept. 25 and Oct. 1*	Pr. 21	B

Job

1:1; 2:1–10	S. btwn. Oct. 2 and 8*	Pr. 22	B
14:1–14	Saturday in Holy Week		A, B, C
19:23–27a	S. btwn. Nov. 6 and 12	Pr. 27	C
23:1–9, 16–17	S. btwn. Oct. 9 and 15*	Pr. 23	B
38:1–7 [34–41]	S. btwn. Oct. 16 and 22*	Pr. 24	B
38:1–11	S. btwn. June 19 and 25	Pr. 7	B
42:1–6, 10–17	S. btwn. Oct. 23 and 29*	Pr. 25	B

Psalms

1	6 Epiphany		C
1	7 Easter		B
1	S. btwn. Sept. 4 and 10	Pr. 18	C
1	S. btwn. Sept. 18 and 24*	Pr. 20	B
1	S. btwn. Oct. 23 and 29	Pr. 25	A
2	Transfiguration of Our Lord		A
4	3 Easter		B
5:1–8	S. btwn. June 12 and 18*	Pr. 6	C
7:1–10	St. James the Elder		A, B, C
8	Holy Trinity		A, C
8	Name of Jesus		A, B, C

(Psalms)

34:1–8	S. btwn. Aug. 7 and 13	Pr. 14	B
34:1–8 [19–22]	S. btwn. Oct. 23 and 29*	Pr. 25	B
34:1–10, 22	All Saints		A
34:9–14	S. btwn. Aug. 14 and 20	Pr. 15	B
34:15–22	S. btwn. Aug. 21 and 27	Pr. 16	B
36:5–10	2 Epiphany		C
36:5–11	Monday in Holy Week		A, B, C
37:1–9	S. btwn. Oct. 2 and 8	Pr. 22	C
37:1–11, 39–40	7 Epiphany		C
40:1–11	2 Epiphany		A
40:5–10	Annunciation of Our Lord		A, B, C
41	7 Epiphany		B
42 and 43	S. btwn. June 19 and 25*	Pr. 7	C
42 and 43	Vigil of Easter		A, B, C
43	S. btwn. Oct. 30 and Nov. 5	Pr. 26	A
43	Vigil of Easter		C
44:1–3, 20–26	St. Philip and St. James		A, B, C
45	Annunciation of Our Lord		A, B, C
45:1–2, 6–9	S. btwn. Aug. 28 and Sept. 3*	Pr. 17	B
45:10–15	Mary, Mother of Our Lord		A, B, C
45:10–17	S. btwn. July 3 and 9*	Pr. 9	A
46	Christ the King	Pr. 29	C
46	Reformation Day		A, B, C
46	S. btwn. May 29 and June 4*	Pr. 4	A
46	Vigil of Easter		A, B, C
47	Ascension of Our Lord		A, B, C
48	S. btwn. July 3 and 9*	Pr. 9	B
49:1–12	S. btwn. July 31 and Aug. 6	Pr. 13	C
50:1–6	Transfiguration of Our Lord		B
50:1–8, 22–23	S. btwn. Aug. 7 and 13*	Pr. 14	C
50:7–15	S. btwn. June 5 and 11	Pr. 5	A
51:1–10	S. btwn. Sept. 11 and 17	Pr. 19	C
51:1–12	5 Lent		B
51:1–12	S. btwn. July 31 and Aug. 6*	Pr. 13	B
51:1–17	Ash Wednesday		A, B, C
52	S. btwn. July 17 and 23*	Pr. 11	C
54	S. btwn. Sept. 18 and 24	Pr. 20	B
56	St. Matthias		A, B, C
57	St. Mark		A, B, C
62:5–12	3 Epiphany		B
63:1–8	3 Lent		C
65	S. btwn. Oct. 23 and 29*	Pr. 25	C
65	Thanksgiving		A
65:[1–8] 9–13	S. btwn. July 10 and 16	Pr. 10	A
66:1–9	S. btwn. July 3 and 9	Pr. 9	C
66:1–12	S. btwn. Oct. 9 and 15*	Pr. 23	C
66:8–20	6 Easter		A
67	6 Easter		C
67	Conversion of St. Paul		A, B, C
67	S. btwn. Aug. 14 and 20	Pr. 15	A
68:1–10, 32–35	7 Easter		A
69:7–10 [11–15] 16–18	S. btwn. June 19 and 25	Pr. 7	A
70	S. btwn. Nov. 6 and 12	Pr. 27	A
70	Wednesday in Holy Week		A, B, C
71:1–6	4 Epiphany		C
71:1–6	S. btwn. Aug. 21 and 27*	Pr. 16	C
71:1–14	Tuesday in Holy Week		A, B, C
72:1–7, 10–14	Epiphany of Our Lord		A, B, C
72:1–7, 18–19	2 Advent		A
73:23–28	St. Mary Magdalene		A, B, C
77:1–2, 11–20	S. btwn. June 26 and July 2*	Pr. 8	C
78:1–2, 34–38	Holy Cross Day		A, B, C
78:1–4, 12–16	S. btwn. Sept. 25 and Oct. 1*	Pr. 21	A
78:1–7	S. btwn. Nov. 6 and 12*	Pr. 27	A

(Psalms)

106:1–6, 19–23	S. btwn. Oct. 9 and 15*	Pr. 23	A
107:1–3, 17–22	4 Lent		B
107:1–3, 23–32	S. btwn. June 19 and 25	Pr. 7	B
107:1–7, 33–37	S. btwn. Oct. 30 and Nov. 5*	Pr. 26	A
107:1–9, 43	S. btwn. July 31 and Aug. 6*	Pr. 13	C
111	4 Epiphany		B
111	S. btwn. Aug. 14 and 20*	Pr. 15	B
111	S. btwn. Oct. 9 and 15	Pr. 23	C
112	S. btwn. Aug. 28 and Sept. 3	Pr. 17	C
112	St. Barnabas		A, B, C
112:1–9 [10]	5 Epiphany		A
113	S. btwn. Sept. 18 and 24	Pr. 20	C
113	Visitation		A, B, C
114	Easter Evening		A, B, C
114	S. btwn. Sept. 11 and 17*	Pr. 19	A
114	Vigil of Easter		A, B, C
116:1–2, 12–19	Maundy Thursday		A, B, C
116:1–2, 12–19	S. btwn. June 12 and 18*	Pr. 6	A
116:1–4, 12–19	3 Easter		A
116:1–9	S. btwn. Sept. 11 and 17	Pr. 19	B
116:12–19	St. John		A, B, C
118:1–2, 14–24	Easter Day		A, B, C
118:1–2, 19–29	Sunday of the Passion (palms)		A, B, C
118:14–29	2 Easter		C
119:1–8	6 Epiphany		A
119:1–8	S. btwn. Oct. 30 and Nov. 5	Pr. 26	B
119:9–16	5 Lent		B
119:33–40	7 Epiphany		A
119:33–40	S. btwn. Sept. 4 and 10	Pr. 18	A
119:33–40	St. Matthew		A, B, C
119:97–104	S. btwn. Oct. 16 and 22*	Pr. 24	C
119:105–112	S. btwn. July 10 and 16*	Pr. 10	A
119:129–136	S. btwn. July 24 and 30	Pr. 12	A
119:137–144	S. btwn. Oct. 30 and Nov. 5*	Pr. 26	C
121	2 Lent		A
121	S. btwn. Oct. 16 and 22	Pr. 24	C
122	1 Advent		A
123	S. btwn. July 3 and 9	Pr. 9	B
123	S. btwn. Nov. 13 and 19*	Pr. 28	A
124	Holy Innocents		A, B, C
124	S. btwn. Aug. 21 and 27*	Pr. 16	A
124	S. btwn. Sept. 25 and Oct. 1*	Pr. 21	B
124	St. Luke		A, B, C
125	S. btwn. Sept. 4 and 10*	Pr. 18	B
126	5 Lent		C
126	3 Advent		B
126	S. btwn. Oct. 23 and 29	Pr. 25	B
126	Thanksgiving		B
127	S. btwn. Nov. 6 and 12*	Pr. 27	B
128	S. btwn. July 24 and 30*	Pr. 12	A
130	5 Lent		A
130	S. btwn. Aug. 7 and 13*	Pr. 14	B
130	S. btwn. June 26 and July 2*	Pr. 8	B
130	S. btwn. June 5 and 11	Pr. 5	B
130	Vigil of Pentecost		A, B, C
131	8 Epiphany		A
131	S. btwn. May 24 and 28	Pr. 3	A
132:1–12 [13–18]	Christ the King*		B
133	2 Easter		B
133	S. btwn. Aug. 14 and 20*	Pr. 15	A
133	S. btwn. June 19 and 25*	Pr. 7	B
136:1–4, 23–26	St. Thomas		A, B, C
136:1–9, 23–26	Vigil of Easter		A, B, C
137	S. btwn. Oct. 2 and 8*	Pr. 22	C

138	5 Epiphany		C
138	S. btwn. Aug. 21 and 27	Pr. 16	A
138	S. btwn. July 24 and 30	Pr. 12	C
138	S. btwn. June 5 and 11*	Pr. 5	B
139:1–6, 13–18	S. btwn. Sept. 4 and 10*	Pr. 18	C
139:1–6, 13–18	2 Epiphany		B
139:1–6, 13–18	S. btwn. May 29 and June 4*	Pr. 4	B
139:1–12, 23–24	S. btwn. July 17 and 23*	Pr. 11	A
141	Nativity of St. John the Baptist		A, B, C
143	Vigil of Easter		A, B, C
145:1–5, 17–21	S. btwn. Nov. 6 and 12*	Pr. 27	C
145:1–8	S. btwn. Sept. 18 and 24	Pr. 20	A
145:8–14	S. btwn. July 3 and 9	Pr. 9	A
145:8–9, 14–21	S. btwn. July 31 and Aug. 6	Pr. 13	A
145:10–18	S. btwn. July 24 and 30	Pr. 12	B
146	S. btwn. June 5 and 11*	Pr. 5	C
146	S. btwn. Nov. 6 and 12	Pr. 27	B
146	S. btwn. Oct. 30 and Nov. 5*	Pr. 26	B
146	S. btwn. Sept. 25 and Oct. 1	Pr. 21	C
146	S. btwn. Sept. 4 and 10	Pr. 18	B
146:5–10	3 Advent		A
147:1–11, 20c	5 Epiphany		B
147:12–20	2 Christmas		A, B, C
148	1 Christmas		A, B, C
148	5 Easter		C
149	All Saints Day		C
149	S. btwn. Sept. 4 and 10*	Pr. 18	A
150	2 Easter		C

Proverbs

1:20–33	S. btwn. Sept. 11 and 17*	Pr. 19	B
8:1–4, 22–31	Holy Trinity		C
8:1–8, 19–21; 9:4b–6	Vigil of Easter		A, B, C
9:1–6	S. btwn. Aug. 14 and 20	Pr. 15	B
22:1–2, 8–9, 22–23	S. btwn. Sept. 4 and 10*	Pr. 18	B
25:6–7	S. btwn. Aug. 28 and Sept. 3	Pr. 17	C
31:10–31	S. btwn. Sept. 18 and 24*	Pr. 20	B

Ecclesiastes

1:2, 12–14; 2:18–23	S. btwn. July 31 and Aug. 6	Pr. 13	C
3:1–13	New Year's Eve		A, B, C

Song of Solomon

2:8–13	S. btwn. Aug. 28 and Sept. 3*	Pr. 17	B
2:8–13	S. btwn. July 3 and 9*	Pr. 9	A

Isaiah

1:1, 10–20	S. btwn. Aug. 7 and 13*	Pr. 14	C
1:10–18	S. btwn. Oct. 30 and Nov. 5	Pr. 26	C
2:1–5	1 Advent		A
5:1–7	S. btwn. Aug. 14 and 20*	Pr. 15	C
5:1–7	S. btwn. Oct. 2 and 8	Pr. 22	A
6:1–8	Holy Trinity		B
6:1–8 [9–13]	5 Epiphany		C
7:10–14	Annunciation of Our Lord		A, B, C
7:10–16	4 Advent		A
9:1–4	3 Epiphany		A
9:2–7	Christmas Eve (I)		A, B, C
11:1–10	2 Advent		A
12	S. btwn. Nov. 13 and 19*	Pr. 28	C
12:2–6	3 Advent		C
12:2–6	Vigil of Easter		A, B, C
25:1–9	S. btwn. Oct. 9 and 15	Pr. 23	A
25:6–9	All Saints		B

(Isaiah)

25:6–9	Easter Day		B
25:6–9	Easter Evening		A, B, C
30:18–21	St. Philip and St. James		A, B, C
35:1–10	3 Advent		A
35:4–7a	S. btwn. Sept. 4 and 10	Pr. 18	B
35:5–8	St. Luke		A, B, C
40:1–11	2 Advent		B
40:21–31	5 Epiphany		B
42:1–9	Baptism of Our Lord		A
42:1–9	Monday in Holy Week		A, B, C
42:5–12	St. Barnabas		A, B, C
43:1–7	Baptism of Our Lord		C
43:16–21	5 Lent		C
43:18–25	7 Epiphany		B
43:8–13	St. Luke		A, B, C
44:6–8	S. btwn. July 17 and 23	Pr. 11	A
45:1–7	S. btwn. Oct. 16 and 22	Pr. 24	A
49:1–7	2 Epiphany		A
49:1–7	Tuesday in Holy Week		A, B, C
49:8–16a	8 Epiphany		A
49:8–16a	S. btwn. May 24 and 28	Pr. 3	A
50:4–9a	S. btwn. Sept. 11 and 17	Pr. 19	B
50:4–9a	Sunday of the Passion		A, B, C
50:4–9a	Wednesday in Holy Week		A, B, C
51:1–6	S. btwn. Aug. 21 and 27	Pr. 16	A
52:7–10	Christmas Day (III)		A, B, C
52:7–10	St. Mark		A, B, C
52:13–53:12	Good Friday		A, B, C
53:4–12	S. btwn. Oct. 16 and 22	Pr. 24	B
55:1–5	S. btwn. July 31 and Aug. 6	Pr. 13	A
55:1–9	3 Lent		C
55:1–11	Vigil of Easter		A, B, C
55:10–13	S. btwn. July 10 and 16	Pr. 10	A
55:10–13	S. btwn. May 24 and 28	Pr. 3	C
55:10–13	8 Epiphany		C
56:1, 6–8	S. btwn. Aug. 14 and 20	Pr. 15	A
58:1–9a [9b–12]	5 Epiphany		A
58:1–12	Ash Wednesday		A, B, C
58:9b–14	S. btwn. Aug. 21 and 27	Pr. 16	C
60:1–6	Epiphany		A, B, C
61:1–4, 8–11	3 Advent		B
61:10–62:3	1 Christmas		B
61:7–11	Mary, Mother of Our Lord		A, B, C
62:1–5	2 Epiphany		C
62:6–12	Christmas Dawn (II)		A, B, C
63:7–9	1 Christmas		A
64:1–9	1 Advent		B
65:1–9	S. btwn. June 19 and 25	Pr. 7	C
65:17–25	Easter Day		C
65:17–25	S. btwn. Nov. 13 and 19*	Pr. 28	C
66:1–2	St. Matthias		A, B, C
66:10–14	S. btwn. July 3 and 9	Pr. 9	C

Jeremiah

1:4–10	4 Epiphany		C
1:4–10	S. btwn. Aug. 21 and 27*	Pr. 16	C
2:4–13	S. btwn. Aug. 28 and Sept. 3*	Pr. 17	C
4:11–12, 22–28	S. btwn. Sept. 11 and 17*	Pr. 19	C
8:18–9:1	S. btwn. Sept. 18 and 24*	Pr. 20	C
11:18–20	S. btwn. Sept. 18 and 24	Pr. 20	B
14:7–10, 19–22	S. btwn. Oct. 23 and 29	Pr. 25	C
15:15–21	S. btwn. Aug. 28 and Sept. 3	Pr. 17	A
17:5–10	6 Epiphany		C
18:1–11	S. btwn. Sept. 4 and 10*	Pr. 18	C
20:7–13	S. btwn. June 19 and 25	Pr. 7	A

3:13–17	Baptism of Our Lord		A
4:1–11	1 Lent		A
4:12–23	3 Epiphany		A
5:1–12	4 Epiphany		A
5:1–12	All Saints		A
5:13–20	5 Epiphany		A
5:21–37	6 Epiphany		A
5:38–48	7 Epiphany		A
6:1–6, 16–21	Ash Wednesday		A, B, C
6:24–34	8 Epiphany		A
6:24–34	S. btwn. May 24 and 28	Pr. 3	A
6:25–33	Thanksgiving		B
7:21–29	S. btwn. May 29 and June 4	Pr. 4	A
9:9–13	St. Matthew		A, B, C
9:9–13, 18–26	S. btwn. June 5 and 11	Pr. 5	A
9:35–10:8 [9–23]	S. btwn. June 12 and 18	Pr. 6	A
10:7–16	St. Barnabas		A, B, C
10:24–39	S. btwn. June 19 and 25	Pr. 7	A
10:40–42	S. btwn. June 26 and July 2	Pr. 8	A
11:2–11	3 Advent		A
11:16–19, 25–30	S. btwn. July 3 and 9	Pr. 9	A
13:1–9, 18–23	S. btwn. July 10 and 16	Pr. 10	A
13:24–30, 36–43	S. btwn. July 17 and 23	Pr. 11	A
13:31–33, 44–52	S. btwn. July 24 and 30	Pr. 12	A
14:13–21	S. btwn. July 31 and Aug. 6	Pr. 13	A
14:22–33	S. btwn. Aug. 7 and 13	Pr. 14	A
15:[10–20] 21–28	S. btwn. Aug. 14 and 20	Pr. 15	A
16:13–19	Confession of St. Peter		A, B, C
16:13–20	S. btwn. Aug. 21 and 27	Pr. 16	A
16:21–28	S. btwn. Aug. 28 and Sept. 3	Pr. 17	A
17:1–9	Transfiguration of Our Lord		A
18:15–20	S. btwn. Sept. 4 and 10	Pr. 18	A
18:21–35	S. btwn. Sept. 11 and 17	Pr. 19	A
20:1–16	S. btwn. Sept. 18 and 24	Pr. 20	A
21:1–11	Sunday of the Passion (palms)		A
21:23–32	S. btwn. Sept. 25 and Oct. 1	Pr. 21	A
21:33–46	S. btwn. Oct. 2 and 8	Pr. 22	A
22:1–14	S. btwn. Oct. 9 and 15	Pr. 23	A
22:15–22	S. btwn. Oct. 16 and 22	Pr. 24	A
22:34–46	S. btwn. Oct. 23 and 29	Pr. 25	A
23:1–12	S. btwn. Oct. 30 and Nov. 5	Pr. 26	A
23:34–39	St. Stephen		A, B, C
24:36–44	1 Advent		A
25:1–13	S. btwn. Nov. 6 and 12	Pr. 27	A
25:14–30	S. btwn. Nov. 13 and 19	Pr. 28	A
25:31–46	Christ the King	Pr. 29	A
25:31–46	New Year's Eve		A, B, C
26:14–27:66	Sunday of the Passion		A
27:11–54	Sunday of the Passion		A
27:57–66	Saturday in Holy Week		A, B, C
28:1–10	Easter Day		A
28:1–10	Vigil of Easter		A
28:16–20	Holy Trinity		A

Mark

1:1–8	2 Advent		B
1:1–15	St. Mark		A, B, C
1:4–11	Baptism of Our Lord		B
1:9–15	1 Lent		B
1:14–20	3 Epiphany		B
1:21–28	4 Epiphany		B
1:29–39	5 Epiphany		B
1:40–45	6 Epiphany		B
2:1–12	7 Epiphany		B
2:13–22	8 Epiphany		B

(Mark)

2:13–22	S. btwn. May 24 and 28	Pr. 3	B
2:23–3:6	S. btwn. May 29 and June 4	Pr. 4	B
3:20–35	S. btwn. June 5 and 11	Pr. 5	B
4:26–34	S. btwn. June 12 and 18	Pr. 6	B
4:35–41	S. btwn. June 19 and 25	Pr. 7	B
5:21–43	S. btwn. June 26 and July 2	Pr. 8	B
6:1–13	S. btwn. July 3 and 9	Pr. 9	B
6:14–29	S. btwn. July 10 and 16	Pr. 10	B
6:30–34, 53–56	S. btwn. July 17 and 23	Pr. 11	B
7:1–8, 14–15, 21–23	S. btwn. Aug. 28 and Sept. 3	Pr. 17	B
7:24–37	S. btwn. Sept. 4 and 10	Pr. 18	B
8:27–35	St. Peter and St. Paul		A, B, C
8:27–38	S. btwn. Sept. 11 and 17	Pr. 19	B
8:31–38	2 Lent		B
9:2–9	Transfiguration of Our Lord		B
9:30–37	S. btwn. Sept. 18 and 24	Pr. 20	B
9:38–50	S. btwn. Sept. 25 and Oct. 1	Pr. 21	B
10:2–16	S. btwn. Oct. 2 and 8	Pr. 22	B
10:17–31	S. btwn. Oct. 9 and 15	Pr. 23	B
10:35–45	S. btwn. Oct. 16 and 22	Pr. 24	B
10:35–45	St. James the Elder		A, B, C
10:46–52	S. btwn. Oct. 23 and 29	Pr. 25	B
11:1–11	Sunday of the Passion (palms)		B
12:28–34	S. btwn. Oct. 30 and Nov. 5	Pr. 26	B
12:38–44	S. btwn. Nov. 6 and 12	Pr. 27	B
13:1–8	S. btwn. Nov. 13 and 19	Pr. 28	B
13:24–37	1 Advent		B
14:1–15:47	Sunday of the Passion		B
15:1–39 [40–47]	Sunday of the Passion		B
16:1–8	Easter Day		B
16:1–8	Vigil of Easter		B

Luke

1:1–4; 24:44–53	St. Luke		A, B, C
1:26–38	4 Advent		B
1:26–38	Annunciation of Our Lord		A, B, C
1:39–45 [46–55]	4 Advent		C
1:39–57	Visitation		A, B, C
1:46–55	Mary, Mother of Our Lord		A, B, C
1:47–55	3 Advent		A, B
1:47–55	4 Advent		B, C
1:57–67 [68–80]	Nativity of St. John the Baptist		A, B, C
1:68–79	2 Advent		C
1:68–79	Christ the King*	Pr. 29	C
2:[1–7] 8–20	Christmas Dawn (II)		A, B, C
2:1–14 [15–20]	Christmas Eve (I)		A, B, C
2:15–21	Name of Jesus		A, B, C
2:22–40	1 Christmas		B
2:22–40	Presentation of Our Lord		A, B, C
2:41–52	1 Christmas		C
3:1–6	2 Advent		C
3:7–18	3 Advent		C
3:15–17, 21–22	Baptism of Our Lord		C
4:1–13	1 Lent		C
4:14–21	3 Epiphany		C
4:21–30	4 Epiphany		C
5:1–11	5 Epiphany		C
6:12–16	St. Matthias		A, B, C
6:17–26	6 Epiphany		C
6:20–31	All Saints Day		C
6:27–38	7 Epiphany		C
6:39–49	8 Epiphany		C
6:39–49	S. btwn. May 24 and 28	Pr. 3	C
7:1–10	S. btwn. May 29 and June 4	Pr. 4	C

(John)

7:37–39	Day of Pentecost		A
7:37–39	Vigil of Pentecost		A, B, C
8:31–36	Reformation		A, B, C
9:1–41	4 Lent		A
10:1–10	4 Easter		A
10:11–18	4 Easter		B
10:22–30	4 Easter		C
11:1–45	5 Lent		A
11:32–44	All Saints		B
12:1–8	5 Lent		C
12:1–11	Monday in Holy Week		A, B, C
12:12–16	Sunday of the Passion (palms)		B
12:20–33	5 Lent		B
12:20–36	Tuesday in Holy Week		A, B, C
13:1–17, 31b–35	Maundy Thursday		A, B, C
13:21–32	Wednesday in Holy Week		A, B, C
13:31–35	5 Easter		C
14:1–7	St. Thomas		A, B, C
14:1–14	5 Easter		A
14:8–14	St. Philip and St. James		A, B, C
14:8–17 [25–27]	Day of Pentecost		C
14:15–21	6 Easter		A
14:21–27	St. Simon and St. Jude		A, B, C
14:23–29	6 Easter		C
15:1–8	5 Easter		B
15:9–17	6 Easter		B
15:26–27; 16:4b–15	Day of Pentecost		B
16:12–15	Holy Trinity		C
17:1–11	7 Easter		A
17:6–19	7 Easter		B
17:20–26	7 Easter		C
18:1–19:42	Good Friday		A, B, C
18:33–37	Christ the King	Pr. 29	B
19:38–42	Saturday in Holy Week		A, B, C
20:1–2, 11–18	St. Mary Magdalene		A, B, C
20:1–18	Easter Day		A, B, C
20:19–23	Day of Pentecost		A
20:19–31	2 Easter		A, B, C
21:1–19	3 Easter		C
21:20–25	St. John		A, B, C

Acts

1:1–11	Ascension of Our Lord	A, B, C
1:6–14	7 Easter	A
1:15–17, 21–26	7 Easter	B
1:15–26	St. Matthias	A, B, C
2:1–11	Vigil of Pentecost	A, B, C
2:1–21	Day of Pentecost	A, B, C
2:14a, 22–32	2 Easter	A
2:14a, 36–41	3 Easter	A
2:42–47	4 Easter	A
3:12–19	3 Easter	B
4:5–12	4 Easter	B
4:8–13	Confession of St. Peter	A, B, C
4:32–35	2 Easter	B
5:27–32	2 Easter	C
6:8–7:2a, 51–60	St. Stephen	A, B, C
7:55–60	5 Easter	A
8:14–17	Baptism of Our Lord	C
8:26–40	5 Easter	B
9:1–6 [7–20]	3 Easter	C
9:1–22	Conversion of St. Paul	A, B, C
9:36–43	4 Easter	C
10:34–43	Baptism of Our Lord	A
10:34–43	Easter Day	A, B, C

(1 Corinthians)

9:24–27	6 Epiphany		B
10:1–5	Confession of St. Peter		A, B, C
10:1–13	3 Lent		C
11:23–26	Maundy Thursday		A, B, C
12:1–11	2 Epiphany		C
12:3b–13	Day of Pentecost		A
12:12–31a	3 Epiphany		C
12:27–31a	St. Bartholomew		A, B, C
13:1–13	4 Epiphany		C
15:1–11	5 Epiphany		C
15:1–11	Easter Day		B
15:12–20	6 Epiphany		C
15:19–26	Easter Day		C
15:35–38, 42–50	7 Epiphany		C
15:51–58	8 Epiphany		C
15:51–58	S. btwn. May 24 and 28	Pr. 3	C

2 Corinthians

1:18–22	7 Epiphany		B
3:1–6	8 Epiphany		B
3:1–6	S. btwn. May 24 and 28	Pr. 3	B
3:12–4:2	Transfiguration of Our Lord		C
4:1–6	St. Philip and St. James		A, B, C
4:3–6	Transfiguration of Our Lord		B
4:5–12	S. btwn. May 29 and June 4	Pr. 4	B
4:13–5:1	S. btwn. June 5 and 11	Pr. 5	B
5:6–10 [11–13] 14–17	S. btwn. June 12 and 18	Pr. 6	B
5:16–21	4 Lent		C
5:20b–6:10	Ash Wednesday		A, B, C
6:1–13	S. btwn. June 19 and 25	Pr. 7	B
8:7–15	S. btwn. June 26 and July 2	Pr. 8	B
9:6–15	Thanksgiving		A
12:2–10	S. btwn. July 3 and 9	Pr. 9	B
13:11–13	Holy Trinity		A

Galatians

1:1–12	S. btwn. May 29 and June 4	Pr. 4	C
1:11–24	Conversion of St. Paul		A, B, C
1:11–24	S. btwn. June 5 and 11	Pr. 5	C
2:15–21	S. btwn. June 12 and 18	Pr. 6	C
3:23–29	S. btwn. June 19 and 25	Pr. 7	C
4:4–7	1 Christmas		B
4:4–7	Mary, Mother of Our Lord		A, B, C
4:4–7	Name of Jesus		A, B, C
5:1, 13–25	S. btwn. June 26 and July 2	Pr. 8	C
6:[1–6] 7–16	S. btwn. July 3 and 9	Pr. 9	C

Ephesians

1:3–14	2 Christmas		A, B, C
1:3–14	S. btwn. July 10 and 16	Pr. 10	B
1:11–23	All Saints Day		C
1:15–23	Ascension of Our Lord		A, B, C
1:15–23	Christ the King	Pr. 29	A
2:1–10	4 Lent		B
2:4–10	St. Matthew		A, B, C
2:11–22	S. btwn. July 17 and 23	Pr. 11	B
3:1–12	Epiphany of Our Lord		A, B, C
3:14–21	S. btwn. July 24 and 30	Pr. 12	B
4:1–16	S. btwn. July 31 and Aug. 6	Pr. 13	B
4:11–16	St. Thomas		A, B, C
4:25–5:2	S. btwn. Aug. 7 and 13	Pr. 14	B
5:8–14	4 Lent		A
5:15–20	S. btwn. Aug. 14 and 20	Pr. 15	B
6:10–20	S. btwn. Aug. 21 and 27	Pr. 16	B

Philippians

1:3–11	2 Advent		C
1:21–30	S. btwn. Sept. 18 and 24	Pr. 20	A
2:1–13	S. btwn. Sept. 25 and Oct. 1	Pr. 21	A
2:5–11	Name of Jesus		A, B, C
2:5–11	Sunday of the Passion		A, B, C
3:4b–14	5 Lent		C
3:4b–14	S. btwn. Oct. 2 and 8	Pr. 22	A
3:17–4:1	2 Lent		C
4:1–9	S. btwn. Oct. 9 and 15	Pr. 23	A
4:4–7	3 Advent		C
4:4–9	Thanksgiving		C

Colossians

1:1–14	S. btwn. July 10 and 16	Pr. 10	C
1:11–20	Christ the King	Pr. 29	C
1:15–28	S. btwn. July 17 and 23	Pr. 11	C
2:6–15 [16–19]	S. btwn. July 24 and 30	Pr. 12	C
3:1–4	Easter Day		A
3:1–11	S. btwn. July 31 and Aug. 6	Pr. 13	C
3:12–17	1 Christmas		C

1 Thessalonians

1:1–10	S. btwn. Oct. 16 and 22	Pr. 24	A
2:1–8	S. btwn. Oct. 23 and 29	Pr. 25	A
2:9–13	S. btwn. Oct. 30 and Nov. 5	Pr. 26	A
3:9–13	1 Advent		C
4:13–18	S. btwn. Nov. 6 and 12	Pr. 27	A
5:1–11	S. btwn. Nov. 13 and 19	Pr. 28	A
5:16–24	3 Advent		B

2 Thessalonians

1:1–4, 11–12	S. btwn. Oct. 30 and Nov. 5	Pr. 26	C
2:1–5, 13–17	S. btwn. Nov. 6 and 12	Pr. 27	C
3:6–13	S. btwn. Nov. 13 and 19	Pr. 28	C

1 Timothy

1:12–17	S. btwn. Sept. 11 and 17	Pr. 19	C
2:1–7	S. btwn. Sept. 18 and 24	Pr. 20	C
2:1–7	Thanksgiving		B
6:6–19	S. btwn. Sept. 25 and Oct. 1	Pr. 21	C

2 Timothy

1:1–14	S. btwn. Oct. 2 and 8	Pr. 22	C
2:8–15	S. btwn. Oct. 9 and 15	Pr. 23	C
3:14–4:5	S. btwn. Oct. 16 and 22	Pr. 24	C
4:5–11	St. Luke		A, B, C
4:6–11, 18	St. Mark		A, B, C
4:6–8, 16–18	S. btwn. Oct. 23 and 29	Pr. 25	C

Titus

2:11–14	Christmas Eve (I)		A, B, C
3:4–7	Christmas Dawn (II)		A, B, C

Philemon

1–21	S. btwn. Sept. 4 and 10	Pr. 18	C

Hebrews

1:1–4 [5–12]	Christmas Day (III)		A, B, C
1:1–4; 2:5–12	S. btwn. Oct. 2 and 8	Pr. 22	B
2:10–18	1 Christmas		A
2:14–18	Presentation of Our Lord		A, B, C
4:12–16	S. btwn. Oct. 9 and 15	Pr. 23	B

(Hebrews)

4:14–16; 5:7–9	Good Friday		A, B, C
5:1–10	S. btwn. Oct. 16 and 22	Pr. 24	B
5:5–10	5 Lent		B
7:23–28	S. btwn. Oct. 23 and 29	Pr. 25	B
9:11–14	S. btwn. Oct. 30 and Nov. 5	Pr. 26	B
9:11–15	Monday in Holy Week		A, B, C
9:24–28	S. btwn. Nov. 6 and 12	Pr. 27	B
10:4–10	Annunciation of Our Lord		A, B, C
10:5–10	4 Advent		C
10:11–14 [15–18] 19–25	S. btwn. Nov. 13 and 19	Pr. 28	B
10:16–25	Good Friday		A, B, C
11:1–3, 8–16	S. btwn. Aug. 7 and 13	Pr. 14	C
11:29–12:2	S. btwn. Aug. 14 and 20	Pr. 15	C
12:1–3	Wednesday in Holy Week		A, B, C
12:18–29	S. btwn. Aug. 21 and 27	Pr. 16	C
13:1–8, 15–16	S. btwn. Aug. 28 and Sept. 3	Pr. 17	C

James

1:17–27	S. btwn. Aug. 28 and Sept. 3	Pr. 17	B
2:1–10 [11–13] 14–17	S. btwn. Sept. 4 and 10	Pr. 18	B
3:1–12	S. btwn. Sept. 11 and 17	Pr. 19	B
3:13–4:3, 7–8a	S. btwn. Sept. 18 and 24	Pr. 20	B
5:7–10	3 Advent		A
5:13–20	S. btwn. Sept. 25 and Oct. 1	Pr. 21	B

1 Peter

1:3–9	2 Easter		A
1:17–23	3 Easter		A
2:2–10	5 Easter		A
2:19–25	4 Easter		A
3:13–22	6 Easter		A
3:18–22	1 Lent		B
4:1–8	Saturday in Holy Week		A, B, C
4:12–14; 5:6–11	7 Easter		A
4:12–19	Holy Innocents		A, B, C

2 Peter

1:16–21	Transfiguration of Our Lord		A
3:8–15a	2 Advent		B

1 John

1:1–2:2	St. John		A, B, C
1:1–2:2	2 Easter		B
3:1–3	All Saints		A
3:1–7	3 Easter		B
3:16–24	4 Easter		B
4:1–6	St. Simon and St. Jude		A, B, C
4:7–21	5 Easter		B
5:1–6	6 Easter		B
5:9–13	7 Easter		B

Revelation

1:4–8	2 Easter		C
1:4b–8	Christ the King	Pr. 29	B
5:11–14	3 Easter		C
7:9–17	4 Easter		C
7:9–17	All Saints		A
12:7–12	St. Michael and All Angels		A, B, C
21:1–6	5 Easter		C
21:1–6a	All Saints		B
21:1–6a	New Year's Eve		A, B, C
21:10, 22–22:5	6 Easter		C
22:12–14, 16–17, 20–21	7 Easter		C

SCRIPTURAL INDEX OF HYMNS AND SONGS

Genesis

1–2	All things bright and beautiful	.767
	Creating God, your fingers trace	.757
	Many and great, O God, are your works	.794
	Oh, sing to God above	.726
1–3	Shout for joy loud and long	.793
	When long before time	.799
1:1	We all believe in one true God	.374
1:1–2	O Holy Spirit, root of life	.688
1:1–3	At the name of Jesus	.179
	Father eternal, ruler of creation	.413
	God, whose almighty word	.400
1:1–4	God, who made the earth and heaven	.281
1:1–5	God, who stretched the spangled heavens	.463
1:2	Creator Spirit, by whose aid	.164
	Eternal Father, strong to save	.467
	Holy Spirit, ever dwelling	.523
	Lord God, the Holy Ghost	.162
1:3	Let us with a gladsome mind	.521
	Thy strong Word	.233
1:3–5	Maker of the earth and heaven	.266
	Praise the Spirit in creation	.682
	Spirit, Spirit of gentleness	.684
1:26–31	Come away to the skies	.669
	God, who stretched the spangled heavens	.463
2:18–24	As man and woman we were made	.751
	When love is found	.749
3:1–15	Welcome, happy morning!	.153
3:8	In Adam we have all been one	.372
3:15	Praise the Savior, now and ever	.155
3:17–19	From shepherding of stars	.63
	Joy to the world	.39
3:19	Jesus Christ, my sure defense	.340
3:24	Let all together praise our God	.47
	Your Word, O Lord, is gentle dew	.232
4:1–16	In Adam we have all been one	.372
	Glory be to Jesus	.95
5:22–24	Chief of sinners though I be	.306
	God of our life, all–glorious Lord	.270
6–8	Thy holy wings	.741
8:22	Evening and morning	.465
	We plow the fields and scatter	.362
11:9	Father eternal, ruler of creation	.413
	It came upon the midnight clear	.54
12:1–8	I want Jesus to walk with me	.660
	The God of Abraham praise	.544
18:27	Lord, teach us how to pray aright	.438
22:16	The God of Abraham praise	.544
28:10–17	Blessed assurance	.699
28:16–18	How blessed is this place, O Lord	.186
	Only-begotten, Word of God eternal	.375
28:20–22	O God of Jacob	.477

Exodus

3:6, 14	The God of Abraham praise	.544
8:1	When Israel was in Egypt's land	.670
9:9–13	Oh, come, oh, come, Emmanuel	.34
12:1–13	Christ Jesus lay in death's strong bands	.134
12:22–27	At the Lamb's high feast we sing	.210
	The day of resurrection!	.141
13–15	When Israel was in Egypt's land	.670

13:21–22	By gracious powers	.736
	Glories of your name are spoken	.358
	Guide me ever, great Redeemer	.343
	Let all things now living	.557
14:22	At the Lamb's high feast we sing	.210
15:1–18	I will sing to the Lord	.19
15:1–21	Come, you faithful, raise the strain	.132
15:20–21	For all the faithful women	.692
	Glory to God, glory in the highest	.788
16	O Bread of life from heaven	.222
16:35	Glories of your name are spoken	.358
17:6	Glories of your name are spoken	.358
17:12	Hark, the voice of Jesus calling	.381
19:4	Sing praise to God, the highest good	.542
	The God of Abraham praise	.544
23:16–19	As saints of old	.404
23:19	We give thee but thine own	.410
25:17	My God, how wonderful thou art	.524
33:20	Holy, holy, holy	.165
34:22–26	As saints of old	.404

Numbers

6:24–26	Christians, while on earth abiding	.440
	Holy Majesty, before you	.247
	Lord, dismiss us with your blessing	.259
6:25	On Jordan's banks the Baptist's cry	.36
	Oh, sing, my soul, your maker's praise	.319
9:13–16	O Love that will not let me go	.324
10:2–10	O day of rest and gladness	.251
13:30–33	All who would valiant be	.498
24:17	O Morning Star, how fair and bright!	.76

Deuteronomy

4:29	O Christ, our king, creator, Lord	.101
5:15	He leadeth me: oh, blessed thought!	.501
6:5	My God, how wonderful thou art	.524
6:7	Christians, while on earth abiding	.440
6:8	I bind unto myself today	.188
8:7–10	Praise and thanksgiving	.409
9:8–21	The glory of these forty days	.657
9:26	Lord, take my hand and lead me	.333
21:23	Christ Jesus lay in death's strong bands	.134
30:15–20	Oh, that the Lord would guide my ways	.480
32:2	Your Word, O Lord, is gentle dew	.232
32:4	Whatever God ordains is right	.446
32:11–12	O Holy Spirit, root of life	.688
33:12	What a fellowship, what a joy divine	.780
33:26	God moves in a mysterious way	.483

Joshua

1:9	God of grace and God of glory	.415
3:13–14	Guide me ever, great Redeemer	.343
	He leadeth me: oh, blessed thought!	.501
3:14–17	Thine is the glory	.145
6:14	Do not despair, O little flock	.361
24:15	O Jesus, I have promised	.503
	Oh, blest the house	.512

Judges

17	All who would valiant be	.498

(Lamentations)

3:19	Go to dark Gethsemane	.109
3:22–23	God, who has called you to glory	.12
	When all your mercies, O my God	.264
3:22–24	Great is thy faithfulness	.771
	If you but trust in God to guide you	.453

Ezekiel

1:22–26	Ride on, ride on in majesty!	.121
2:1–6	Lord of all nations, grant me grace	.419
21:9–10	Battle Hymn of the Republic	.332
33:6	Awake, O Spirit of the watchmen	.382
34	Savior, like a shepherd lead us	.481
34	The Lord's my shepherd	.451
34	With God as our friend	.371
34:11–16	Look from your sphere of endless day	.402
34:14	Jerusalem the golden	.347
34:16	O Christ, our light, O Radiance true	.380
36:26	God, my Lord, my strength	.484
	Lord of glory, you have bought us	.424
	O Spirit of the living God	.388
37	Veni Sancte Spiritus	.686
	The Word of God is source and seed	.658
47:1–12	Shall we gather at the river	.690

Daniel

1	The glory of these forty days	.657
2:35	The day you gave us, Lord, has ended	.274
4:13	Ye watchers and ye holy ones	.175
6	The glory of these forty days	.657
7:3	Immortal, invisible, God only wise	.526
7:9–10	Who is this host arrayed in white	.314
7:13	Come, thou almighty King	.522
	The God of Abraham praise	.544
7:13–14	Lo! He comes with clouds descending	.27

Hosea

14:5–7	Your Word, O Lord, is gentle dew	.232

Joel

2:28–29	Lord God, the Holy Ghost	.162
	Spirit, Spirit of gentleness	.684
3:18	Shall we gather at the river	.690

Amos

5:24	Let justice flow like streams	.763
7:7–9	Let justice flow like streams	.763

Micah

4:1–4	O day of peace	.762
4:3	God of grace and God of glory	.415
	O God of every nation	.416
5:2	O little town of Bethlehem	.41
	Once in royal David's city	.643
6:8	Now we join in celebration	.203

Habbakuk

2:2–4	Climb to the top of the highest mountain	.7
2:20	God himself is present	.249
	Let all mortal flesh keep silence	.198
	Now the silence	.205

Zephaniah

3:14–20	Jesus, still lead on	.341

Zechariah

4:6	Not alone for mighty empire	.437
9:9	The advent of our God	.22
	Ride on, ride on in majesty!	.121
12:10	Lo! He comes with clouds descending	.27
13:1	Come to Calvary's holy mountain	.301
14:6–7	Your kingdom come, O Father	.384

Malachi

3:1–3	Judge eternal, throned in splendor	.418
4:1	Judge eternal, throned in splendor	.418
4:2	As the sun with longer journey	.655
	Christ, whose glory fills the skies	.265
	From God the Father, virgin-born	.83
	God, whose almighty word	.400
	Hark! The herald angels sing	.60
	O Lord, how shall I meet you	.23
	O one with God the Father	.77
	O Savior, rend the heavens wide	.38
	O Sun of justice	.659
	Praise the Savior, now and ever	.155

Song of the Three Young Men

35–65	All you works of the Lord	.18

Matthew

1:18–25	All earth is hopeful	.629
	I wonder as I wander	.642
	Peace came to earth	.641
1:21–23	Of the Father's love begotten	.42
	Savior of the nations, come	.28
2:1–12	As with gladness men of old	.82
	Bright and glorious is the sky	.75
	Brightest and best of the stars	.84
	He whom shepherds once came praising	.68
	I am so glad each Christmas Eve	.69
	I wonder as I wander	.642
	O chief of cities, Bethlehem	.81
	The first Noel	.56
	There's a star in the East	.645
	We three kings of Orient are	.646
	When Christ's appearing was made known	.85
2:1–3	Songs of thankfulness and praise	.90
	Angels, from the realms of glory	.50
2:9	Your Word, O Lord, is gentle dew	.232
2:11	Angels we have heard on high	.71
	Once again my heart rejoices	.46
	What child is this	.40
2:13–23	Oh, sleep now, holy baby	.639
	By all your saints in warfare	.177:9
3:1–6	By all your saints in warfare	.178:15
	On Jordan's banks the Baptist's cry	.36
3:1–12	All earth is hopeful	.629
3:3	Comfort, comfort now my people	.29
	Prepare the royal highway	.26
3:9	A stable lamp is lighted	.74
3:13–17	Songs of thankfulness and praise	.90
	Spirit of God, descend upon my heart	.486
	To Jordan came the Christ, our Lord	.79
	When Christ's appearing was made known	.85
	When Jesus came to Jordan	.647
3:16–17	Eternal Ruler of the ceaseless round	.373
4:1–11	O Lord, throughout these forty days	.99
	Savior, when in dust to you	.91
	Songs of thankfulness and praise	.90

1 Peter

2 Peter

1 John

3 John

Revelation

PSALM PARAPHRASES

TOPICAL INDEX OF HYMNS AND SONGS

Adoration
See Praise, Adoration; Worship

Advent, 22–38, 625–635
Blessed be the God of Israel 725
He comes to us as one unknown 768
Herald, sound the note of judgment 556
I want to walk as a child of the light 649
Lord Christ, when first you came to earth 421
Lost in the night 394
My soul now magnifies the Lord 180
My soul proclaims your greatness 730
O day of peace 762
O Lord of light, who made the stars 323
Once he came in blessing 312
Rise, my soul, to watch and pray 443
Soon and very soon 744
The clouds of judgment gather 322
The day is surely drawing near 321

Affirmation of Baptism
Come away to the skies 669
"Come, follow me," the Savior spake 455
Come, gracious Spirit, heavenly dove 475
Come, oh, come, O quickening Spirit 478
Eternal God, before your throne 354
Go, my children, with my blessing 721
Lord, take my hand and lead me 333
Mothering God, you gave me birth 769
O Jesus, I have promised 503
Spirit of God, unleashed on earth 387
See Commitment; Holy Baptism; Pentecost, The Holy Spirit

Affliction
See Comfort and Rest; Sorrow, Suffering

All Saints' Day
Blest are they 764
Come, we that love the Lord 742
Eat this bread, drink this cup 706
For all the saints 174
For all your saints, O Lord 176
Oh, what their joy 337
Rejoice in God's saints .689
Shall we gather at the river 690
Sing with all the saints in glory 691
Who is this host arrayed in white 314
Ye watchers and ye holy ones 175
See Saints' Days

Angels
God himself is present .249
Holy God, we praise your name 535
The angel Gabriel from heaven came 632
Ye watchers and ye holy ones 175

You who dwell in the shelter of the Lord 779
See Christmas

Anniversary, Church
Built on a rock 365
Christ is made the sure foundation 367, 747
Christians, while on earth abiding 440
God is here! 719
Lord, you give the great commission 756
Now thank we all our God 533, 534
O God, our help in ages past 320
Only-begotten, Word of God eternal 375
The Church's one foundation 369

Annunciation of Our Lord, The
From east to west 64
My soul now magnifies the Lord 180
My soul proclaims your greatness 730
Of the Father's love begotten 42
Sing of Mary, pure and lowly 634
The angel Gabriel from heaven came 632
The only Son from heaven 86

Arts and Music
Come to us, creative Spirit 758
Earth and all stars! 558
Let all things now living 557
My life flows on in endless song 781
O God beyond all praising 797
O Morning Star, how fair and bright! 76
Oh, that I had a thousand voices 560
Sing praise to the Lord .10
When in our music God is glorified 555, 802
When long before time 799
See Creation, Preservation; Praise, Adoration; Celebration, Jubilation

Ascension, 156–159
Alleluia! Jesus is risen! 674
And have the bright immensities 391
At the name of Jesus 179
Christ is alive! Let Christians sing 363
Come away to the skies 669
Glory to God, we give you thanks 787
Hail thee, festival day! .142
Lord, you give the great commission 756
O Christ, our hope 300
O God of God, O Light of light 536
See Christ the King

Ash Wednesday
Create in me a clean heart 732
Just as I am, without one plea 296
O Sun of justice 659
Out of the depths I cry to you 295
Restore in us, O God 662
See Lent; Forgiveness, Healing; Sorrow, Suffering

Aspiration

Assurance

Atonement

Baptism, Christian

Baptism of Our Lord, The

Beginning of Service, 241–257

Benevolence

Bible

Burial

Celebration, Jubilation, 552–565

Children, Songs for

Alleluia Canon 677
Angels we have heard on high 71
Away in a manger .67, 644
Baptized into your name most holy 192
Children of the heavenly Father 474
Christ the Lord is risen today; Alleluia! 128
Come, let us eat 214
Cradling children in his arm 193
Dona nobis pacem 774
Earth and all stars! 558
For the beauty of the earth 561
Glory to God, glory in the highest 788
Go, my children, with my blessing 721
Hallelujah! We sing your praises 722
Have no fear, little flock 476
I want Jesus to walk with me 660
I want to walk as a child of the light 649
I'm so glad Jesus lifted me 673
In a lowly manger born .417
Jesu, Jesu, fill us with your love 765
Jesus, remember me 740
Let us break bread together 212
Let us talents and tongues employ 754
Lift high the cross 377
Light one candle to watch for Messiah 630
Lord of all hopefulness .469
Lord, take my hand and lead me 333
Now thank we all our God 533, 534
Oh, come, all ye faithful .45
Oh, come, oh, come, Emmanuel 34
Oh, sing to the Lord 795
Oh, sleep now, holy baby 639
Once in royal David's city 643
Our Father, by whose name 357
Praise God. Praise him .529
Prepare the royal highway 26
Rejoice, O pilgrim throng 553
Savior, like a shepherd lead us 481
Shall we gather at the river 690
Seek ye first the kingdom of God 783
Shalom 727
Soon and very soon 744
There is a green hill far away 114
Thy holy wings 741
'Twas in the moon of wintertime 72
We are marching in the light of God 650
Were you there 92
When Israel was in Egypt's land 670
You have put on Christ .694
Your little ones, dear Lord 52

Christ the King, 170–173
All hail the power of Jesus' name! 328, 329
At the name of Jesus 179
Christ is alive! Let Christians sing 363
Christ is the king! 386
Jesus shall reign 530
Jesus, remember me 740
Lift up your heads, O gates 631
O Christ the same 778
O God of God, O Light of light 536
O Jesus, king most wonderful! 537
Soon and very soon 744

The King shall come 33
Thine the amen, thine the praise 801
See Ascension

Christmas, 39–74, 636–645
Glory to God, glory in the highest 788
Glory to God, we give you thanks 787
In a lowly manger born .417
Sing of Mary, pure and lowly 634
The only Son from heaven 86
What feast of love 701
When long before time .799

Church
God is here! 719
Here in this place 718
Lord, who the night you were betrayed 206
Lord, you give the great commission 756
O God, send heralds 283
The Church of Christ, in every age 433
See Community in Christ; Kingdom of God

Church Building
Christ is made the sure foundation 367, 747
How blessed is this place 186
Only-begotten, Word of God eternal 375
See Cornerstone

Church Triumphant
A mighty fortress is our God 228, 229
Come, we that love the Lord 742
Have no fear, little flock 476
Lift high the cross 377
Lo! He comes with clouds descending 27
Rise, O children of salvation 182
The Church's one foundation 369
We are marching in the light of God 650
See Hope

City
All who love and serve your city 436
Come, we that love the Lord 742
O Jesus Christ, may grateful hymns be rising . . .427
Where cross the crowded ways of life 429
Where restless crowds are thronging 430
See Society

Close of Service, 258–263
Almighty God, your Word is cast 234
Come with us, O blessed Jesus 219
How blest are they who hear God's Word 227
I leave, as you have promised, Lord 349
Lord, dismiss us with your blessing 259
Now thank we all our God 533, 534
O Lord, now let your servant 339
O Savior, precious Savior 514
Only-begotten, Word of God eternal 375
Peace, to soothe our bitter woes 338
Praise and thanks and adoration 470

Praise the Lord, rise up rejoicing 196
Sent forth by God's blessing 221
Sing praise to God, the highest good 542
See Sending

Comfort and Rest

Abide with me 272
Children of the heavenly Father 474
Christ, mighty Savior 729
Day by day 746
God moves in a mysterious way 483
Healer of our every ill 738
Hope of the world 493
How sweet the name of Jesus sounds 345
I, the Lord of sea and sky 752
If God himself be for me 454
If you but trust in God to guide you 453
In the hour of trial 106
Jesus, priceless treasure 457, 458
Loving Spirit 683
O Christ the same 778
O God, my faithful God 504
Peace, to soothe our bitter woes 338
Precious Lord, take my hand 731
The King of love my shepherd is 456
The Lord's my shepherd 451
There in God's garden 668
There is a balm in Gilead 737
Thy holy wings 741
Whatever God ordains is right 446
When in the hour of deepest need 303
When peace, like a river 346
Who trusts in God, a strong abode 450
You who dwell in the shelter of the Lord 779
See Assurance; Sorrow, Suffering; Trust, Guidance

Commemorations and Occasions
See specific days for additional listings

Saints
For all the faithful women 692
For all your saints, O Lord 176
Oh, happy day when we shall stand 351

Martyrs
Jerusalem the golden 347
Oh, what their joy 337
Sing with all the saints in glory 691

Missionaries
Lift high the cross 377
Lord, you give the great commission 756
O Zion, haste 397

Renewers of the Church
Lord, whose love in humble service 423
Rejoice in God's saints 689
Rise, shine, you people! 393

Renewers of Society
Christ is alive! Let Christians sing 363
Great God, your love has called us 666
Lord of all nations, grant me grace 419

Pastors and Bishops
Bow down your ear, almighty Lord 286
Hope of the world 493
Lord, you give the great commission 756

Theologians
Be thou my vision 776
God has spoken by his prophets 238
O Holy Spirit, enter in 459

Artists and Scientists
Come to us, creative Spirit 758
Creating God, your fingers trace 757
God, who stretched the spangled heavens 463
When in our music God is glorified 555, 802

Unity
Blest be the tie that binds 370
In Christ there is no east or west 359
Oh, praise the gracious power 750

Dedication, Anniversary
How blessed is this place, O Lord 186
I love your kingdom, Lord 468
God is here! 719

Harvest
See Harvest

Day of Penitence
See Forgiveness, Healing; Sorrow, Suffering

National Holiday
See National Songs; Society

Peace
See Peace

Day of Thanksgiving
See Thanksgiving

Stewardship of Creation
See Creation, Preservation; Harvest; Stewardship

New Year's Eve
See New Year

Commissioning, Lay Ministry
See Commitment; Ministry; Service

Commitment, 486–513, 783–785
Arise, your light has come! 652
Be thou my vision 776
Children of the heavenly Father 474
Fight the good fight 461
God is here! 719
Gracious Spirit, heed our pleading 687
I lay my sins on Jesus 305
I, the Lord of sea and sky 752
In the hour of trial 106

Jesus, thy boundless love to me 336
Lord, let my heart be good soil 713
Lord, speak to us, that we may speak 403
Lord, you give the great commission 756
May we your precepts, Lord, fulfill 353
O Lord, now let your servant 339
O Love that will not let me go 324
Rise up, O saints of God! 383
Rise, my soul, to watch and pray 443
Spirit, Spirit of gentleness 684
Take my life, that I may be 406
"Take up your cross," the Savior said 398
We all are one in mission 755
With the Lord begin your task 444

Communion of Saints
See Community in Christ; Hope; Heaven, Eternal Life

Community in Christ, 353–375, 747–751
A mighty fortress is our God 228, 229
As the grains of wheat .705
Father, we thank you 704
For all the faithful women 692
God is here! 719
God! When human bonds are broken 735
God, my Lord, my strength 484
Grains of wheat 708
Here in this place 718
Jesu, Jesu, fill us with your love 765
Let justice flow like streams 763
Let us talents and tongues employ 754
Like the murmur of the dove's song 685
Lord, receive this company 255
My soul, now praise your maker! 519
Now we offer 761
O God of Jacob 477
O God, O Lord of heaven and earth 396
Oh, blest the house 512
Oh, sing, my soul, your maker's praise 319
One bread, one body 710
Shalom 724
Spirit of God, sent from heaven abroad 285
We all are one in mission 755
Where charity and love prevail 126
See Kingdom of God

Confession of Sin
See Forgiveness, Healing

Confirmation
See Affirmation of Baptism; Commitment; Pentecost, The Holy Spirit

Consecration
God is here! 719
Take my life, that I may be 406
See Commitment

Cornerstone
Great God, a blessing from your throne 185
See Church Building

Creation, Preservation, 767–771
All creatures of our God and King 527
Creating God, your fingers trace 757
Eternal Ruler of the ceaseless round 373
For the beauty of the earth 561
For the fruit of all creation 563, 760
God, who stretched the spangled heavens 463
Great God, our source .466
How marvelous God's greatness 515
Joyful, joyful we adore thee 551
Let all things now living 557
Let the whole creation cry 242
Many and great, O God, are your works 794
Oh, sing to God above .726
Oh, worship the King 548
Praise the Lord of heaven! 541
Praise the Spirit in creation 682
Shout for joy loud and long 793
Sing to the Lord of harvest 412
Spirit, Spirit of gentleness 684
This is my Father's world 554
We plow the fields and scatter 362
When long before time .799

Cross-bearing
Beneath the cross of Jesus 107
In the cross of Christ I glory 104
Jesus, I will ponder now 115
Let us ever walk with Jesus 487
O God, my faithful God 504
"Take up your cross," the Savior said 398
Weary of all trumpeting 785
See Commitment

Deaconesses, Deacons, Diaconal Ministers
Great God, your love has called us 666
Jesu, Jesu, fill us with your love 765
Lord, whose love in humble service 423
See Commitment; Ministry; Pastors; Service

Death
Even as we live each day 350
God loved the world 292
Guide me ever, great Redeemer 343
He leadeth me: oh, blessed thought! 501
I know of a sleep in Jesus' name 342
I want to walk as a child of the light 649
In the morning when I rise 777
Jesus Christ, my sure defense 340
Jesus lives! The victory's won! 133
Kyrie, God Father 168
My faith looks up to thee 479
O God, whose will is life and good 435
O Lord, now let your servant 339
O sacred head, now wounded 116, 117
Precious Lord, take my hand 731

The King of love my shepherd is 456
The Lord's my shepherd 451
This joyful Eastertide 676
We are the Lord's 399
You who dwell in the shelter of the Lord 779
See Burial; Heaven, Eternal Life; Hope

Dedication of a Church
Built on a rock 365
Christ is made the sure foundation 367, 747
Glories of your name are spoken 358
God is here! 719
How blessed is this place, O Lord 186
I love your kingdom, Lord 368
Only-begotten, Word of God eternal 375
Open now thy gates of beauty 250

Discipleship
See Witness; Commitment; Ministry; Service

Earth
See Creation, Preservation

Easter, 128–155, 671–679
Alabaré 791
Alleluia! Sing to Jesus .158
At the Lamb's high feast we sing 210
Baptized in water 693
Christ is alive! Let Christians sing 363
Come away to the skies 669
Come, risen Lord 209
For all the faithful women 692
Hosanna to the living Lord! 258
I know that my Redeemer lives! 352
Jesus Christ, my sure defense 340
Now the feast and celebration 789
O blessed spring 695
O Christ, our hope 300
Shout for joy loud and long 793
Sing with all the saints in glory 691
Stay with us 743
Thine the amen, thine the praise 801
We know that Christ is raised 189
We were baptized in Christ Jesus 698
We who once were dead 207

Easter, Vigil of
Baptized in water 693
Christ is risen! Alleluia! 131
Come away to the skies 669
Come, you faithful, raise the strain 132
Let all things now living 557
Rejoice, angelic choirs, rejoice! 146
Shout for joy loud and long 793
The day of resurrection! 141
The strife is o'er, the battle done 135
We know that Christ is raised 189
We were baptized in Christ Jesus 698
When Israel was in Egypt's land 670
You have put on Christ .694

Education
Be thou my vision 776
Christ is made the sure foundation 367, 747
Come, Holy Ghost, our souls inspire 472, 473
Earth and all stars!! 558
Father of mercies, in your Word 240
God has spoken by his prophets 238
God's Word is our great heritage 239
Gracious Spirit, heed our pleading 687
Holy Spirit, truth divine 257
Lead on, O King eternal! 495
Listen, God is calling 712
Lord, speak to us, that we may speak 403
O God of light 237
O God of youth 510
Open your ears, O faithful people 715
You are the way 464

Entrance
See Beginning of Service; Gathering

Epiphany, 75–90, 646–654
Angels from the realms of glory 50
Be thou my vision 776
Christ, whose glory fills the skies 265
Each morning brings us 800
Holy Child within the manger 638
Now the silence 205
O Christ, you are the light and day 273
O God of God, O Light of light 536
O God of light 237
O Splendor of the Father's light 271
Oh, for a thousand tongues to sing 559
Oh, praise the gracious power 750
Rise, shine, you people! 393
We all are one in mission 755
Word of God, come down on earth 716
You have come down to the lakeshore 784

Eternal Life
See Hope; Heaven, Eternal Life

Evangelism
Hallelujah! We sing your praises 722
Herald, sound the note of judgment 556
Jesus shall reign 530
Listen, God is calling 712
Oh, for a thousand tongues to sing 559
O God of mercy, God of light 425
Shine, Jesus, shine 651
Spirit of God, sent from heaven abroad 285
The Church of Christ, in every age 433
The Spirit sends us forth to serve 723
See Witness

Evening, 272–282, 728–731
Abide with us, our Savior 263
Be thou my vision 776
Dona nobis pacem 774
Evening and morning 465

God, my Lord, my strength 484
I want to walk as a child of the light 649
Let all things now living 557
Lord, as a pilgrim 485
Lord of all hopefulness 469
Lord, take my hand and lead me 333
My soul now magnifies the Lord 180
O Christ, our king, creator, Lord 101
O Jesus, joy of loving hearts 356
O Jesus, king most wonderful!! 537
O Lord, now let your servant 339
O Sun of justice 659
Shine, Jesus, shine 651
Stay with us 743
Thy holy wings 741
When twilight comes 663

Faith

Amid the world's bleak wilderness 378
Blest are they 764
Faith of our fathers 500
God is here! 719
God moves in a mysterious way 483
God! When human bonds are broken 735
How firm a foundation .507
I heard the voice of Jesus say 497
I want Jesus to walk with me 660
Jesus Christ, my sure defense 340
My faith looks up to thee 479
O Jesus, joy of loving hearts 356
O Master, let me walk with you 492
O Spirit of life 680
Rock of Ages, cleft for me 327
This joyful Eastertide 676
We walk by faith and not by sight 675
You are the way 464
See Justification; Trust, Guidance

Family

Bind us together 748
Children of the heavenly Father 474
Christians, while on earth abiding 440
For the beauty of the earth 561
God! When human bonds are broken 735
I am so glad each Christmas Eve 69
In all our grief 739
Oh, blest the house 512
Our Father, by whose name 357
When love is found 749

Fellowship

See Community in Christ

Feminine Images for God

Around you, O Lord Jesus 496
Baptized in water 693
Jesus, Savior, pilot me .334
I was there to hear your borning cry 770
Like the murmur of the dove's song 685
Loving Spirit 683

Mothering God, you gave me birth 769
My God, how wonderful thou art 524
My soul, now praise your maker! 519
Now rest beneath night's shadow 282
O Bread of life from heaven 222
O Holy Spirit, root of life 688
O Word of God incarnate 231
Thy holy wings 741
Wash, O God, our sons and daughters 697
When twilight comes 663
Your heart, O God, is grieved 96

Forgiveness, Healing, 732–741

Awake, awake, and greet the new morn 633
Awake, O sleeper 745
Christians, while on earth abiding 440
Go, my children, with my blessing 721
God loved the world 292
God, whose almighty word 400
Great God, your love has called us 666
I trust, O Christ, in you alone 395
I've just come from the fountain 696
Lord, whose love in humble service 423
O Christ, the healer, we have come 360
O God, whose will is life and good 435
O Son of God, in Galilee 426
O Sun of justice 659
Out of the depths I cry to you 295
Restore in us, O God 662
The Word of God is source and seed 658
There in God's garden .668
When twilight comes 663
Word of God, come down on earth 716
Your hand, O Lord, in days of old 431
See also Repentance, Forgiveness, 303–312

Freedom

All earth is hopeful 629
Battle Hymn of the Republic 332
By the Babylonian rivers 656
God! When human bonds are broken 735
I, the Lord of sea and sky 752
Let justice flow like streams 763
Lift every voice and sing 562
Lord, you give the great commission 756
My country, 'tis of thee 566
O day of peace 762
Oh, praise the gracious power 750
Our Paschal Lamb, that sets us free 679
Praise to you, O God of mercy 790
Rise, shine, you people! 393
We are marching in the light of God 650
We come to the hungry feast 766
What wondrous love is this 385
When Israel was in Egypt's land 670
With high delight let us unite 140

Funerals

See Burial; Death; Easter; Heaven, Eternal Life;
Hope; Sorrow, Suffering

Gathering, 717–720

Christ is made the sure foundation 367, 747
Come, O Holy Spirit, come 681
Draw us in the Spirit's tether 703
Gracious Spirit, heed our pleading 687
Jesus, come! for we invite you 648
Lift up your heads, O gates 631
Like the murmur of the dove's song 685
O Spirit of life 680
The thirsty fields drink in the rain 714
Veni Sancte Spiritus 686
Word of God, come down on earth 716
See Beginning of Service

Good Friday

Ah, holy Jesus 123
Jesus, remember me 740
Lamb of God, pure and sinless 111
My song is love unknown 94, 661
O sacred head, now wounded 116, 117
Sing, my tongue 118
The royal banners forward go 124, 125
There in God's garden .668
Were you there 92
When I survey the wondrous cross 482
See Holy Week, The Three Days

Grace

Alas! And did my Savior bleed 98
All my hope on God is founded 782
Amazing grace, how sweet the sound 448
Come, thou Fount of every blessing 499
Creating God, your fingers trace 757
Give to our God immortal praise! 520
God is here! 719
Great God, your love has called us 666
Healer of our every ill 738
I was there to hear your borning cry 770
Mothering God, you gave me birth 769
O Jesus, joy of loving hearts 356
Our Father, we have wandered 733
Praise, my soul, the King of heaven 549
Restore in us, O God 662
Salvation unto us has come 297
There's a wideness in God's mercy 290
Thy holy wings 741
Wide open are your hands 489

Growth

Amid the world's bleak wilderness 378
As the sun with longer journey 655
For the fruit of all creation 563, 760
Go, my children, with my blessing 721
Lord, let my heart be good soil 713
Lord, your hands have formed 727
On what has now been sown 261
Our Father, by whose name 357
Sent forth by God's blessing 221
The Word of God is source and seed 658
We know that Christ is raised 189
We plow the fields and scatter 362

When seed falls on good soil 236
You are the seed 753
Your Word, O Lord, is gentle dew 232

Guidance
See Trust, Guidance

Harvest

Accept, O Lord, the gifts we bring 759
As saints of old 404
Come, you thankful people, come 407
For the fruit of all creation 563, 760
Great is thy faithfulness 771
Praise and thanksgiving 409
Sing to the Lord of harvest 412
We plow the fields and scatter 362
See Creation, Preservation

Healing
See Forgiveness, Healing

Heaven, Eternal Life

A multitude comes from the east and the west . .313
Alabaré 791
Alleluia! Jesus is risen! .674
Arise, my soul, arise! 516
Blessed assurance 699
Come, we that love the Lord 742
I am the Bread of life 702
I want to walk as a child of the light 649
In heaven above 330
Jerusalem, my happy home 331
Jerusalem, whose towers touch the skies 348
Jesus, remember me 740
Let me be yours forever 490
O Morning Star, how fair and bright! 76
Oh, happy day when we shall stand 351
Oh, what their joy 337
Shall we gather at the river 690
Sing with all the saints in glory 691
Soon and very soon 744
The God of Abraham praise 544
Thine the amen, thine the praise 801
What wondrous love is this 385
Who is this host arrayed in white 314

Holiness
*See Justification; Pentecost, The Holy Spirit; Trust,
Guidance*

Holy Baptism, 187–195, 693–698

Bind us together 748
Come away to the skies .669
Glories of your name are spoken 358
Go, my children, with my blessing 721
I was there to hear your borning cry 770
I'm so glad Jesus lifted me 673
Loving Spirit 683
Shall we gather at the river 690

Spirit of God, unleashed on earth .... .387
The King of love my shepherd is .... .456
Thine the amen, thine the praise .... .801
Thy holy wings .... .741
To Jordan came the Christ, our Lord .... .79
When Jesus came to Jordan .... .647

Holy Communion, 196–226, 699–711
Alleluia! Jesus is risen! .... .674
Alleluia! Sing to Jesus .... .158
Arise, my soul, arise! .... .516
Around you, O Lord Jesus .... .496
Go, my children, with my blessing .... .721
Hallelujah! We sing your praises .... .722
Here in this place .... .718
It happened on that fateful night .... .127
Jesus, come! for we invite you .... .648
Let us talents and tongues employ .... .754
Lord, enthroned in heavenly splendor .... .172
Lord, receive this company .... .255
Mothering God, you gave me birth .... .769
Now the feast and celebration .... .789
O Jesus, joy of loving hearts .... .356
Of the glorious body telling .... .120
Only-begotten, Word of God eternal .... .375
Our Paschal Lamb, that sets us free .... .679
Stay with us .... .743
Thine the amen, thine the praise .... .801
We come to the hungry feast .... .766
When twilight comes .... .663
With God as our friend .... .371
See Praise, Adoration

Holy Cross Day
Lift high the cross .... .377
Oh, praise the gracious power .... .750
Sing, my tongue .... .118
There in God's garden .... .668
We sing the praise of him who died .... .344
Weary of all trumpeting .... .785
When I survey the wondrous cross .... .482

Holy Innocents, Martyrs
By all your saints in warfare .... .177
Oh, sleep now, holy baby .... .639

Holy Spirit
See Commitment; Pentecost, The Holy Spirit; Witness

Holy Trinity, The, 165–169
Come, all you people .... .717
Come, thou almighty King .... .522
Creating God, your fingers trace .... .757
Creator Spirit, heavenly dove .... .284
Eternal God, before your throne .... .354
Glory to God, we give you thanks .... .787
God the Father, be our stay .... .308
God, whose almighty word .... .400
Holy God, we praise your name .... .535
Holy Spirit, truth divine .... .257
I bind unto myself today .... .188

Mothering God, you gave me birth .... .769
My Lord of light .... .796
Thy strong Word .... .233
We all believe in one true God .... .374

Holy Week, The Three Days, 108–127, 663–670

Home
See Family

Hope (Christian Hope), 313–352, 742–746
All earth is hopeful .... .629
Alleluia! Jesus is risen! .... .674
As pants the hart for cooling streams .... .452
Blessed assurance .... .699
By gracious powers .... .736
Christ is risen! Shout hosanna! .... .672
Come away to the skies .... .669
Each winter as the year grows older .... .628
Glories of your name are spoken .... .358
Healer of our every ill .... .738
In the morning when I rise .... .777
Jesus lives! The victory's won! .... .133
Jesus, come! for we invite you .... .648
Kyrie, God Father .... .168
Let us ever walk with Jesus .... .487
Lord our God, with praise we come .... .244
My heart is longing .... .326
O blessed spring .... .695
O Christ the same .... .778
O day full of grace .... .161
O day of peace .... .762
O Savior, rend the heavens wide .... .38
O Son of God, in Galilee .... .426
Precious Lord, take my hand .... .731
Rise, O children of salvation .... .182
Shall we gather at the river .... .690
Sing with all the saints in glory .... .691
Spirit of God, unleashed on earth .... .387
The King shall come .... .33
Thine the amen, thine the praise .... .801
This joyful Eastertide .... .149, 676
We worship you, O God of might .... .432
Your kingdom come, O Father .... .384
See Heaven, Eternal Life

Hospitals
See Forgiveness, Healing

House of God
See Church Building; Dedication of a Church

Humility
Come down, O Love divine .... .508
Great God, your love has called us .... .666
Jesu, Jesu, fill us with your love .... .765
Lord Jesus, think on me .... .309
Lord, teach us how to pray aright .... .438
Lord, whose love in humble service .... .423
To you, omniscient Lord of all .... .310

Hunger

For the fruit of all creation 563, 760
Hallelujah! We sing your praises 722
I, the Lord of sea and sky 752
Let us talents and tongues employ 754
Lord, whose love in humble service 423
Praise and thanksgiving 409
We come to the hungry feast 766
You satisfy the hungry heart 711

Immortality

See Hope; Heaven, Eternal Life

Incarnation

Christ is alive! Let Christians sing 363
Father eternal, ruler of creation 413
He comes to us as one unknown 768
Let all mortal flesh keep silence 198
O Holy Spirit, root of life 688
Son of God, eternal Savior 364
Songs of thankfulness and praise 90
The Word of God is source and seed 658
When long before time 799
Word of God, come down on earth 716
See Christmas

Inner Life

Be thou my vision 776
Breathe on me, breath of God 488
Come down, O Love divine 508
Dear Lord and Father of mankind 506
Eternal Spirit of the living Christ 441
He comes to us as one unknown 768
He leadeth me: oh, blessed thought! 501
Here, O my Lord, I see thee 211
How sweet the name of Jesus sounds 345
Jesus, the very thought of you 316
Jesus, thy boundless love to me 336
Mothering God, you gave me birth 769
O blessed spring 695
O Jesus, king most wonderful! 537
O Spirit of life 680
Restore in us, O God 662
Spirit of God, descend upon my heart 486

Installation

*See Commitment; Deaconesses, Deacons, Diaconal
Ministers; Pastors*

Invitation

Come to Calvary's holy mountain 301
Eat this bread 709
Hark, the voice of Jesus calling 381
Here in this place 718
I heard the voice of Jesus say 497
Jesus calls us; o'er the tumult 494
Jesus sinners will receive 291
Listen, God is calling 712
Softly and tenderly Jesus is calling 734
There's a wideness in God's mercy 290

Today your mercy calls us 304
You have come down to the lakeshore 784

Invocation

Come down, O Love divine 508
Come, Holy Ghost, our souls inspire 472, 473
Come, O Holy Spirit, come 681
Come, thou almighty King 522
Eternal God, before your throne 354
Holy God, we praise your name 535
O Holy Spirit, enter in .459
Veni Sancte Spiritus 686
*See Beginning of Service; Gathering; Pentecost, The
Holy Spirit*

Joy

All things bright and beautiful 767
Arise, my soul, arise! 516
Blest are they 764
I received the living God 700
I'm so glad Jesus lifted me 673
Joy to the world 39
Joyful, joyful, we adore thee 551
My life flows on in endless song 781
O Morning Star, how fair and bright! 76
Oh, sing to God above .726
Oh, sing to the Lord 795
Shout for joy loud and long 793
See Celebration, Jubilation

Judgment

All earth is hopeful 629
Hark! A thrilling voice is sounding! 37
Herald, sound the note of judgment 556
Judge eternal, throned in splendor 418
Lo! He comes with clouds descending 27
My Lord, what a morning 627
O Lord of light, who made the stars 323
O Spirit of the living God 388
Soon and very soon 744
The clouds of judgment gather 322
The day is surely drawing near 321
The King shall come 33
The Lord will come and not be slow 318
Wake, awake, for night is flying 31

Justice

See Society

Justification, 290–302

Awake, O sleeper 745
Great God, your love has called us 666
If God himself be for me 454
Let me be yours forever 490
Lord of glory, you have bought us 424
My heart is longing 326
My song is love unknown 94, 661
My soul, now praise your maker! 519
The head that once was crowned 173
There in God's garden .668

Joyful, joyful we adore thee 551
Lord of all nations, grant me grace 419
Lord, speak to us, that we may speak 403
Lord, thee I love with all my heart 325
Love divine, all loves excelling 315
My song is love unknown 94, 661
O God, I love thee 491
O Spirit of life 680
Oh, love, how deep 88
One there is, above all others 298
Son of God, eternal Savior 364
Thee will I love, my strength 502
Ubi caritas et amor 665
What wondrous love is this 385
When love is found 749
Word of God, come down on earth 716

Marriage, 287–289
As man and woman we were made 751
Bind us together 748
Come, my way, my truth, my life 513
Eternal God, before your throne 354
Jesus, come! for we invite you 648
Joyful, joyful we adore thee 551
Now thank we all our God 533, 534
O Morning Star, how fair and bright! 76
Soul, adorn yourself with gladness 224
When love is found 749
See Family

Mary, Mother of Our Lord
At the cross, her station keeping 110
Cold December flies away 53
For all the faithful women 692
Lo, how a rose is growing 58
My soul now magnifies the Lord 180
My soul proclaims your greatness 730
Sing of Mary, pure and lowly 634
The angel Gabriel from heaven came 632
Ye watchers and ye holy ones 175

Maundy Thursday
A new commandment 664
Great God, your love has called us 666
It happened on that fateful night 127
Jesu, Jesu, fill us with your love 765
Lord, who the night you were betrayed 206
Lord, whose love in humble service 423
Love consecrates the humblest act 122
O Lord, we praise you .215
Of the glorious body telling 120
Stay here 667
Ubi caritas et amor 665
When twilight comes 663
Where charity and love prevail 126
See Holy Week, The Three Days

Means of Grace
*See Forgiveness, Healing; Holy Baptism; Holy
Communion; Word, The*

Mercy
Great is thy faithfulness 771
Let us with a gladsome mind 521
Love divine, all loves excelling 315
O God of mercy, God of light 425
Our Father, we have wandered 733
Out of the depths I cry to you 295
Softly and tenderly Jesus is calling 734
There's a wideness in God's mercy 290
Today your mercy calls us 304
When all your mercies, O my God 264

Ministry
Arise, your light has come! 652
For the fruit of all creation 563, 760
God is here! 719
Great God, your love has called us 666
Holy Spirit, ever dwelling 523
I, the Lord of sea and sky 752
Jesus calls us; o'er the tumult 494
Lord, whose love in humble service 423
Lord, you give the great commission 756
Rise up, O saints of God! 383
The Church of Christ, in every age 433
The Son of God, our Christ 434
*See Commitment; Deaconesses, Deacons, Diaconal
Ministers; Pastors; Service*

Mission, Missions
*See Commitment; Pilgrimage; Society; Witness; The
Word*

Morning, 264–271, 725–727
Day by day 746
Each morning brings us 800
Evening and morning 465
Great is thy faithfulness 771
Holy, holy, holy 165
In the morning when I rise 777
Let us break bread together 212
My Lord, what a morning 627
When morning gilds the skies 545, 546
With the Lord begin your task 444

Music
See Arts and Music

Name of Jesus, The
All hail the power of Jesus' name! 328, 329
At the name of Jesus 179
Greet now the swiftly changing year 181
How sweet the name of Jesus sounds 345
I want to walk as a child of the light 649
In the morning when I rise 777
Oh, for a thousand tongues to sing 559
O Savior, precious Savior 514

Nation
All my hope on God is founded 782
Before you, Lord, we bow 401

For the fruit of all creation 563, 760
God the omnipotent! 462
Judge eternal, throned in splendor 418
Lift every voice and sing 562
Not alone for mighty empire 437
O day of peace 762
O God of earth and altar 428
O God of every nation 416
See National Songs; Society

National Songs, 566–569

Nature
See Creation, Preservation; Stewardship

Neighbor
See Commitment; Love; Society; Service

New Year
By gracious powers 736
Greet now the swiftly changing year 181
In thee is gladness 552
It came upon the midnight clear 54
O Christ the same 778
O God, our help in ages past 320

Obedience
See Service

Occasions
See Commemorations and Occasions

Offerings
See Offertory; Stewardship

Offertory
Accept, O Lord, the gifts we bring 759
As saints of old 404
As the grains of wheat 705
Come to us, creative Spirit 758
Create in me a clean heart 732
Draw us in the Spirit's tether 703
For the fruit of all creation 563, 760
Grains of wheat 708
Let us talents and tongues employ 754
Lord of all good 411
Lord, receive this company 255
Now we offer 760
One bread, one body 710
We come to the hungry feast 766
We give thee but thine own 410
We place upon your table, Lord 217
What child is this 40

Ordination
See Ministry; Pastors; Pentecost, The Holy Spirit

Palm Sunday (Sunday of the Passion)
See Holy Week, The Three Days

Passion of Christ
See Holy Week, The Three Days

Passion, Sunday of the
See Holy Week, The Three Days

Pastors, 283–286
Come, Holy Ghost, our souls inspire 472, 473
Come, oh, come, O quickening Spirit 478
Creator Spirit, by whose aid 164
God is here! 719
Great God, your love has called us 666
Holy Spirit, ever dwelling 523
I, the Lord of sea and sky 752
Lord, you give the great commission 756
You are the seed 753
You have come down to the lakeshore 784
See Deaconesses, Deacons, Diaconal Ministers;
Ministry; Service

Peace
Creating God, your fingers trace 757
Dona nobis pacem 774
God the omnipotent! 462
Grant peace, we pray, in mercy, Lord 471
Great God, our source 466
Let justice flow like streams 763
Lord of our life 366
My life flows on in endless song 781
O day of peace 762
O God of every nation 416
O God of love, O King of peace 414
Oh, praise the gracious power 750
Peace came to earth 641
Shalom 724
We come to the hungry feast 766
Weary of all trumpeting 785
What a fellowship, what a joy divine 780
See Comfort and Rest; Society

Penitence
See Forgiveness, Healing

Pentecost, The Holy Spirit, 160–164, 680–688
Come, gracious Spirit, heavenly dove 475
Come down, O Love divine 508
Come, oh, come, O quickening Spirit 478
Creator Spirit, heavenly dove 284
God is here! 719
Holy Spirit, ever dwelling 523
Lord, listen to your children praying 775
Lord, you give the great commission 756
O Holy Spirit, enter in 459
Spirit of God, sent from heaven abroad 285
Spirit of God, unleashed on earth 387

Pilgrimage

All who would valiant be 498
As the sun with longer journey 655
Come, we that love the Lord 742
Day by day 746
Guide me ever, great Redeemer 343
I want Jesus to walk with me 660
I want to walk as a child of the light 649
Jesus, Savior, pilot me .334
Jesus, still lead on 341
Lift every voice and sing 562
Lord, as a pilgrim on earth I go 485
Lord, dismiss us with your blessing 259
O God of Jacob 477
O Word of God incarnate 231
Savior, like a shepherd lead us 481
The King of love my shepherd is 456
The Lord's my shepherd 451
Through the night of doubt and sorrow 355
We are marching in the light of God 650
What a fellowship, what a joy divine 780

Praise, Adoration, 514–551, 786–802

All glory be to God on high 166
All hail the power of Jesus' name! 328, 329
All my hope on God is founded 782
All people that on earth do dwell 245
Alleluia! Jesus is risen! 674
Alleluia, alleluia, give thanks 671
Blessed assurance 699
Christ is made the sure foundation 367, 747
Come to us, creative Spirit 758
Come, all you people 717
Gloria (Taizé) 640
Gloria, gloria, gloria 637
Glory be to God the Father! 167
God himself is present .249
God is here! 719
Hallelujah! We sing your praises 722
Holy Majesty, before you 247
Holy Spirit, ever dwelling 523
Hosanna to the living Lord! 258
How sweet the name of Jesus sounds 345
In the presence of your people 720
Let the whole creation cry 242
Lift high the cross 377
Lift up your heads, O gates 631
Lord our God, with praise we come 244
Lord, with glowing heart 243
My heart is longing 326
My soul now magnifies the Lord 180
My soul proclaims your greatness 730
Oh, sing to God above .726
Praise and thanks and adoration 470
Praise and thanksgiving be to God 191
Rejoice, the Lord is king! 171
Surely it is God who saves me 635
Thy strong Word 233
We praise you, O God 241
We sing the praise of him who died 344
When all your mercies, O my God 264
You servants of God 252
See Celebration, Jubilation

Prayer, 438–444, 772–775

Jesus, remember me 740
Lord, keep us steadfast in your Word 230
Seek ye first the kingdom of God 783
Stay here 667
With God as our friend .371

Presentation of Our Lord, The

In his temple now behold him 184
Peace came to earth 641

Processions

Hail thee, festival day! .142
Lift high the cross 377
Oh, praise the gracious power 750
Rejoice, O pilgrim throng! 553
The royal banners forward go 124, 125
We are marching in the light of God 650

Proclamation

See Witness; Word, The

Providence

See Creation, Preservation; Thanksgiving

Reception

See Affirmation of Baptism; Community in Christ

Reconciliation

Awake, O sleeper 745
Dear Christians, one and all 299
Forgive our sins as we forgive 307
God! When human bonds are broken 735
Healer of our every ill 738
Lord of all nations, grant me grace 419
Lord, who the night you were betrayed 206
Now we join in celebration 203
O day of peace 762
Oh, praise the gracious power 750
See Atonement; Forgiveness, Healing; Justification

Redeemer

See Justification

Races and Cultures

Christ is alive! Let Christians sing 363
Grains of wheat 708
Great God, your love has called us 666
In Christ there is no east or west 359
Jesu, Jesu, fill us with your love 765
Let us break bread together 212
One bread, one body 710
Sent forth by God's blessing 221
See Community in Christ; Society

Reformation Day

A mighty fortress is our God 228, 229
Built on a rock 365

Christ is made the sure foundation 367, 747
Dear Christians, one and all 299
God is here! 719
God's Word is our great heritage 239
Listen, God is calling 712
Lord, keep us steadfast in your Word 230
O God, O Lord of heaven and earth 396
Salvation unto us has come 297
The Church's one foundation 369
See Community in Christ; Justification

Repentance, Forgiveness, 303–312
See Forgiveness, Healing

Rest
See Comfort and Rest

Restoration
See Affirmation of Baptism; Commitment;
Forgiveness, Healing

Resurrection
See Easter; Heaven, Eternal Life; Hope

Rogation
See Creation, Preservation; Thanksgiving

Sacraments
See Holy Baptism; Holy Communion

Saints' Days
By all your saints in warfare 177, 178
For all the faithful women 692
For all your saints, O Lord 176
Rejoice in God's saints .689
Rise, O children of salvation 182
Sing with all the saints in glory 691

St. Andrew, Apostle
Jesus call us; o'er the tumult 494

St. Thomas, Apostle
We walk by faith and not by sight 675
You are the way 464

St. Stephen, Deacon and Martyr
The Son of God goes forth to war 183

St. John, Apostle and Evangelist
All praise to you, eternal Lord 48

Confession of St. Peter, The
Christ is made the sure foundation 367, 747

Conversion of St. Paul, The
O Lord, send forth your Spirit 392

St. Peter and St. Paul, Apostles
The head that once was crowned 173

St. Mary Magdalene
For all the faithful women 692
Hallelujah! Jesus lives! .147

Mary, Mother of Our Lord
My soul now magnifies the Lord 180
My soul proclaims your greatness 730
Sing of Mary, pure and lowly 634
The angel Gabriel from heaven came 632
Ye watchers and ye holy ones 175

St. Michael and All Angels
God himself is present 249
Let all mortal flesh keep silence 198
Ye watchers and ye holy ones 175
You who dwell in the shelter of the Lord 779

Salvation
See Grace; Justification; Reconciliation

Sanctification
See Commitment; Pentecost, The Holy Spirit; Trust,
Guidance

Schools
See Education

Scriptures
Bright and glorious is the sky 75
Father of mercies, in your Word 240
He comes to us as one unknown 768
How blest are they who hear God's Word 227
O God of light 237
O Word of God incarnate 231
Open your ears, O faithful people 715

Second Coming of Christ
See Hope; Judgment; Last Things; Watchfulness

Sending, 721–724
Awake, O sleeper 745
Let us talents and tongues employ 754
Listen, God is calling 712
O Holy Spirit, root of life 688
Send me, Jesus 773
We all are one in mission 755
You are the seed 753
See Close of Service

Service
As saints of old 404
Draw us in the Spirit's tether 703
Filled with the Spirit's power 160
For the fruit of all creation 563, 760
God is here! 719
God of grace and God of glory 415
God, whose giving knows no ending 408
Great God, your love has called us 666
In Christ there is no east or west 359

Jesu, Jesu, fill us with your love 765
Lord, whose love in humble service 423
Lord, you give the great commission 756
Love consecrates the humblest act 122
O God of youth 510
O Master, let me walk with you 492
Son of God, eternal Savior 364
The Spirit sends us forth to serve 723
We all are one in mission 755
We give thee but thine own 410
See Ministry

Sickness
See Forgiveness, Healing

Sin, Confession of
See Forgiveness, Healing

Society, 413–437, 762–766
Arise, your light has come! 652
Before you, Lord, we bow 401
Christ is alive! Let Christians sing 363
Creating God, your fingers trace 757
Each winter as the year grows older 628
Eternal Ruler of the ceaseless round 373
God the omnipotent! 462
God, who stretched the spangled heavens 463
Great God, our source 466
Great God, your love has called us 666
Here in this place 718
Hope of the world 493
I, the Lord of sea and sky 752
In Adam we have all been one 372
In Christ there is no east or west 359
Lift every voice and sing 562
Lord, you give the great commission 756
My soul proclaims your greatness 730
O God, O Lord of heaven and earth 396
Oh, praise the gracious power 750
Praise to you, O God of mercy 790
Rise up, O saints of God! 383
Son of God, eternal Savior 364
Thy strong Word 233
When Israel was in Egypt's land 670

Social Justice
See Society

Sorrow, Suffering
By gracious powers 736
By the Babylonian rivers 656
Day by day 746
God! When human bonds are broken 735
Healer of our every ill 738
I want Jesus to walk with me 660
If God himself be for me 454
If you but trust in God to guide you 453
In all our grief 739
In the hour of trial 106
In the morning when I rise 777

My life flows on in endless song 781
Oh, sing my soul, your maker's praise 319
Out of the depths I cry to you 295
Precious Lord, take my hand 731
Soon and very soon 744
Stay with us 743
There in God's garden 668
There is a balm in Gilead 737
Weary of all trumpeting 785
When in the hour of deepest need 303
See Comfort and Rest

Stewardship, 404–412, 757–761
Draw us in the Spirit's tether 703
God is here! 719
I, the Lord of sea and sky 752
Let us talents and tongues employ 754
O God of mercy, God of light 425
Son of God, eternal Savior 364
We come to the hungry feast 766
We plow the fields and scatter 362
When in our music God is glorified 555, 802
You have come down to the lakeshore 784
See Commitment; Creation, Preservation; Offertory

Suffering
See Sorrow, Suffering

Sunday
God is here! 719
O day of rest and gladness 251
The first day of the week 246
See Easter

Teachers
See Education; Commitment

Temptation
By gracious powers 736
I want Jesus to walk with me 660
If you but trust in God to guide you 453
In the hour of trial 106
O Jesus, I have promised 503
What a friend we have in Jesus 439

Thanksgiving
All my hope on God is founded 782
All things bright and beautiful 767
Come, you thankful people, come 407
For the fruit of all creation 563, 760
Great is thy faithfulness 771
Let all things now living 557
Many and great, O God, are your works 794
My life flows on in endless song 781
Now thank we all our God 533, 534
O God beyond all praising 797
Praise and thanksgiving 409
Praise to you, O God of mercy 790
Sing to the Lord of harvest 412

We praise you, O God 241
When all your mercies, O my God 264
See Celebration, Jubilation; Praise, Adoration

Transfiguration of Our Lord, The
Alleluia, song of gladness 654
Beautiful Savior 518
How good, Lord, to be here! 89
I want to walk as a child of the light 649
Jesus on the mountain peak 653
Oh, wondrous type! Oh, vision fair 80
Shine, Jesus, shine 651

Travelers
Eternal Father, strong to save 467
I want Jesus to walk with me 660
See Pilgrimage

Trial
See Comfort and Rest; Sorrow, Suffering

Trinity
See Holy Trinity

Trust, Guidance, 445–485, 776–782
Beneath the cross of Jesus 107
By gracious powers 736
Day by day 746
Do not despair, O little flock 361
Eternal Spirit of the living Christ 441
God of our life, all-glorious Lord 270
Guide me ever, great Redeemer 343
He leadeth me: oh, blessed thought! 501
Healer of our every ill .738
How firm a foundation .507
I bind unto myself today 188
I lay my sins on Jesus 305
I trust, O Christ, in you alone 395
I want Jesus to walk with me 660
In the cross of Christ I glory 104
In thee is gladness 552
Jesus calls us; o'er the tumult 494
Jesus, Savior, pilot me .334
Jesus, still lead on 341
Lead on, O King eternal! 495
Lift every voice and sing 562
Lord of our life 366
Lord, take my hand and lead me 333
Lord, thee I love with all my heart 325
Loving Spirit 683
My heart is longing 326
My hope is built on nothing less 293, 294
O God, our help in ages past 320
O one with God the Father 77
Oh, sing, my soul, your maker's praise 319
On my heart imprint your image 102
Out of the depths I cry to you 295
Precious Lord, take my hand 731
Stay with us 743

Surely it is God who saves me 735
There is a balm in Gilead 737
Thy holy wings 741
We are the Lord's 399
We walk by faith and not by sight 675
With the Lord begin your task 444

Unity
As the grains of wheat .705
Awake, O sleeper 745
Bind us together 748
Christ is the king! 386
Christ is made the sure foundation 747
Draw us in the Spirit's tether 703
God is here! 719
Grains of wheat 708
Father, we thank you 704
Let us break bread together 212
Let us talents and tongues employ 754
Like the murmur of the dove's song 685
Lord, keep us steadfast in your word 230
Lord, receive this company 255
Lord, who the night you were betrayed 206
Oh, praise the gracious power 750
O Lord, we praise you .215
One bread, one body 710
Shalom 724
We all are one in mission 755
See Community in Christ

Visitation, The
The angel Gabriel from heaven came 632
The only Son from heaven 86

Warfare, Christian
By all your saints in warfare 177, 178
Fight the good fight 461
Lead on, O King eternal! 495
Onward, Christian soldiers 509
Stand up, stand up for Jesus 389
The Son of God goes forth to war 183
We are the Lord's 399
Weary of all trumpeting 785

Watchfulness
As the sun with longer journey 655
Awake, my soul, and with the sun 269
Light one candle to watch for Messiah 630
Oh, that the Lord would guide my ways 480
Rise, my soul, to watch and pray 443
Rise up, O saints of God! 383
Soon and very soon 744
Stay here 667
Wake, awake, for night is flying 31

Witness, 376–403, 752–756
A new commandment 664
Arise, your light has come! 652
At the name of Jesus 179
Creating God, your fingers trace 757

Crown him with many crowns 170
Filled with the Spirit's power 160
For the fruit of all creation 563, 760
God is here! 719
God the omnipotent! 462
Gracious Spirit, heed our pleading 687
Hallelujah! We sing your praises 722
Herald, sound the note of judgment 556
Here in this place 718
Holy Spirit, ever dwelling 523
In Adam we have all been one 372
Jesus shall reign 530
Listen, God is calling 712
Look, the sight is glorious 156
Lord, keep us steadfast in your Word 230
O day full of grace 161
O God, send heralds 283
Oh, for a thousand tongues to sing 559
Oh, praise the gracious power 750
Praise the Spirit in creation 682
Shine, Jesus, shine 651
Spirit of God, sent from heaven abroad 285
Spread, oh, spread, almighty Word 379
Strengthen for service, Lord 218
Surely it is God who saves me 735
The Church of Christ, in every age 433
The Son of God, our Christ 434
The Spirit sends us forth to serve 723
Through the night of doubt and sorrow 355
We all believe in one true God 374
You servants of God 252
See Evangelism; Word, The

Word, The, 227–240, 712–716
Open now thy gates of beauty 250
He comes to us as one unknown 768
O Spirit of life 680
Seek ye first the kingdom of God 783
The Word of God is source and seed 658
See Witness

Work, Daily
All who love and serve your city 436
As saints of old 404
Awake, my soul, and with the sun 269
Draw us in the Spirit's tether 703
Evening and morning 465
Forth in thy name, O Lord, I go 505
God is here! 719
Lord of all hopefulness .469
Now we offer 761
Praise and thanksgiving 409
Praise to you, O Christ, our Savior 614
We all are one in mission 755
With the Lord begin your task 444
See Society

World
See Creation, Preservation; Society

Worship
All people that on earth do dwell 245
Come to us, creative Spirit 758
Evening and morning 465
Go, my children, with my blessing 721
Let all mortal flesh keep silence 198
Lord, whose love in humble service 423
Now the silence 205
O Savior, precious Savior 514
Oh, worship the King 548
Only-begotten, Word of God eternal 375
Thine the amen, thine the praise 801
When in our music God is glorified 555, 802
*See Beginning of Service; Gathering; Praise,
Adoration*

TEXT AND MUSIC SOURCES

TUNES — METRICAL

S M (Short Meter-6 6 8 6)

S M and refrain

S M D (Short Meter Double-6 6 8 6 6 6 8 6)

C M (Common Meter-8 6 8 6)

C M and refrain

C M and repeat

C M D (Common Meter Double-8 6 8 6 8 6 8 6)

L M (Long Meter-8 8 8 8)

L M and alleluia

L M and refrain

L M D (Long Meter Double-8 8 8 8 8 8 8 8)

4 4 6 and refrain

4 5 7 4 5 7 and refrain

4 5 10 4 5 10 and refrain

5 5 5 4 D

5 5 8 D

5 5 6 D

5 5 6 5 6 5 6 5 and refrain

5 5 7 5 5 8

5 5 8 8 5 5

5 6 5 6 5

5 6 5 6 5 6 5 5

5 6 5 6 5 6 7

6 4 6 4 D

6 4 6 4 and refrain

6 5 6 5

6 5 6 5 D

6 5 6 5 6 5 D

6 5 6 5 6 6 6 5

6 6 4 6 6 6 4

6 6 5 6 6 5 7 8 6

6 6 6 6 4 4 4 4

6 6 6 6 and refrain

6 6 6 6 6 6

6 6 6 6 6 6 D

6 6 6 6 8 8

ALTERNATE TUNES

FIRST LINES AND COMMON TITLES

This index is arranged by the titles that appear in *Lutheran Book of Worship* and *With One Voice*. Indented lines indicate first lines or titles by which certain hymns and songs may also be known.

ISBN 0-8066-2348-9

90000